Network-based
Language Teaching

THE CAMBRIDGE APPLIED LINGUISTICS SERIES

Series editors: Michael H. Long and Jack C. Richards

This series presents the findings of recent work in applied linguistics which are of direct relevance to language teaching and learning and of particular interest to applied linguistics, researchers, language teachers, and teacher trainers.

In this series:

Network-based Language Teaching

Concepts and Practice

Edited by

Mark Warschauer

America-Mideast Educational & Training Services

and

Richard Kern

University of California at Berkeley

CAMBRIDGE
UNIVERSITY PRESS

PUBLISHED BY THE PRESS SYNDICATE OF THE UNIVERSITY OF CAMBRIDGE
The Pitt Building, Trumpington Street, Cambridge, United Kingdom

CAMBRIDGE UNIVERSITY PRESS
The Edinburgh Building, Cambridge CB2 2 RU, United Kingdom   http://www.cup.ac.uk
40 West 20th Street, New York, NY 10011-4211, USA   http://www.cup.org
10 Stamford Road, Oakleigh, Melbourne 3166, Australia
Ruiz de Alarcón 13, 28014 Madrid, Spain

© Cambridge University Press 2000

First published 2000

Printed in the United States of America.

Typeface Sabon 10½/12 pt.   *System* QuarkXPress 4.04 [AG]

A catalogue record for this book is available from the British Library

Library of Congress Cataloguing in Publication data

Network-based language teaching : concepts and practice / editors,
Mark Warschauer, Richard Kern.
   p.   cm.
ISBN 0-521-66136-6 (hb). – ISBN 0-521-66742-9 (pb)
1. Language and languages – Study and teaching – Computer network
resources.   I. Warschauer, Mark.   II. Kern, Richard (Richard
Geyman)
P53.285.N48   2000
418′.00285 – dc21   99-12566
                                                        CIP

ISBN 0 521 661366 hardback
ISBN 0 521 667429 paperback

October 11, 2000

Contents

Contributors

Carol A. Chapelle, Iowa State University
Dorothy M. Chun, University of California, Santa Barbara
Boyd Davis, University of North Carolina, Charlotte
Agnès Fauverge, University of Cambridge
Richard Kern, University of California, Berkeley
Carla Meskill, State University of New York at Albany
Jill Pellettieri, California State University, San Marcos
Jan L. Plass, University of New Mexico
Krassimira Ranglova, University of Sofia, Bulgaria
Jean Marie Schultz, University of California, Berkeley
Heidi Shetzer, University of California, Santa Barbara
Ralf Thiede, University of North Carolina, Charlotte
Mark Warschauer, America-Mideast Educational & Training Services,
    Cairo
Jan Wong, University of Cambridge
Christoph Zähner, University of Cambridge

Series editors' preface

For many second and foreign language learners, experience of the target language has traditionally been limited to opportunities created by the teacher in the classroom, drawing on such resources as textbooks, tapes or CDs, and videos. In recent years alternative modes of delivery in teaching have been developed such as distance learning and self-access learning, seeking on the one hand to economize on teaching resources, and on the other to recognize principles of learner-centeredness in teaching. However, perhaps the most dramatic changes in the mode in which second language teaching and learning is accomplished have come about as a result of developments in computer-based teaching and learning. The Internet in particular has become a new medium of communication that is shaping both the processes and the products of communication. Because computers have opened up new opportunities for communication between both learners and teachers and among second language users themselves, many language teachers see great potential in computer-mediated teaching and learning. The present book offers a comprehensive account of teaching that makes use of computers connected to one another in either local or global networks, network-based language teaching.

Although a number of recent books provide an overview of developments in computer-mediated language teaching, the present book has a wider agenda. It presents not only descriptive accounts of network-based language teaching in a variety of foreign and second language teaching contexts, but also careful empirical investigations of the nature and effects of such innovations. These studies seek to establish whether network-based language teaching is compatible with educational theory as well as current understanding of the nature of second language acquisition.

Among the range of issues explored in the book are the nature of the interaction and discourse that occurs during computer-mediated communication, the use of technology-mediated activities in a literature-based curriculum and their impact on classroom processes and discourse, ethnographic study of on-line learning in college language and writing classrooms, L2 learners' use of style shifting during electronic conferencing, the role of the computer in fostering improvement in students' writing, the development of second language competencies and skills through the Web, and the impact of this new mode of learning on the beliefs of teachers and learners.

The book thus provides a valuable addition to the Cambridge Applied Linguistics Series, through clarifying the nature of network-based language teaching, illustrating the diverse range of potential applications of this new technology, and identifying significant research issues and implications.

Michael H. Long
Jack C. Richards

Preface

The rapidly expanding use of computer networking in many parts of the world is transforming the way we communicate with each other, conduct business, and produce knowledge. In the context of language education, computer networks make it possible for learners to access and/or publish texts and multimedia materials and to extend their communicative experience to worlds far beyond the classroom. These possibilities have led to great expectations of how computer networks will enhance language learning. Historically, however, educators' expectations of how new technologies may transform learning have not necessarily been borne out in practice. This book offers an initial step forward evaluating educators' expectations about computer networking by presenting recent research on what happens when language learners are brought together with texts and with other speakers of a language in networked environments.

This book originated when the two of us first met at the National Foreign Language Resource Center Symposium on Local and Global Electronic Networking in Foreign Language Learning and Research at the University of Hawaii at Manoa in July 1995. At the time it struck us that the field was long on pedagogical suggestions for exploiting networking technology but short on research. Despite a growing body of general research on computer-mediated communication, relatively few studies have been published that deal specifically with second language learning contexts. This book attempts to fill that void by bringing together in one volume the best current research on language learning using computer networks.

We have done our best to identify the main issues deserving of study in this area and to include contributions that cover this spectrum of issues. We have sought out research studies that are systematic in design and that have results of importance for applied linguistics and language pedagogy. Readers of this book will not find a simple overriding answer as to whether or not teaching with computers "works." Instead, they will find careful research as to what types of processes and outcomes are achieved when language learners use computer networks in particular circumstances, and what implications this has for how we might design and implement network-based language teaching according to particular pedagogical goals.

Any such book is a collaborative effort. As editors, we are especially grateful to the authors whose work appears in this collection. Their patience, perseverance, and willingness to revise and coordinate their chapters deserve special recognition. We are also grateful to the editorial staff at Cambridge University Press, especially Deborah Goldblatt, Mary Vaughn, and Mary Carson, for their professional work on the manuscript. We thank Mike Long and Jack Richards for recognizing the importance of the topic and helping to bring this book into the Cambridge Applied Linguistics Series. We would also like to acknowledge the University of Hawaii and the University of California, Berkeley, for their support of our research. Finally, we thank our families, Mark's wife, Keiko Hirata, and Richard's wife and daughters, Louise Erickson and Maria and Olivia Kern, for their love and support during the several years when we were planning, writing, revising, and editing this book.

Mark Warschauer
Richard Kern

1 Introduction

Theory and practice of network-based language teaching

Richard Kern
Mark Warschauer

Since the early 1960s, language teachers have witnessed dramatic changes in the ways that languages are taught. The focus of instruction has broadened from the teaching of discrete grammatical structures to the fostering of communicative ability. Creative self-expression has come to be valued over recitation of memorized dialogues. Negotiation of meaning has come to take precedence over structural drill practice. Comprehension has taken on new importance, and providing comprehensible input has become a common pedagogical imperative. Culture has received renewed interest and emphasis, even if many teachers remain unsure how best to teach it. Language textbooks have begun to distinguish spoken and written language forms, and commonly incorporate authentic texts (such as advertisements and realia) alongside literary texts. It is in the context of these multifarious changes that one of the most significant areas of innovation in language education – computer-assisted language learning (CALL) – has come of age. Nowadays, audiotape-based language labs are gradually being replaced by language media centers, where language learners can use multimedia CD-ROMs and laser discs, access foreign language documents on the World Wide Web, and communicate with their teachers, fellow classmates, and native speakers by electronic mail. If language teaching has become more exciting, it has also become considerably more complex.

This book deals with one form of CALL, what we call *network-based language teaching* (NBLT). NBLT is language teaching that involves the use of computers connected to one another in either local or global networks. Whereas CALL has traditionally been associated with self-contained, programmed applications such as tutorials, drills, simulations, instructional games, tests, and so on, NBLT represents a new and different side of CALL, where human-to-human communication is the focus. Language learners with access to the Internet, for example, can now potentially communicate with native speakers (or other language learners) all over the world twenty-four hours a day, seven days a week, from school, home, or work. That learners can communicate either on a one-to-one or a many-to-many basis in local-area network conferences further multiplies their opportunities for communicative practice. Finally, the fact that computer-mediated communication occurs in a written, electronically archived form gives students additional opportunities to plan their discourse and to notice and reflect on language use in the messages they compose and read.

Given these possibilities, it is not surprising that many language teachers have enthusiastically embraced networking technology and have developed creative ways of using networked computers with their students (see Warschauer, 1995, for 125 such examples). On the other hand, many other teachers remain skeptical of the value of computer use in general. A 1995 survey of instructional use of technology in twelve academic areas (Cotton, 1995), for example, showed that 59% of foreign language programs and 65% of ESL programs used no form of computer technology in their courses – placing language teaching at the bottom of the list of academic areas surveyed.

To date, there has been relatively little published research that explores the relationship between the use of computer networks and language learning. The simple question to which everyone wants an answer – Does the use of network-based language teaching lead to better language learning? – turns out not to be so simple. The computer, like any other technological tool used in teaching (e.g., pencils and paper, blackboards, overhead projectors, tape recorders), does not in and of itself bring about improvements in learning. We must therefore look to particular *practices of use* in particular contexts in order to begin to answer the question. Furthermore, these practices of use must be described as well as evaluated in terms of their specific social context. Who were the learners? What exactly did they do? For what purpose? In what setting? With what kinds of language? In what patterns of social interaction? What were the particular outcomes in terms of quantity/quality of language use, attitudes, motivation?

This book is written for researchers, graduate students, and teachers who are interested in research in the theory and practice of network-based language teaching. The book has two main purposes: (1) to frame a conceptual rationale for network-based teaching in terms of trends in language acquisition theory and educational theory, and (2) to present a variety of recent empirical studies that will help scholars and educators to make informed decisions about both pedagogical practices and future research.

In this first chapter, we situate NBLT within the history of approaches to second language education as well as the particular history of computer-assisted language learning. We also discuss some of the particular research issues associated with network-based language teaching, and identify gaps in our knowledge that chapters in this volume help to fill.

Shifting perspectives on language learning and teaching

Although the changes in language teaching described at the beginning of this chapter are often characterized in terms of a polar shift from structural to communicative perspectives on language teaching, we perceive a more complex overlapping of three theoretical movements – structural, cognitive, and sociocognitive – in the recent history of language teaching. Because each of these three theoretical perspectives has influenced how computer technology has been used in language teaching, we will begin by briefly tracing the development of these perspectives.

Structural perspective

For much of the twentieth century (as well as preceding centuries), language teaching emphasized the formal analysis of the system of structures that make up a given language. The grammar-translation method, for example, trained students to memorize verb paradigms, apply prescriptive rules, parse sentences, and translate texts. From the 1920s through the 1950s, influenced by the work of American structural linguists (e.g., Bloomfield, 1933), various structural methods of language instruction were developed, culminating in the audiolingual method of the 1940s and 1950s. Although audiolingual teaching focused on spoken rather than written language skills, it shared two principal assumptions with the grammar-translation method: that language teaching syllabi should be organized by linguistic categories and that the sentence was the primary unit of analysis and practice. Strongly influenced by the work of behavioral psychologists such as John Watson and B. F. Skinner, structural methodologists conceived of language learning as habit formation and thus saturated students with dialogues and pattern drills designed to condition learners to produce automatic, correct responses to linguistic stimuli. Contrastive analyses of the structural differences between the native and target languages (e.g., Lado, 1957; Moulton, 1962; Stockwell, Bowen, & Martin, 1965) provided the basis for the careful selection, gradation, and presentation of structures. Practice, not abstract knowledge, was the key.

Approaches to the teaching of reading and writing also reflected the emphasis on structure. During the audiolingual period, reading was largely seen as an aid to the learning of correct structures; students were instructed to read out loud in order to practice correct pronunciation. Second-language writing instruction focused on students' production of formally correct sentences and paragraphs. At more advanced levels, contrastive rhetoric was used to provide examples of L1/L2 essay structure differences. In sum, the emphasis in speaking, reading, and writing was on the achieved linguistic product, not on cognitive or social processes.

Cognitive/constructivist perspective

By the early 1960s, the audiolingual method began to be criticized as being overly mechanical and theoretically unjustified. Noam Chomsky

(1959) had rejected B. F. Skinner's behaviorist notion of language learning, arguing that because a speaker of a language can produce (and understand) an infinite number of well-formed utterances, language competence could not possibly be explained by a model based on imitation and habit formation. Instead, Chomsky (1957; 1965) proposed a transformational-generative grammar that mediated between deep structures and surface structures of language. The development of an individual's grammatical system was guided by innate cognitive structures – not behavioral reinforcement. In the language teaching world, Chomsky's theory contributed to a gradual shift in goals from instilling accurate language habits to fostering learners' mental construction of a second language system. Errors came to be seen in a new light – not as bad habits to be avoided but as natural by-products of a creative learning process that involved simplification, generalization, transfer, and other general cognitive strategies. Language learning had thus come to be understood not as conditioned response but as an active process of generating and transforming knowledge.

Although this new perspective at first led to renewed attention to the teaching of grammar rules (e.g., the cognitive code learning method), it later led to an emphasis on providing comprehensible input in lieu of an explicit focus on grammar (Krashen, 1982). Yet the purpose of providing comprehensible input, at least in Krashen's view, was not to foster authentic social interaction (indeed, Krashen felt that learners' speech was largely irrelevant to language learning), but rather to give individuals an opportunity to mentally construct the grammar of the language from extensive natural data.

The influence of cognitive approaches was seen quite strongly in the teaching of reading and writing. Following developments in first language reading and writing research, second language educators came to see literacy as an individual psycholinguistic process. Readers were taught a variety of cognitive strategies, both *top-down* (e.g., using schematic knowledge) and *bottom-up* (e.g., using individual word clues), in order to improve their reading processes. Second language writing instruction shifted its emphasis from the mimicking of correct structure to the development of a cognitive, problem-solving approach, focused on heuristic exercises and collaborative tasks organized in staged processes such as idea generation, drafting, and revising.

Sociocognitive perspective

At about the same time that cognitively oriented perspectives on language acquisition were gaining popularity, Dell Hymes, an American sociolinguist, and Michael Halliday, a British linguist, reminded educators that language is not just a private, "in the head" affair, but rather a socially constructed phenomenon. Hymes, who coined the term *communicative competence* in response to Chomsky's mentalistic characterization of linguistic competence, insisted on the social *appropriateness* of language use, remarking, "There are rules of use without which the rules of grammar would be useless" (Hymes, 1971, p. 10). For Hymes, syntax and language forms were best understood not as autonomous, acontextual structures, but rather as meaning resources used in particular conventional ways in particular speech communities. Grammaticality was not separable from social acceptability, nor was cognition separable from communication.

Halliday posited three principal functions of language use – ideational, interpersonal, and textual. In doing so, he brought attention to the fact that language teaching had really only dealt with the first of these – ideational (i.e., use of referential language to express content) – while the interpersonal function (i.e., use of language to maintain social relations) and the textual function (i.e., to create situationally relevant discourse) had largely been neglected.

During the 1980s, communicative competence became the buzzword of the language teaching profession. What needed to be taught was no longer just linguistic competence but also sociolinguistic competence, discourse competence, and strategic competence (Canale and Swain, 1980; Canale, 1983). With interactive communicative language use as the call of the day, communicative processes became as important as linguistic product, and instruction became more learner-centered and less structurally driven. In a sociocognitive approach, learning is viewed not just in terms of changes in individuals' cognitive structures but also in terms of the social structure of learners' discourse and activity (Crook, 1994, p. 78). From this point of view, cognitive and social dimensions overlap in a "dialectical, co-constitutive relationship" (Nystrand, Greene, & Wiemelt, 1993, p. 300). Or, as Holquist (1990) puts it, "Discourse does not reflect a situation, it *is* a situation" (p. 63).

From this perspective, language instruction was viewed not just in terms of providing comprehensible input, but rather as helping students enter into the kinds of authentic social discourse situations and discourse communities that they would later encounter outside the classroom. Some saw this to be achieved through various types of task-based learning, in which students engaged in authentic tasks and projects (see, for example, Breen, 1987; Candlin, 1987; Prabhu, 1987; Long & Crookes, 1992). Others emphasized content-based learning, in which students learned language and content simultaneously (e.g., Snow, 1991; Flowerdew, 1993).

In sociocognitive approaches, reading and writing came to be viewed as processes embedded in particular sociocultural contexts. Reading instruction focused not only on individual learning strategies but also on

TABLE I. PEDAGOGICAL FOCI IN STRUCTURAL, COGNITIVE,
AND SOCIOCOGNITIVE FRAMEWORKS

	Structural
Who are some key scholars?	Leonard Bloomfield, Charles Fries, Robert Lado
How is language viewed?	As an autonomous structural system.
How is language understood to develop?	Through transmission from competent users. Internalization of structures and habits through repetition and corrective feedback.
What should be fostered in students?	Mastery of a prescriptive norm, imitation of modeled discourse, with minimal errors.
How is instruction oriented?	Toward well-formed language products (spoken or written). Focus on mastery of discrete skills.
What is the primary unit of analysis?	Isolated sentences.
How are language texts (spoken or written) primarily treated?	As displays of vocabulary and grammar structures to be emulated.
Where is meaning located?	In utterances and texts (to be extracted by the listener or reader).

helping learners become part of literate communities through extensive discussion of readings and the linking of reading and writing (see, for example, Bernhardt, 1991; Eskey, 1993; Leki, 1993). Writing instruction focused not only on the development of individual strategies but also on learning appropriate ways to communicate to particular audiences. In the field of English for academic purposes, for example, there has been a shift in emphasis from expressive writing toward helping students to integrate themselves into academic discourse communities through discussion and analysis of the nature of academic writing (e.g., Swales, 1990). Literacy has been increasingly seen as a key to developing not only language knowledge but also sociocultural and intercultural competence.

Table 1 summarizes the respective instructional foci commonly associated with structural, cognitive, and sociocognitive approaches to language teaching.

Cognitive	Sociocognitive
Noam Chomsky, Stephen Krashen	Dell Hymes, M. A. K. Halliday
As a mentally constructed system.	As a social and cognitive phenomenon.
Through the operation of innate cognitive heuristics on language input.	Through social interaction and assimilation of others' speech.
Ongoing development of their inter-language. Ability to realize their individual communicative purposes.	Attention to form (including genre, register, and style variation) in contexts of real language use.
Toward cognitive processes involved in the learning and use of language. Focus on development of strategies for communication and learning.	Toward negotiation of meaning through collaborative interaction with others. Creating a discourse community with authentic commu-nicative tasks.
Sentences as well as connected discourse.	Stretches of connected discourse.
Either as "input" for unconscious processing or as objects of problem solving and hypothesis testing.	As communicative acts ("doing things with words").
In the mind of the learner (through activation of existing knowledge).	In the interaction between inter-locutors, writers and readers; con-strained by interpretive rules of the relevant discourse community.

Changing nature of computer use in language teaching

It is within this shifting context of structural, cognitive, and sociocog-nitive orientations that we can understand changes in how computers have been used in language teaching, and in particular the role of network-based language teaching today. Interestingly, shifts in perspectives on language learning and teaching have paralleled developments in tech-nology from the mainframe to the personal to the networked computer. As will be seen, they also correspond roughly to three metaphors of computer-based educational activities posited by Charles Crook (1994): namely, a tutorial metaphor (computer-as-tutor), a construction metaphor (computer-as-pupil), and a toolbox metaphor (computer-as-tool).

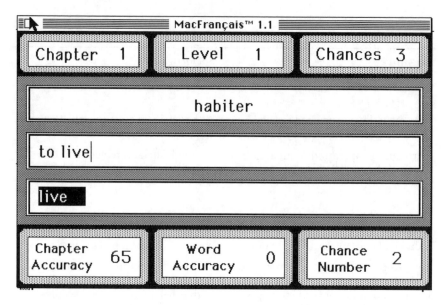

Figure 1   Screen shot from MacFrançais (Raymond, 1988).

Structural approaches to CALL

The earliest CALL programs, consisting of grammar and vocabulary tutorials, drill and practice programs, and language testing instruments, strictly followed the computer-as-tutor model. Developed originally for mainframe computers in the 1960s and 1970s, though still used in different variations today, these programs were designed to provide immediate positive or negative feedback to learners on the formal accuracy of their responses. This was consistent with the structuralist approach, which emphasized that repeated drilling on the same material was beneficial or even essential to learning.

As an example of a simple drill program, consider MacFrançais shown in Figure 1. The student selects the appropriate chapter, level, and number of desired chances. A target French word appears in the first line (here *habiter*), and the student types in a translation in line 2 ("live"). The program does not accept this answer, however, so it highlights the student's initial response in line 3, leaving line 2 blank again. The student then types in the full infinitive "to live" in line 2, which is accepted, and the prompt then changes to the next word to be tested.

Drill programs of this type generally stirred little excitement among learners and teachers, however, because they merely perpetuated existing instructional practices, albeit in a repackaged form. Moreover, until recently, these programs tended to be technically unsophisticated, generally allowing only one acceptable response per item. These factors, combined with the rejection of purely behavioristic approaches to language learning at both theoretical and pedagogical levels, as well as the development of more sophisticated personal computers, propelled CALL into its second generation.

Cognitive approaches to CALL

In line with cognitive/constructivist views of learning, the next generation of CALL programs tended to shift agency to the learner. In this model, learners construct new knowledge through exploration of what Seymour Papert has described as microworlds, which provide opportunities for problem solving and hypothesis testing, allowing learners to utilize their existing knowledge to develop new understandings. Extending a tradition of thought popularized by John Dewey and Alfred Whitehead that learning occurs through creative action, Papert (1980) and his colleagues at the MIT Media Laboratory flip the earlier *computer-as-tutor* metaphor on its head, seeing computers as things to be controlled by, rather than controlling, learners. The computer provides tools and resources, but it is up to the learner to *do* something with these in a simulated environment (e.g., in Papert's Turtle Logo program, learners program a turtle to carry out their instructions).

A more recent and sophisticated application in this tradition is the multimedia videodisc program *A la rencontre de Philippe* (Furstenberg, Murray, Malone, & Farman-Farmaian, 1993), developed by the Athena Language Learning Project at the MIT Laboratory for Advanced Technology in the Humanities. *Philippe* is a game for intermediate and advanced French learners that incorporates full-motion video, sound, graphics, and text, allowing learners to "walk around" and explore simulated environments by following street signs or floor plans, as shown in Figure 2. Filmed in Paris, the video footage creates a sense of realism, and the branching of the story lines maintains the player's interest. To help language learners understand the sometimes challenging spoken French, the program provides optional comprehension tools, such as transcriptions of all audio segments and a glossary, as well as a video album that includes samples of many of the language functions one would teach in a communicative approach such as expressing feelings, saying hello and goodbye, and using gestures appropriately. Students can easily create their own custom video albums, which they store on their own computer diskettes.[1]

---

1 Other multimedia programs using high-quality video and branching technology to create vivid microworlds for language learning include *Dans un quartier de Paris* (Furstenberg, in press), *Nouvelles dimensions* (Noblitt, 1994), and *Nuevas dimensiones* (Noblitt, Rosser, & Martínez-Lage, 1997).

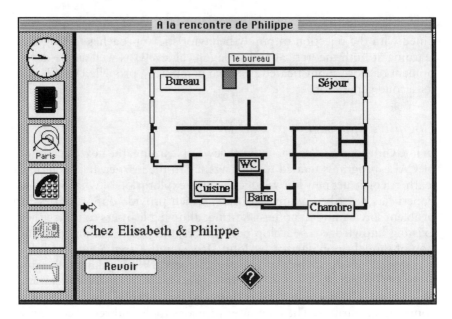

Figure 2   Screen shot from A la rencontre de Phillipe *(Furstenberg et al., 1993).*

This cognitive, constructivist generation of CALL was a significant advance over earlier tutorial and drill programs. But by the early 1990s, many educators felt that CALL was still failing to live up to its full potential (Kenning & Kenning, 1990; Pusack & Otto, 1990; Rüschoff, 1993). Critics pointed out that the computer was being used in an ad hoc and disconnected fashion and thus was "making a greater contribution to marginal rather than to central elements" of the language teaching process (Kenning & Kenning, 1990, p. 90). Moreover, as Crook (1994) points out, computer activities based on either a tutor or a pupil metaphor potentially distance the teacher from what students are doing individually and autonomously and can thus compromise the collaborative nature of classroom learning. Despite the apparent advantages of multimedia CALL, today's computer programs are not yet intelligent enough to be truly interactive. Although programs such as *Philippe* put the learner in an active stance and provide an effective illusion of communicative interaction, the learner nevertheless acts in a principally consultative mode within a closed system, and does not engage in genuine negotiation of meaning. Computer programs that are capable of evaluating the appropriateness of a user's writing or speech, diagnosing learner difficulties, and intelligently choosing among a range of communicative response options are not expected to exist for quite some time.[2] Thus, although Intelligent CALL (Underwood, 1989) may be the next and ultimate usage of computers for language learning, that phase remains a distant dream.

Sociocognitive approaches to CALL

Sociocognitive approaches to CALL shift the dynamic from learners' interaction *with* computers to interaction with other humans *via* the computer. The basis for this new approach to CALL lies in both theoretical and technological developments. Theoretically, there has been the broader emphasis on meaningful interaction in authentic discourse communities. Technologically, there has been the development of computer networking, which allows the computer to be used as a vehicle for interactive human communication.

Many uses of networked computers fit into Crook's (1994) computer-as-toolkit model. This metaphor emphasizes the role that computers can play as mediational tools that shape the ways we interact with the world (e.g., accessing and organizing information through databases, spreadsheets, and word processors). Word processors, for example, facilitate the invention, revision, and editing processes of writing, allowing quick, easy (and reversible) reshaping of text. In the 1980s, John Higgins developed a series of text reconstruction programs such as Storyboard and Double-Up, which allowed learners to manipulate texts in various ways. The purpose of these programs was to allow learners to reconstruct the original texts and, in the process, to develop their own constructions of language. Hypertextual writing assistants such as *Atajo* (Domínguez, Noblitt, & Pet, 1994) and *Système-D* (Noblitt, Pet, & Solá, 1992), and concordancers such as MicroConcord (Scott and Johns, 1993) have been valuable tools for helping learners to use language with greater lexical and syntactic appropriateness.

Computer networking allows a powerful extension of the computer-as-tool in that it now facilitates access to other people as well as to information and data. Computer networking in the language classroom stems from two important technological (and social) developments: (1) computer-mediated communication (CMC) and (2) globally linked hypertext.

CMC has existed in primitive form since the 1960s, but its use has became widespread only since the late 1980s.[3] CMC allows language

---

2 Artificial intelligence (AI) of a more modest degree does currently exist, but the cost and technical demands of implementing AI in language learning software have so far exceeded available resources.

3 For in-depth discussion of the linguistic and interactional characteristics of computer-mediated communication, as well as historical background, see Herring (1996) and Murray (1995).

learners with network access to communicate with other learners or speakers of the target language in either asynchronous (not simultaneous) or synchronous (simultaneous, in real time) modes. Through tools such as e-mail, which allows participants to compose messages whenever they choose, or Internet Relay Chat or MOOs, which allow individuals all around the world to have a simultaneous conversation by typing at their keyboards, CMC permits not only one-to-one communication but also one-to-many communication. It therefore allows a teacher or student to share a message with a small group, the whole class, a partner class, or an international discussion list involving hundreds or thousands of people. Participants can share not only brief messages but also lengthy documents, thus facilitating collaborative reading and writing.

Globally linked hypertext and hypermedia, as represented in the World Wide Web, represents a revolutionary new medium for organizing, linking, and accessing information. Among its important features are (1) informational representation through multilinear strands linked electronically, (2) integration of graphic, audio, and audiovisual information together with texts, (3) rapid global access, and (4) ease and low cost of international publication. The World Wide Web offers an abundance of informational resources whose utility for language learning is just beginning to be tapped. Using the World Wide Web, students can search through millions of files around the world within minutes to locate and access authentic materials (e.g., newspaper and magazine articles, radio broadcasts, short videos, movie reviews, book excerpts) that correspond to their own personal interests. They can also use the Web to publish their texts or multimedia materials to share with partner classes or with the general public. These features can facilitate an approach to using technology in which authentic and creative communication is integrated into all aspects of the course. Furthermore, the World Wide Web has tremendous potential for creating and providing access to multiuser, interactive multimedia environments, although so far there have been few development projects in this area (see Chun & Plass, this volume).

These new technologies do not only *serve* the new teaching/learning paradigms, they also help *shape* the new paradigms. The very existence of networked computers creates possibilities for new kinds of communication. Because these new forms of communication are now so widespread, it is imperative that language students be exposed to them in the classroom. This is particularly important in English-language teaching, because so much international on-line communication is conducted in that language, but it is likely to become increasingly important in the teaching of other languages as well, as cyberspace continues to become more multilingual. A pedagogy of networked computers must therefore take a broad view, examining not only the role of information technology in language learning but also the role of language learning in an in-

TABLE 2. THE ROLE OF CALL IN STRUCTURAL, COGNITIVE, AND SOCIOCOGNITIVE FRAMEWORKS

	Structural	*Cognitive*	*Sociocognitive*
What is the principal role of computers?	To provide unlimited drill, practice, tutorial explanation, and corrective feedback.	To provide language input and analytic and inferential tasks.	To provide alternative contexts for social interaction; to facilitate access to existing discourse communities and the creation of new ones.

formation technology society. If our goal is to help students enter into new authentic discourse communities, and if those discourse communities are increasingly located on-line, then it seems appropriate to incorporate on-line activities for their social utility as well as for their perceived particular pedagogical value.

To summarize, the computer can play multiple roles in language teaching. It originated on the mainframe as a tutor that delivers language drills or skill practice. With the advent of multimedia technology on the personal computer, it serves as a space in which to explore and creatively influence microworlds. And with the development of computer networks, it now serves as a medium of local and global communication and a source of authentic materials. This multiplicity of roles has taken CALL far beyond the early "electronic workbook" variety of software that dominated the second and foreign language marketplace for years and has opened up new avenues in foreign language teaching. These trends are summarized in Table 2.

Research on network-based language teaching

Just as the paradigms of CALL have changed, so has research on the role of computers in the language classroom. Early CALL research focused mostly on the language performance of students who had used CALL programs, attempting to determine whether those programs were superior to other methods for maximizing structural accuracy. The cognitive paradigm engendered research that looked at the development of individual processes, strategies, and competencies, using measures such as motivational surveys, observations, recordings of keystrokes, and think-aloud protocols. The sociocognitive paradigm and an emphasis on learning through computer networks have brought about a focus on the way that

TABLE 3. RESEARCH IMPLICATIONS FOR VARIOUS CALL APPROACHES

	Structural	*Cognitive*	*Sociocognitive*
Orientation	product	cognitive processes	social and cognitive processes
Methodology	quantitative: experimental-control comparisons	both quantitative and qualitative	principally qualitative: discourse analysis, analysis of sociocultural context
Principal kinds of data	quantities/frequencies of words, errors, structures	think-aloud protocols, questionnaires, computer-recorded data (e.g., keystrokes)	transcriptions of social interactions, ethnographic observations, and interviews

discourse and discourse communities develop during use of computer networks.

Table 3 summarizes the implications for research methods of the various CALL approaches. Research on network-based language teaching, while potentially spanning all of these approaches, has so far been largely limited to structural goals and methods.

Because NBLT is an emerging area, the corpus of NBLT research includes few published studies that examine in depth the development of discourse and discourse communities in on-line environments. Those studies that have been published have tended to focus on the most quantifiable and easily measured aspects of on-line communication. For example, a number of studies (e.g., Kern, 1995; Sullivan & Pratt, 1996; Warschauer, 1996) have quantitatively compared amount of participation in face-to-face and computer-assisted discussion and have found more balanced participation among students (and between students and teacher) in the computer mode. Other studies have attempted to quantify the language functions used in on-line communication, concluding to little surprise that learners use a variety of functions in computer-mediated communication (Chun, 1994; Warschauer, 1996). Researchers have also quantitatively examined the linguistic features of on-line discussion and found that it is lexically and syntactically more complex than face-to-face discussion (Warschauer, 1996). These are all examples of a product-oriented, structuralist approach to NBLT research.

This volume attempts to expand the body of NBLT research into several important areas that have been so far relatively neglected. These areas are *context, interaction,* and *multimedia networking.*

The contexts in which networked-based teaching and learning occur have not, by and large, been studied in sufficient depth. As Gee (1996) explains, discourse represents not just language but "saying(writing)-doing-being-valuing-believing combinations" (p. 127). To understand the full impact of new forms of interacting in the language classroom, we must look beyond the texts of interaction to the broader contextual dynamics that shape and are shaped by those texts. This entails holistic, qualitative research that goes beyond inventories of linguistic features and attempts to account for the way classroom cultures take shape over time. Although a number of educators have attempted to look at such phenonema, much of the published work to date in this regard has consisted of informal reports by teachers of what they have observed in their classes.

Chapters 2 and 3 of this book present descriptive studies that discuss the overall context of network-based language teaching in foreign and second language contexts. In Chapter 2, Carla Meskill and Krassimira Ranglova present research on the implementation of new technology-enhanced EFL teaching in Bulgaria. They show that the use of computer networks was part of a broader reconceptualization of the language program that resulted in a more "sociocollaborative" approach to learning. The chapter is a sterling example of the fact that technology is not just a machine, or even just the use of a machine, but rather a broad form of social organization. In Chapter 3, Mark Warschauer presents the results of an ethnographic study of four computer-intensive language and writing classes in Hawaii: two ESL classes, one indigenous language class, and one English class (in which the majority of students were second language learners). Warschauer's study shows that the particular implementation of network-based teaching is highly dependent on sociocultural context, including, but not limited to, the attitudes and beliefs of the teacher. The study also illustrates the significance of new conceptions of literacy when considering network-based teaching.

The nature of interaction has been one of the most important areas of research in second language learning (for a review, see Pica, 1994). It has been suggested that computer-mediated communication provides an ideal medium for students to benefit from interaction, because the written nature of the discussion allows greater opportunity to attend to and reflect on the form and content of the communication. Yet most of the research on the linguistic nature of CMC has focused on counting or categorizing individual students' comments rather than qualitatively analyzing how and in what ways students actually negotiate meaning with each other.

Chapters 4, 5, and 6 begin to overcome this shortcoming. In Chapter 4, Jill Pellettieri uses a framework from Gass and Varonis to examine task-based real-time computer interaction between adult learners of

Spanish. By analyzing the modifications that learners make in response to negotiation signals as well as corrective feedback, she provides evidence that computer-mediated interaction provides a useful mechanism for helping learners achieve higher levels of metalinguistic awareness. Whereas Pellettieri uses frameworks developed from oral interaction, Boyd Davis and Ralf Thiede in Chapter 5 use frameworks derived from writing research. They examine the interaction among L2 and L1 writers in asynchronous computer conferences to investigate the nature and degree of language learners' imitation and accommodation of writing styles. Their linguistic analysis indicates that L2 students shifted their style in response to L1 interlocuters.

In Chapter 6, Jean Schultz focuses not so much on the linguistic interaction itself during electronic conferencing, but rather on its results, comparing how L2 learners make use of peer editing feedback that has been provided in computer-mediated or oral discussion. The results indicate a complex interrelationship of students' level, activity, and medium, rather than a simple conclusion of superiority or inferiority for computer-mediated feedback. She concludes with thought-provoking observations regarding the differences between written and oral communication.

A final area that has been insufficiently investigated to date is the particular impact of combining a variety of media in networked-based learning. This area is so new that almost no research has yet been published. Authors in this book examine this issue from several angles: in Chapter 7, Dorothy Chun and Jan Plass examine concepts of networked multimedia in light of theory and research in second language acquisition. They then discuss criteria for the design of networked multimedia environments, illustrating with a prototype project under development based on SLA theory and research. In Chapter 8, Heidi Shetzer and Mark Warschauer return to the earlier theme of new on-line literacies, providing a theoretical framework for how literacy and communication practices change in on-line and hypertextual environments. They also provide discussion of pedagogical implications of adopting an electronic literacy approach to language teaching. In Chapter 9, Christoph Zähner, Agnès Fauverge, and Jan Wong present the results of a pilot study on the use of broadband audio- and audiovisual conferencing to help college students learn French. Their study indicates the potential of audiovisual networking for long-distance task-based learning. These three papers bring us full circle, back to the issues of context and interaction, now redefined in terms of multimedia environments.

Finally, in Chapter 10, Carol Chapelle situates the studies in this volume and previous research on network-based language teaching within the broader perspective of the history and future of how we conduct research on computer-assisted language learning.

Conclusion

Network-based language teaching does not represent a particular technique, method, or approach. It is a constellation of ways by which students communicate via computer networks and interpret and construct on-line texts and multimedia documents, all as part of a process of steadily increasing engagement in new discourse communities. How that engagement takes place depends on a number of factors, including the nature of interaction via computer, the sociocultural context that shapes that interaction, and the way that students communicate and learn in multimedia modes. We hope that the chapters in this volume provide some initial steps toward a better understanding of these issues.

References

Bernhardt, E. B. (1991). *Reading development in a second language: Theoretical, empirical, and classroom perspectives.* Norwood, NJ: Ablex.

Bloomfield, L. (1933). *Language.* New York: Holt, Rinehart & Winston.

Breen, M. P. (1987). Learner contributions to task design. In C. N. Candlin & D. Murphy (Eds.), *Lancaster practical papers in English language education,* Vol. 7, *Language learning tasks* (pp. 23–46). Englewood Cliffs, NJ: Prentice Hall.

Canale, M. (1983). From communicative competence to communicative language pedagogy. In J. C. Richards & R. W. Schmidt (Eds.), *Language and communication* (pp. 2–27). London: Longman.

Canale, M., & Swain, M. (1980). Theoretical bases of communicative approaches to second language teaching and testing. *Applied Linguistics, 1*(1), 1–47.

Candlin, C. N. (1987). Towards task-based language learning. In C. N. Candlin & D. Murphy (Eds.), *Lancaster practical papers in English language education,* Vol. 7, *Language learning tasks* (pp. 5–22). Englewood Cliffs, NJ: Prentice Hall.

Chomsky, N. (1957). *Syntactic structures.* The Hague: Mouton.

Chomsky, N. (1959). A review of B. F. Skinner's "Verbal behavior." *Language, 35*(1), 26–58.

Chomsky, N. (1965). *Aspects of the theory of syntax.* Cambridge, MA: MIT Press.

Chun, D. (1994). Using computer networking to facilitate the acquisition of interactive competence. *System, 22*(1), 17–31.

Cotton, C. (1995). Technology-mediated learning: Are we there yet? *Syllabus, 8*(9), 26–27.

Crook, C. (1994). *Computers and the collaborative experience of learning.* London: Routledge.

Domínguez, F., Noblitt, J. S., & Pet, W. A. J. (1994). *Atajo: Writing assistant for Spanish.* Boston: Heinle & Heinle.

Eskey, D. (1993). Reading and writing as both cognitive process and social behavior. In J. G. Carson & I. Leki (Eds.), *Reading in the composition classroom: Second language perspectives* (pp. 221–233). Boston: Heinle & Heinle.

Flowerdew, J. (1993). Content-based language instruction in a tertiary setting. *English for Specific Purposes, 12,* 121–138.

Furstenberg, G., Murray, J. H., Malone, S., & Farman-Farmaian, A. (1993). *A la rencontre de Philippe.* New Haven: Yale University Press.

Furstenberg, G. (in press). *Dans un quartier de Paris.* New Haven: Yale University Press.

Gee, J. P. (1996). *Social linguistics and literacies,* 2nd ed. London: Taylor & Francis.

Herring, S. C. (Ed.) (1996). *Computer-mediated communication: Linguistic, social and cross-cultural perspectives.* Amsterdam: John Benjamins.

Holquist, M. (1990). *Dialogism: Bakhtin and his world.* London: Routledge.

Hymes, D. (1971). Competence and performance in linguistic theory. In R. Huxley & E. Ingram (Eds.), *Language acquisition: Models and methods* (pp. 3–28). London: Academic Press.

Kenning, M.-M., & Kenning, M. J. (1990). *Computers and language learning: Current theory and practice.* New York: Ellis Horwood.

Kern, R. (1995). Restructuring classroom interaction with networked computers: Effects on quantity and quality of language production. *Modern Language Journal, 79,* 457–476.

Krashen, S. D. (1982). *Principles and practice in second language acquisition.* New York: Prentice Hall.

Lado, R. (1957). *Linguistics across cultures.* Ann Arbor: University of Michigan Press.

Leki, I. (1993). Reciprocal themes in ESL reading and writing. In J. G. Carson & I. Leki (Eds.), *Reading in the composition classroom: Second language perspectives* (pp. 9–32). Boston: Heinle & Heinle.

Long, M. H., & Crookes, G. (1992). Three approaches to task-based syllabus design. *TESOL Quarterly, 26*(1), 27–56.

Moulton, W. G. (1962). *The sounds of English and German.* Chicago: University of Chicago Press.

Murray, D. E. (1995). *Knowledge machines: Language and information in a technological society.* London: Longman.

Noblitt, J. S. (1994). *Nouvelles dimensions.* Boston: Heinle & Heinle.

Noblitt, J. S., Pet, W. J. A., & Solá, D. F. (1992). *Système-D: Writing assistant for French.* Boston: Heinle & Heinle.

Noblitt, J. S., Rosser, H., Martínez-Lage, A. (1997). *Nuevas dimensiones multimedia program.* Boston: Heinle & Heinle.

Nystrand, M., Greene, S., & Wiemelt, J. (1993). Where did composition studies come from?: An intellectual history. *Written Communication, 10*(3), 267–333.

Papert, S. (1980). *Mindstorms: Children, computers, and powerful ideas.* New York: Basic Books.

Pica, T. (1994). Research on negotiation: What does it reveal about second-language learning conditions, processes, and outcomes? *Language Learning, 44*(3), 493–527.

Prabhu, N. S. (1987). *Second language pedagogy.* Oxford: Oxford University Press.

Pusack, J. P., & Otto, S. K. (1990). Applying instructional technologies. *Foreign Language Annals, 23*(5), 409–417.

Raymond, P. C. (1988). *MacFrançais* (version 1.1). Midland, TX: Cletus Software.

Rüschoff, B. (1993). Language learning and information technology: State of the art. *CALICO Journal, 10*(3), 5–17.

Scott, M., & Johns, T. (1993). *MicroConcord.* Oxford: Oxford University Press.

Snow, M. A. (1991). Teaching language through content. In M. A. Snow (Ed.), *Teaching English as a second or foreign language* (pp. 315–328). Boston: Newbury House.

Stockwell, R. P., Bowen, J. D., & Martin, J. W. (1965). *The grammatical structures of English and Spanish.* Chicago: University of Chicago Press.

Sullivan, N., & Pratt, E. (1996). A comparative study of two ESL writing environments: A computer-assisted classroom and a traditional oral classroom. *System, 24*(4), 491–501.

Swales, J. M. (1990). *Genre analysis: English in academic and research settings.* Cambridge: Cambridge University Press.

Underwood, J. (1989). On the edge: Intelligent CALL in the 1990s. *Computers and the Humanities, 23*, 71–84.

Warschauer, M. (1996). Comparing face-to-face and electronic communication in the second language classroom. *CALICO Journal, 13*(2–3), 7–26.

Warschauer, M. (Ed.) (1995). *Virtual connections: Online activities and projects for networking language learners.* Honolulu: Second Language Teaching and Curriculum Center, University of Hawaii.

2 *Sociocollaborative language learning in Bulgaria*

Carla Meskill

Krassimira Ranglova

New technologies and access to them have brought a whirlwind increase in the number of available designs for learning. Such development has brought to the education sector innumerable possibilities for rethinking language and literacy and, in turn, redesigning instruction (New London Group, 1996). Consideration of potential redesigns, however, must be guided by two interdependent considerations: first, current, best instructional theory and practice; second, careful consideration of the situational variables that pertain to contexts of technology use. This chapter discusses the redesign of an English as a foreign language (EFL) curriculum at the University of Sofia, Bulgaria. Central to the rethinking and redevelopment of the resulting technologies-based curriculum was careful consideration of (1) current best language teaching practice; and (2) technologies that could be called into service of such activity.

Background

The development and implementation processes of the literature- and technologies-based curriculum in Bulgaria enjoyed an opportunity unique to former Communist-bloc countries; that is, because of imposed isolation of the academic community up until democratization in 1989, foreign language instructional practices were not influenced by the major rethinking and restructuring experienced by the international language teaching community from the 1960s to the 1980s. Consequently, up to the time of Bulgaria's reopened communications with the rest of the world, EFL curricula followed fairly closely the traditional British model, one that emphasized the study of philology, literary canon, and language appreciation. As such, the status quo did little to prepare English majors to learn and use English in productive and meaningful ways. Likewise,

This project was funded in part through a University Affiliations Grant, United States Information Agency (USIA) (#IA-ASLB-631090453). The opinions expressed herein do not necessarily reflect the position or policy of the funding agency, and no official endorsement should be inferred.

access to computers had been limited to computer-science faculty and students. EFL students, although required to spend a significant amount of time every week in an audiolingual audiotape laboratory, had no other access to technologies to support their learning.

Since the early 1990s, the English department at the University of Sofia has seen burgeoning activity on the part of faculty who have been taking advantage of access to information and professional contacts outside the country. Several initiatives, including the USIA-sponsored exchange that supported this curriculum innovation project, have worked to increase faculty opportunity for professional development as well as access to and implementation of instructional technologies. The EFL curriculum redesign project discussed in this chapter concentrated on the integration and use of technologies both as tools for teaching and learning and as a way to expand faculty understandings of current language teaching pedagogies.

Pedagogical groundings for change

Recent theoretical and pedagogical trends in the field of second language acquisition favor socially mediated forms of instructional activity over the drilling, testing, and language appreciation activities that once predominated. Active *use* of language by learners is no longer believed to be merely a venue for students to practice the syntax and vocabulary of the language they study. On the contrary, process writing, response-based reading, and the active negotiation of meaning with others are now widely considered the primary loci of syntactic development and, ultimately, overall competence in use and understanding of the target language (Wagner-Gough & Hatch, 1975; Savignon, 1983, 1991; Ellis, 1984). A language learner's engagement in meaningful, motivated communication activity using the target language is considered the best route to becoming both literate and fluent in that language (Stevik, 1980; Brown, 1994). Practice, therefore, sees student- and meaning-centered activity in motivated, content-rich environments as the best route for nonnative speakers to learn English language and literacy. The redesign of the Bulgarian EFL curriculum, therefore, was based on current sociocognitive theory and practice.

Response-based literature teaching and learning

Central to the revised EFL curriculum was a radical shift away from a curriculum that emphasized lecture and philology to a student-centered one that emphasizes the integration of the five skills as they are actively used and acquired. The organizational basis for the student-centered curriculum became the contemporary short story. A response-based approach to teaching and learning with literature formed the basis of classroom and homework activity.

The traditional role of literature in the language classroom has been as the embodiment of target language literacy and culture. Canonical works of literature from the target culture are typically read, analyzed, and explicated for purposes of appreciation with a subsidiary goal being to augment students' understanding of target language vocabulary and usage. This tradition, while certainly exposing learners to important aspects of language and culture, falls far short of contributing to the acquisition processes now widely valued as primary in the language teaching community. Literature, especially contemporary literature, has more to offer than a singular representation of the target language and culture. Indeed, it is the potential for active, critical, interpretative involvement on the part of individual students that renders literature a powerful tool for second language teaching. Moreover, just as language learning activity can no longer be confined to the study of unique interpretations, in the age of extensive global communications for which English is the lingua franca, instruction can no longer be limited to treating a single, canonical English as reflected in culturally sanctioned literary forms.

A response-based approach to literature regards learners as active meaning makers whose personal experiences affect their interpretations of the texts they read. Therefore, it advocates practice that encourages student exploration of multiple meanings and perspectives and the development of personal, defensible interpretations (Iser, 1974, 1978; Holland, 1975; Rosenblatt, 1978; Langer, 1991; Cox & Many, 1992). The processes of literary understanding are both socially and personally mediated; that is, equal value is placed on personally and socially constructed meaning derived from literary texts, with class and small-group discussion serving as a venue for presentation, expansion, and revision of personal readings. A great deal of emphasis, therefore, is on dialogic processes whereby meaning and interpretation get discovered and articulated (Miller, 1993).

In short, response-based practice views literature as a vehicle to promote critical and creative thinking through student discourse. Literature is viewed not as an embodiment of the aesthetic side of the target culture but as a springboard for learners to explore the worlds and feelings of provocative narrative art. In so doing, learners of another language are using the target language in a highly charged, extensive, and meaningful way.

Development of the revised EFL curriculum centered on contemporary U.S. and British short stories. Readings were selected based on their relevance to students' interests, the degree to which the text represented authentic use of English (especially in dialogues), and their potential for provoking personal responses (a list of the short stories selected is given in Appendix A). Active listening, speaking and pronunciation practice, process writing activities, discussion sessions, and exploratory, deductive grammar activities were built around these pieces of literature. A critical component of the curriculum's design is the additional voices of U.S. graduate students who communicate via e-mail with EFL students about the short stories on a regular basis. This ongoing transatlantic dialogue serves to support and extend the in-class discussions in Sofia.

Roles for technologies

Traditional uses of technologies – ones that adhere to a "transmission model" of teaching and learning – cast machines in the role of delivery systems for instruction; that is, audio, video, and computers are considered to be like teachers and textbooks and are used accordingly. Responsibility for a set of information and the transmission of that information is perceived as residing in the medium, with the learner cast in the role of recipient of a body of knowledge on which she is drilled and tested. In the transmission paradigm, students work independently with technologies with the goal of arriving at a specified level of mastery of a given knowledge set. This project was guided by a more recently evolved paradigm for technologies use, one that reverses the roles of learners and machines inherent in the transmission model – that is, technologies become *slaves* to student learning rather than *masters* of it (Higgins, 1988).

A technology-*mediated* model places machines within carefully crafted social contexts for learning where student-constructed knowledge is central. The role of the technology is as a tool, resource, and catalyst for socially constructed knowledge and understanding (Snyder & Palmer, 1986; Penfield, 1987; Papert, 1993). Learning is teacher-orchestrated and student-centered, with technology tools stimulating and supporting off-line thinking, discourse, and learning. Machines serve to cue, support, and encourage collaborative activity in their role as "object to think with" (Winograd & Flores, 1988). For this curriculum, technologies were enslaved to active, meaningful language learning activity.

Curricular integration

Central to the success of technologies use in second and foreign language study is how thoughtfully technologies are integrated into both the social context of learning and its content. In this case, the short story serves as the foundational content of the revised curriculum. It was around and through the selected short stories that language learning activities were conceptualized, designed, and implemented. The following sections provide illustrations of how content matter and tasks involving audiotape, computer concordancing, word processing, and telecommunications were integrated in the literature-based curriculum.

Audiotape

Tape recordings of selected dialogues and descriptive narratives from the short stories were made by U.S. students in the State University of New York at Albany graduate program in TESOL. Criteria for selecting passages to be recorded were (1) dramatic opportunity for emphasis on stress and intonation; (2) centrality to the overall ethos of the short story; and (3) degree to which the text, especially dialogue, was representative of plausible discourse in contemporary U.S. settings. These recorded texts were incorporated into the listening, speaking, and pronunciation development portion of the revised EFL curriculum. They were used on a weekly basis for whole-class listening as practice in comprehending native-speaker discourse. Learners were guided to attend to and imitate specific phonetic and prosodic features of the text. Recordings were also used as a springboard for discussing students' thoughts and responses to the characters, plot, and themes of the story under study.

Example: Students listen to a dialogue between the characters in "A Father-to-Be." They are assigned to listen for intonation patterns in the dialogue that indicate distrust and reassurances. They sketch these patterns on paper, and in turn practice their contours out loud. Subsequent discussion elicits students' perceptions of these characters' motivations and intentions.

Concordancing and style checking

An integral part of the course redesign reflects changing theory and approach as regards the role of the language learner. In the case of on-line concordancing and style checking, the student becomes a discoverer rather than a passive recipient of knowledge about the language under study. In the revised curriculum, rules, patterns, tendencies, and exceptions in English syntax and semantics are discovered and explicated by students as an important part of the learning process. A concordancing program and style checker, in conjunction with extensive English language corpora, were used by learners as a means of exploring English in use, and to formulate and test out their original hypotheses concerning English use and usage. Because the corpora (chiefly the International Computer Archive of Modern and Medieval English (ICAME) corpus) included samples of discourse from a range of English-speaking countries, registers, and environments, students could, in addition to determining rules and patterns, perform cross-dialectic research as part of their inquiry. Consequently, students came to interact actively with accessible language data, were exposed to a wide range of authentic language input, and took in as much as each considered necessary for a given query. They compared, analyzed, and readjusted their current, personally developing understandings. Questions about language use and usage grew out of short story readings and discussions. Students generated their hypotheses and researched answers collaboratively. Their responses (descriptions and explications of language in use and its rules) became part of a class-generated grammar book that would be expanded upon by first-year EFL students in subsequent semesters.

Example: In the short story "Hunters in the Snow," students came across what they had previously learned to be a stative verb but in the progressive tense ("I was seeing things in a different perspective"). Turning to the on-line corpora, they found a half-dozen additional instances of this use. From the short-story and corpora contexts, they in turn formulated and tested out their hypothesis: "see" in the progressive denotes a temporary state of understanding that differs from an earlier state. This student-initiated "discovery" was then entered into their class grammar book under special notes on the progressive tense.

Word processing

Participating students used word processing extensively. All first drafts of journal entries, essays, and grammar book entries were word processed, then revised using peers' and teachers' comments and recommendations. Word processing was also used to prepare oral presentation handouts.

Example: Students developed drafts of their weekly journal entries. These entries were composed of their personal thoughts about and reflections on the short story they were reading. Each student chose and printed out selections to share with class members. These were distributed and responded to both orally and in writing. Based on this feedback, students expanded and revised their drafts into more formal treatments of the aspect of the story they wished to develop.

E-mail collaborations

Many questions concerning the language and culture in these short stories arose out of independent reflections and classroom discussions. EFL students worked collaboratively to formalize these questions in writing to address to the class's partner group, TESOL graduate students in the United States. Limited access to telecommunications on the Sofia campus required that a secretary/correspondent be assigned by the class. This student compiled and typed in the class's questions and sent these via e-mail to students in Albany, New York. U.S. students' responses to the Bulgarians' questions were printed out, brought back to the classroom, and incorporated into literature-based discussions, the course grammar book, and students' individual writings.

Example: During one class discussion, students speculated on the significance of the Flannery O'Connor short story title, "Everything That Rises Must Converge." The group collaboratively developed working hypotheses about the meaning of this title and sent these to their e-mail partners for comment and clarification. U.S. students replied with their own interpretations. These were brought back to the EFL class for further discussion (see Appendix B for examples).

Summary of EFL curriculum redesign

Table 1 represents the revised EFL curriculum and how its approach differs from that of the traditional EFL curriculum at the University of Sofia. The technologies and assessment methods for the new curriculum also appear in the far right columns.

Evaluation of the technologies-based curriculum

Evaluation of the new curriculum has been ongoing since the mid-1990s. The "experimental" (new curriculum) classes have been team-taught by three instructors. Instructors have participated in evaluating the viability and effectiveness of the revised curriculum. Formal assessment of the processes and outcomes of the curriculum's implementation was designed to determine the following:

- How did the overall language achievement of the experimental group (those participating in the revised curriculum) compare with those being taught by traditional methods?
- How did teachers respond to the revised curriculum? Was there conceptual change on their part concerning instructional approaches to language teaching or the role technologies can play in teaching and learning?
- How did students respond to the revised curriculum? Was there conceptual change on their part concerning their roles as learners of another language?
- How did the revised curriculum and its technology tools change the nature of classroom discourse?
- What constraints (conceptual and logistic) presented themselves during the implementation of this curriculum?

TABLE 1. EFL REVISED CURRICULUM

	Traditional approach	Revised approach	Technologies	Assessment
Grammar	Lecture on form and function; textbook-based	Problem solving; discovery learning	Style checkers, concordancers; digitized corpora; e-mail	Student presentations; development of class grammar book; final exam
Listening & Speaking	Lecture/note taking; answering comprehension check questions	Recordings of short-story renditions; interaction through class discussions and collaborative tasks	Audiotape; e-mail	Involvement and performance in class discussions, tasks, writings, final exam
Writing	Write on specified topics following model compositions	Process writing based on individual responses to short stories, class discussions, and peer correspondence	Word processing; e-mail	Peer and teacher review of drafts and final essays; final exams
Reading	Read for selected work from literary cannon for comprehension and vocabulary; lectures	Read for response and developing interpretations of contemporary fiction; student-centered, response-based conversation	Print; e-mail	Involvement and performance in class discussions, tasks, writings; final exams

TABLE 2. MEAN TEST GAINS: CONTROL VS. EXPERIMENTAL

	Control n = 14	Experimental n = 14	Difference between means
Dictation	8.8571	8.7857	.0714
Listening	14.9286	14.9286	.0000
Reading and Vocabulary	19.2857	22.5000	3.2143*
Grammar	14.7857	16.4286	1.6429*
Writing	13.9286	17.7143	3.7857*

p < .05

Data used in this evaluation included pre- and postsemester test scores of students in an experimental and in a traditional program; instructor and student logs; records of e-mail interactions; completed student assignments; a survey of students; interviews with instructors and students; and open-ended questionnaires of students and teachers.

Student achievement

The University of Sofia admissions test of English, a rigorous series of proficiency measures, was used as a pre-course measure in assessing the effectiveness of the curriculum. This test, like the campus's year-end final exam, includes both traditional reading/translation portions and tests of students' communicative competence as reflected in active listening, speaking, and writing. Students with the highest scores on this test were admitted as "first-year" English majors. The group was then randomly assigned either to traditional EFL sections or to the experimental (revised curriculum). Both courses met 8 hours per week over the academic year. Both groups of students were required to take an equally comprehensive end-of-year achievement test. Summative achievement scores for both groups are composed of scores from an equally rigorous, comprehensive final exam. Pre–post gains for both groups appear in Table 2; they were compared using a two-tailed t-test, with significance level set at $p < .05$.

Although scores on the dictation and listening portions of the final examination reveal no statistically significant difference between the two groups, the other test sections – Reading and Vocabulary, Grammar, and Writing – do. Instructors from both groups reasoned that the number of audiotapes and the requirements for students to listen to these outside of class were greater for the control group. The textbook used in the traditional class had accompanying listening-comprehension tapes that were assigned weekly in the language laboratory. The experimental group's contact with the short story recordings was on a more limited basis (in the classroom) and, unlike the audiotape activity of the control group, focused more on content and discussion than on discrete listening-comprehension tasks, a form of practice more in keeping with the mode of listening comprehension that the final exam required (including dictation).

The significant gains on the part of the experimental group in reading and writing as measured by these examinations suggest that the revised curriculum helped learners develop their reading skills and expand their vocabulary a great deal. Perhaps the most noteworthy difference between the groups – scores on the grammar portion – suggest that student-centered, exploratory forms of grammar study may be more effective forms of instruction than lecture presentations. Moreover, the fact that students in the experimental group were required to *use* English – that is, to formulate and respond to meaningful utterances in realistic tasks on a continual basis – may have contributed to this notable difference in end-of-course measures of English grammar.

In terms of oral-skills assessment, both groups were evaluated as part of their final examinations. In keeping with the student-centered aspect of the revised curriculum, students assembled portfolios of their written work and prepared oral presentations of this work in lieu of the traditional oral text explication that was required for the control group.

Final course grades based on these two forms of assessment were higher for the experimental group than for the control group. However, as these forms of assessment differed in format, a direct comparison of scores is not realistic. Anecdotal reports on the part of both teams of participating teachers indicate, nevertheless, that the oral-skills performance of the experimental group was consistently superior to that of the control group.

Formative evaluation throughout the year in the form of questionnaires and class debriefing sessions consistently indicated that students and teachers in the revised curriculum sections were over time adapting well to these new forms of learning and teaching. Additionally, participating instructors maintained a log of their thoughts and observations throughout the year. The following sections outline resulting issues and responses on the part of participating teachers and students.

Teachers' responses

Implementation of the new curriculum required reconceptualization of fundamental issues and processes in learning language on the part of participating students and their instructors. Teachers and students had to, in the words of one of the participating instructors, "radically alter" their understandings of what it is to acquire another language, what that process entails, and the best route to achieving communicative competence. In practice, this represented a major change from the teacher-centered, language appreciation activity to which all were accustomed. Most notably, the revised curriculum involved new roles for the teacher. Participating teachers relinquished their traditional authority in the classroom in favor of student-centered activity. No longer in the role of lecturer, instructors developed discussion-leading skills. They took risks by assigning students to undertake work independent of their once unquestioned authority. Their commitment to a response-based approach required that they guide students to sources, rather than acting as *the* source, and that they actively participate in and support student autonomy and collaborative work.

In terms of technologies, the revised curriculum also pushed participating teachers to reconceptualize audiotape and computers as tools and resources, rather than as mechanisms that deliver instruction. The integration of e-mail collaborations with U.S. students also brought teachers to accept and value the voices of outside informants. Traditional forms of authority were relinquished on both fronts: teaching and technologies.

Instructors of the revised curriculum report that their students came to these new forms of instruction unaccustomed to independent thinking and writing. Bulgarian schools had taught them to memorize and reproduce what others think and write. They therefore came to the revised curriculum completely unaccustomed to being asked to express a personal opinion. Consequently, participating students were, according to their instructors, "in shock for some time" at the beginning of the year when asked to play a very different, active role in learning. However, instructors report that over the course of the year, participating students uniformly came to appreciate the value of independent and participatory learning.

In terms of their own adjustments, instructors report that, although initially quite difficult, relinquishing authority in favor of student-centered activity brought about such immediately discernible benefits that they fell into the new role with ease. One instructor reported that "student enthusiasm and involvement in their work was contagious, something I had never experienced as an instructor." Supporting literature-based class discussions was perceived as a relatively easy adjustment; as one instructor noted, "it was a delightful surprise to find students had so many interesting things to say when given the opportunity." Instructors reported that they were very impressed by the seriousness with which students took and completed language learning tasks and by what they felt were very substantial gains in their students' English skills over the course of the year.

Students' responses

Results from an end-of-year course questionnaire indicate that 92% of the participating students were "very enthusiastic" about the short story readings and discussions. Students reported that they found sharing their responses and interpretations "extremely helpful" in terms of motivation, confidence, and their overall English-language development. They found responding to contemporary literature a powerful opportunity to use the language productively and meaningfully and that this form of active participation, although novel at first, became a great source of motivation.

Although students uniformly reported favoring the ease of drafting, revision, and the "look" of their final work when word processed, only 73% reported that they "enjoyed" the writing portion of the curriculum. "Free" writing based on one's personal thoughts and interpretations is a very foreign concept, one with which some students apparently remained uncomfortable. Instructors speculate that these students found the lack of direct guidance (assigned topics and a structure for presentation) too challenging. Moreover, only half of the participating students responded that they found peer feedback (receiving comments on written work from classmates) helpful. This reaction also reflects a preexisting orientation and a high degree of comfort with uncritical, model-based composing.

Students in the revised course reported that doing research on the computer in collaboration with classmates did a great deal to strengthen their "confidence with communication in English" (89%). They enjoyed the autonomy they experienced in undertaking activities that led them to discover aspects of English that became part of their individual developing competence. Through problem-solving activities, they reported that they learned "how to strategize around using various sources." They also reported a great deal of satisfaction at being "directly involved and active in the learning and teaching process." Some observed that the strategies they developed through this independent work would continue to serve their English-language growth.

The first group of students to participate in the redesigned curriculum collaboratively composed the following statement regarding their experience:

At the beginning of our first year, we were quite confused as to what we were supposed to do. The methods employed in the Programme were completely new to us: no authoritarian guidance, extensive work with computer data, opportunity for individual and group research, heated discussions on contemporary short stories, writing tons of essays and getting constant feedback from colleagues by means of peer-editing and e-mail exchange with American colleagues from SUNYA [State University of New York at Albany]. Once we got used to the procedure, however, we found out how much we could profit from it.

The year ending with written and oral presentation of our work on grammar, vocabulary and literature essays, we were absolutely convinced of the necessity to adopt fully this new style of work and learning in the academic work we were to do at the University. We developed the skill to analyze linguistic data, cooperate with colleagues, and even the courage to trust our own ideas and intuitions and to test our most daring hypotheses. The new approach to

language made us aware of the idiomaticity of English; discovering colloca-
tional patterns of words gave us insight into "living" English.

Now that we have switched back to the standard course [second year], which
is based on a coursebook and aims at a rather artificial, test-oriented preparation, we find our current work completely displeasing. The challenge to discover things for ourselves is missing. Motivation to learn is missing, too. We
can now appreciate fully the advantages of the innovative programme in our
first year. We feel the new approach is best for purposes of comprehensive
language acquisition.

Classroom discourse

A major change brought about by the revised curriculum was the dynamic
of classroom processes and discourse. In the traditional curriculum, teachers ask students to read out loud and respond to single-answer information questions about course texts. The teacher does the vast majority of
the talking: directing students' attention, asking questions, explicating,
and lecturing about the English language. Activity is very much teacher-
centered, with students playing the role of passive recipients. In the revised curriculum, learners are the center of both in-class and out-of-class
activities, these being shaped in large part through their own thinking
and initiative. It is students who shape in-class literature discussions, develop research projects with the concordancers and style checkers, engage in reflective writing, develop class presentations, and write e-mail
queries and responses. In doing so, they use authentic, motivated, task-
based English. The teacher serves as moderator who unobtrusively guides
discussions and provides help when called on to do so. Participating instructors report that the amount and quality of student discourse as they
undertook these activities was "astounding." In observing this high-level
English-language activity between and among their students, instructors
themselves became motivated to "stay out of the way" and to participate
in, rather than dictate, instructional activities.

Through e-mail exchanges, U.S. students provided the Sofia classes
with cultural and language usage information not typically available in
reference books. More important, perhaps, these e-mail communications
contributed greatly to the threadedness and community flavor of the
experimental course. Communiqués provided a sense of relevance and
meaningfulness to students' work and queries by virtue of native-speaker
"voices" becoming part of class discussions and resources for independent activity (research, writing, presentations). The Bulgarian EFL students
were, for example, noted using U.S. students' responses as ammunition
in defending their own interpretations and understandings of the course
short stories.

The U.S. e-mail partners' contributions became a legitimate, integral addition to classroom discourse. The availability of these "external" experts also worked toward focusing attention away from a single authority (instructor/textbook) and, in doing so, opened up possibilities for students to be more confident of their own independent thinking. The U.S. students' contributions had a leveling effect that worked to empower the EFL learners; that is, U.S. students' responses were frequently tentative (see Appendix B). They offered what explanations they could, often with qualification. They were, therefore, to some extent engaging *with* the EFL students in discovery learning; they were modeling collaborative thinking and problem solving and native-speaker forms of discourse for this.

An earlier study on the role of student communications printouts in the response-based literature classroom pointed up the richness of this "captured dialogue" as it is used as a catalyst and support mechanism for classroom discourse (Meskill, Swan, & Frazer, 1997). Printouts of students' on-line communications are essentially "spoken" thoughts, questions, and replies that are in a static, readable form. When printouts of on-line communications were brought to literature discussions, they served as springboard, focal point, and even court of appeals.

Constraints

During the development of the revised curriculum, there was concern for the fact that both instructors and students in the new curriculum would be operating under very new and different assumptions about learning; the fact that they would be introduced to using technologies as part of the course was also of concern. These envisaged constraints figured heavily into the curriculum's design and implementation. The chief strategy in overcoming them was to emphasize learner motivation through involvement and empowerment. As discussed earlier, the strategy was successful in that both students and instructors, after some initial discomfort with these novel roles and assumptions, adapted not only well, but enthusiastically, to the learner-centered nature of the experimental course. The technologies used in the course were cast in the role of tools to support independent and collaborative work. Using audiotape and computers in this way underscored and enhanced the learner-centeredness of these students' instructional experiences and contributed a great deal to their motivation. What were considered likely constraining factors to the curriculum's implementation actually turned out to be what the course most successfully worked to change.

The constraints that did work against the implementation of the curriculum involved the technologies themselves, particularly in terms of access. First, the audiotape recordings that were made in the United

States were of too poor a quality to be used for whole-class listening as much as had been originally intended. Where the revised curriculum had planned for these audiotapes (one selection from each of the short stories) to be used on a weekly basis, some were not used at all because of inadequate fidelity. Second, although it had been anticipated that students would have regular access to e-mail on the Sofia campus, this was not, and still is not, the case. Instead of students writing individual questions to U.S. partners and carrying on "pen-pal"–type correspondences, the class as a whole submitted whole-group questions via a secretary who traveled across the city to another institution in order to send and receive e-mail communications. On the one hand, this can be interpreted as a tremendous detriment to the project; on the other, instructors report that the collaborations around composing, reading, and responding to these e-mail communications by the whole group were quite valuable. The voices and opinions of the native speakers on the subjects of everyday language and culture in this way truly became a part of the dynamic and activity of the class.

Discussion

Unlike the majority of empirical studies on technology's contribution to teaching and learning, this project enjoyed yearlong periods of implementation and data collection, rather than the "one- or two-shot deal" common to instructional technologies studies. The longitudinal, mixed-method nature of this project's evaluation is, therefore, in keeping with current calls for more extensive, comprehensive, and context-based approaches to studying computer-assisted language learning (CALL) *in use* (Crookall, Coleman, & Oxford, 1992; Chapelle, Jamieson, & Park, 1996). In addition to collecting both formative and summative data on participant reactions and English-language development, the project tracked the implementation process over a significant period of time. Of note is that, even though using the computer was very new, there was no initial wave of enthusiasm over the introduction of new technologies in the course work; in other words, there was no novelty effect. On the contrary, it was at the start of the course that students reported misgivings about the nature of the course and its tools. However, this trepidation turned to an enthusiasm that grew progressively over the course of the year. Parallel to, and not independent of, this enthusiasm was a steadily increasing sense of individual propriety and achievement on the part of participating learners. As students became increasingly confident in themselves as active users of English, so their instructors became more confident in the philosophy, methods, and technology tools of the revised curriculum.

Technology and curricular change

Outcomes of the revised curriculum consistently point to the viability of technologies as tools to support language learning goals and the socio-collaborative processes that promote them. More instructive, however, may be the role that technologies came to play in catalyzing philosophical change on the part of students and their teachers. The revised curriculum brought about fairly radical changes in participants' views of language learning and teaching. To a great extent, the technologies utilized played a key role in bringing about new ways of using and thinking about language, especially in terms of student autonomy, student-student collaboration, and teacher participation. Through literature-based and technologies-based activities involving both independent and collaborative work, students came to model back to their teachers what knowing a language means and some powerful ways to gain that knowledge. The telecommunications component in these new practices, moreover, worked to bring instructors out of the traditional role of single knower into one that places them within a wide target-language-speaking community, members of which had, in effect, "equal time" in expressing personal and collaborative understandings of the literature. The project is, therefore, an example not only of the ways in which telecommunications opens the world to teachers and students of another language but also of how the introduction of the world outside of the classroom can come to impact beliefs and practices.

Additionally, the revised curriculum has had a wider, systemic impact. Based on the "misfit" between traditional tests and testing procedures and the new curriculum, the EFL program at Sofia is redesigning tests to better reflect the ways in which English is now being learned. This is an extraordinary instance where practice is determining evaluation, rather than the widespread tradition of tests determining teaching practices.

Conclusion

The widening, practical availability of technologies in tandem with the democratization of nations around the globe suggests new possibilities on many fronts. For language education, access to people and materials through technology opens doors for teaching professionals and their students. Where learning another language was once confined to activity isolated from actual productive *use* of that language in its cultural context, new approaches to second language teaching, in conjunction with technologies called into its service, may make obsolete the traditional combination of "book learning" and the language appreciation lecture. This project demonstrates the processes and outcomes of the revised curriculum whereby learners become not only connected to the language and culture under study through telecommunications but also directly *involved* in constructing new understandings in collaboration with others. As professional educators turn to technologies as tools of their craft, reconsideration of instructional goals, roles, and processes must naturally follow. Technologies represent a prime opportunity to stimulate and support the redesign of language learning and teaching.

Appendix A: Short stories used in revised curriculum

"Shopping for One," by Anne Cassidy
"Two Kinds," by Amy Tan
"In the Hours of Darkness," by Edna O'Brien
"The Time Keeper," by Elspeth Davie
"Heat," by Joyce Carol Oates
"Thucydides," by Rachel Gould
"Hunters in the Snow," by Tobia Wolff
"Everthing That Rises Must Converge," by Flannery O'Connor
"The Girls in Their Summer Dresses," by Irwin Shaw
"A Father-to-Be," by Saul Bellow
"The Office," by Alice Munro
"Marrying the Hangman," by Sheila Weller

Appendix B: Sample e-mail dialogue

I've asked some of my brilliant and not-so-brilliant friends to give me some ideas about Flannery O'Connor's short story titled "Everything that Rises Must Converge". I'd love to say that the following came from a deep discussion with these pals. Well, not really. We didn't have a clue, but we did have a few good laughs. I do know the following: A few years before Flannery O'Connor wrote her short story, a friend, Robert Giroux, sent her a French Anthology written by Teilhard de Chardin titled "Tout ce qui monte converge". It could be that this American author didn't have any American cultural thoughts in mind and simply liked the French title, so she used it. Maybe in the next few days I can come up with something else, but I seriously doubt it.

helen

I felt compelled to do a little research for this question because I know next to nothing about Flannery O'Connor and I have never read the story "Everything That Rises Must Converge". Helen was correct: O'Connor did take the title from Pierre Teilhard de Chardin, a French Jesuit paleontologist, whom she greatly admired. In fact, although she was thrilled with this title when she found it, she became less enthused about it as time went on and left the final decision about whether or not to use it to her editor, Robert Giroux. Knowing now that the title comes from a French writer makes me skeptical about whether there is any American cultural significance attached to it. In any case, Teilhard believed in what he called the Omega Point, a "scientific explanation of human evolution" in which humans were continually evolving toward a greater "consciousness". I'm not exactly sure what this means (and neither was O'Connor by the way), but I'll give you a quote from Teilhard himself which may help explain the title: "Remain true to yourselves, but move ever upward toward greater consciousness and greater love! At the summit you will find yourselves united with all those who, from every direction, have made the same ascent. For everything that rises must converge".

Apparently, most of the stories in O'Connor's collection contain characters which are in this type of evolution toward some "supreme consciousness", or Omega Point, and perhaps this is why O'Connor chose the title she did.

Jennifer

P.S. I got my information from "Understanding Flannery O'Connor" by Margaret Earley Whitt.

What I extract from all of this is that not only is "Everything That Rises Must Converge" the title of this short story in particular, but a pervasive theme in many of her stories, as it pertains to class, generation, and race. "Rising" and "converging" takes place in all three of these domains. For example, in this short story we see the generational struggle between the mother and Julian; racial tension between the blacks and whites; and the class struggle/tension evidenced by the attitudes of whites towards blacks, and the mother's strangle hold on her "roots". But, nowhere are all three of these more beautifully illustrated than on the bus when the mother finds that she and a young black woman are donning the same exact hat: generation, class, and race rising and converging at that strategic point.

The same struggles exist in her other short stories, thus the permeating and pervasive "rising" and "converging". For example, in "Greenleaf" the struggle within a race is exhibited by jealousy toward the opportunities and upward mobility of "white trash". In "Revelation" the struggle is clear between class AND race as Mrs. Turpin declares that blacks "got to be right up there with the white folks".

So, what does any of this have to do with the question at hand? (I'm a lit. person and it's kind of nice to be in my element again . . .) Basically, given the nature of her work, and the prevalent themes and motifs, I wonder if she didn't "borrow" the expression with more in mind than we realize. I do not believe this solitary expression to be limited to this piece solely: it takes on a life of its own throughout her work. I wonder if any of you feel the same way?

In O'Connor's world of civil rights, integration, and die-hard Southern values, everything that rose did eventually converge. She poignantly transforms this world on paper by breathing her Southern-world life (and experiences) into her characters.

Maybe, maybe not??

I agree that although the story takes place in America and is written about a specific group of Americans, the theme is universal (wasn't the title taken from a French work?). If something is rising, it is overcoming. Water overcomes its physical connection to the earth by changing. "Heat" acts upon the water, exciting its molecules and it vaporizes; it undergoes a metamorphosis that changes it to vapor so that it can rise. The rising vapors converge, droplet by droplet, to form clouds. And we all know the power of clouds.

People are the same way. If you're down and low and being stepped on, you get hot, you get mad, you get courage. Your particles change, too, and you rise above what had been keeping you down. And there are others like you up in the stratosphere that have endured the same, so you bond to become stronger, wiser. I think that is why everything that rises must converge. They need to become a force to be reckoned with. They need to support one another.

–Jodie

The title refers to, like Jen and Christine said, a search for inner peace and working towards a goal. In our lives, we strive to be the best people we can be and I believe this title shows us that everything in our lives is interconnected. We cannot separate or isolate any part of our existence because anything we focus on to become successful in life, is related to our "being" as a person.

All our successes and failures in life have significance to each other and, ultimately, will all come together for us in the end.

or I could be wrong!

Mona

The only thing I can think of is to add another metaphor. When I read the words "everything that rises must converge" the image of a mountain appeared in my mind, which is logical. It may be helpful to those students trying to grasp an abstract concept that is expressed in English. The struggle, the climb, is toward the summit, the same point. We may be climbing up different parts or sides of the mountain, at different paces, in different company and with different support systems, if any, so the journey will be a different experience for each of us, but at the same time, it's the same journey. We are all headed to the same place as long as we have the strength, ability, faith and will to keep climbing. I just reached the point in thinking this through that I realized: what happens when we start reaching the top? There isn't room for all of us. Hmmm . . . Okay, how about this – we might not reach the top, certainly all of us won't, but that's not the point (no pun intended). It's the struggle, the getting there, that counts.

I hope that's relevant.

Celene

Sample questions from the EFL students

POPULAR CULTURE

What would it mean if someone said about someone else: "He is like unwashed Bela Lugosi"?

SOCIAL ISSUES

We read about contemporary American society. I hope I don't sound offensive. Excuse my ignorance! So. what about the minority problem? How do Americans feel about it? Do Americans make attempts to integrate the minorities in society?

LANGUAGE USE

Do you still use "date" in the meaning of some kind of a bloke?

References

Brown, H. (1994). *Principles of language learning and teaching.* Englewood Cliffs, NJ: Prentice Hall Regents.

Chapelle, C., Jamieson, J., & Park, Y. (1996). Second language classroom research traditions: How does CALL fit? In M. Pennington (Ed.), *The power of CALL* (pp. 33–53.) Houston, TX: Athelstan.

Cox, C., & Many, J. (1992). Stance towards a literary work: Applying the transactional theory to children's responses. *Reading Psychology, 13,* 37–72.

Crookall, D., Coleman, D., & Oxford, R. (1992). Computer-mediated language learning environments: Prolegomenon to a research framework. *Computer Assisted Language Learning, 5*(1–2), 93–120.

Ellis, R. (1984). *Classroom second language development: A study of classroom interaction and language acquisition.* Oxford: Pergamon Press.

Higgins, J. (1988). *Language, learners and computers: Human intelligence and artificial unintelligence.* London: Longman.

Holland, N. (1975). *Five readers reading.* New York: Oxford University Press.

Iser, W. (1974). *The implied reader: Patterns of communication in prose fiction from Bunyan to Beckett.* Baltimore: Johns Hopkins University Press.

Iser, W. (1978). *The act of reading.* Baltimore: Johns Hopkins University Press.

Langer, J. (1991). Discussion as exploration: Literature and the horizon of possibilities. Report Series 6.3. Albany: National Research Center on Literature Teaching and Learning, State University of New York at Albany.

Meskill, C., Swan, K., & Frazer, M. (1997). Tools for supporting response-based literature teaching and learning: A multimedia exploration of the beat generation. Report 2.29. Albany: National Research Center on Literature Teaching and Learning, State University of New York at Albany.

Miller, S. (1993). Creating change: Towards a dialogic pedagogy. Report Series 2.18. Albany: National Research Center on Literature Teaching and Learning, State University of New York at Albany.

New London Group (1996). A pedagogy of multiliteracies: Designing social futures. *Harvard Educational Review,* 66, 60–92.

Papert, S. (1993). *The children's machine: Rethinking school in the age of the computer.* New York: Basic Books.

Penfield, J. (1987). *The media: Catalysts for communicative language learning.* Reading, MA: Addison-Wesley.

Rosenblatt, L. (1978). *The reader, the text, the poem.* Carbondale: Southern Illinois University Press.

Savignon, S. (1983). *Communicative competence: Theory and classroom practice.* Reading, MA: Addison-Wesley.

Savignon, S. (1991). Communicative language teaching: The state of the art. *TESOL Quarterly,* 25, 261–277.

Snyder, T., & Palmer, J. (1986). *In search of the most amazing thing: Children, education and computers.* Reading, MA: Addison-Wesley.

Stevik, E. (1980). *Teaching languages: A way and ways.* Rowley, MA: Newbury House.

Wagner-Gough, J., & Hatch, E. (1975). The importance of input data in second language studies. *Language Learning,* 25, 997–307.

Winograd, T., & Flores, F. (1988). *Understanding computers and cognition: A new foundation for design.* Reading, MA: Addison-Wesley.

3 On-line learning in second language classrooms

An ethnographic study

Mark Warschauer

The great enthusiasm about the potential of computer networks for language learning has not yet been matched by research on what actually occurs in on-line classrooms. Much of the published literature on the topic consists of anecdotal teacher reports. The small number of systematic studies that have been published have reported on narrow slices of data, such as the outcome of particular class sessions (e.g., Kern, 1995) or students' use of particular discourse features (e.g., Chun, 1992). Yet, language learning is a complex social and cultural phenomenon, even more so when it involves new technologies that connect the classroom to the world. Short-term quantitative studies may fail to account for the complex interaction of social, cultural, and individual factors that shape the language learning experience. Researchers in education and applied linguistics are increasingly turning to interpretative qualitative approaches, such as ethnography (see, for example, the fall 1995 special issue of *TESOL Quarterly*), but thus far few ethnographic studies have been conducted on uses of technology in the language classroom.

This chapter reports on a 2-year ethnographic study of on-line learning in four college language and writing classrooms in Hawaii. I undertook the study in order to attempt to achieve a holistic, contextualized understanding of the actual implementation of on-line learning. By immersing myself over a prolonged period in the culture of the classrooms and institutions, I sought to determine "the *immediate and local meanings of actions,* as defined from the actors' point of view" (Erickson, 1986, p. 119; emphasis in original). In other words, I attempted to understand how the students and teachers themselves perceived the experiences, rather than trying to fit their behaviors or comments into predesigned research categories.

In the study, I chose classrooms that reflect the cultural and linguistic diversity of Hawaii, focusing in particular on students who could be described as struggling to achieve equal access to language and technology. The classes included (1) an undergraduate English as a second language (ESL) writing class of Pacific Island, Asian, and South American students in a small Christian college; (2) a graduate ESL writing class of Asian students in a public university; (3) a writing-intensive undergraduate

Hawaiian language class of Native Hawaiian students in a public university; and (4) an undergraduate English writing class of immigrant, international, and ethnically diverse American students at a community college. The research methods I used were similar across classes, and included longitudinal open-ended interviews with students and teachers; audio- and video-taping of class sessions; analysis of students' e-mail messages and other electronic texts; and participant observation in the classes. The nature of my participation varied; I assisted in all classes in helping the students during computer-based activities, and in the Hawaiian class I also participated as a language learner.

The entire study has been reported at monograph length elsewhere (Warschauer, 1999). In this chapter, I will summarize the main findings. These relate to (1) the effect of sociocultural context on use of technologies, (2) the importance of electronic literacies, and (3) the purpose of literacy activities.

Sociocultural context

One of the most striking findings of the study was how implementation of new technologies varied from classroom to classroom, influenced by the general institutional context and the particular beliefs of each individual teacher. This is best illustrated by briefly discussing each college and class.

ESL at Miller College[1]

Miller College is a small Christian institution tied to what might be described as a conservative, evangelical Christian church. The purpose of the college, as stated in the college catalog, is to help prepare students for a life of service to Christ and to the church. Most of the students become missionaries during or after their studies, at least for a period of time. The college has a number of strict rules of behavior controlling students' dress and moral conduct.

The teacher of the ESL class I observed, Mary Sanderson, had herself studied in another institution of the same church and was a devoted follower. She was a strict believer in order and discipline, both on campus and in class. Her general attitude toward order and discipline extended to her approach toward writing as well. For Mary, a good essay was one that included, according to one of her handouts, "an introduction of three sentences with a thesis statement at the end; 2–3 development paragraphs

---

1 All names of teachers, students, and institutions are pseudonyms unless otherwise noted.

(with 5+ sentences per paragraph) with keyword and 'most important' transitions in each paragraph; comparison transition in the body of each paragraph; and a conclusion of at least three sentences."

Mary used technology in order to help enforce an atmosphere of discipline and order in the classroom and in writing. Students had on-line quizzes that they had to complete the first 5 minutes of class to help ensure that they were not late. They used the World Wide Web, at least in the first half of the semester, not to search for information, but rather to take further grammar quizzes. They used computer-mediated communication in the classroom to share their paragraphs with their classmates so they could be checked for correct inclusion of topic sentences. They also wrote "letters" to long-distance key pals (i.e., e-mail pen pals), but these were in fact brief essays that were first corrected for a grade by the teacher, and then reedited and sent.

ESL at the University of Hawaii[2]

The University of Hawaii is a large public university with a liberal faculty and an ethnically diverse student body. The university's English Language Institute is administered by a radical Freirian educator. Most of the teachers in the institute are graduate students who are similarly interested in devolving power to students.

Luz Santos taught a graduate ESL writing course in the institute. Luz, herself a foreign student, believed that learning to write involved gaining access to new discourse communities. In her class she emphasized practices that would allow international students to critically explore ways of thinking, researching, and writing in American scholarly institutions.

Luz used electronic communication in a way that she hoped would further these goals. Students used computer-assisted discussion to share their ideas about discourse conventions in the United States, comparing, for example, notions of plagiarism in the United States and in their own countries. They wrote e-mail journals to the teacher to further explore the same topics. They joined academic listservs so as to participate in new discourse communities. They were asked to publish Web pages with their biodata and copies of a paper in order to further the process of connecting themselves to the broader academic community.

Hawaiian language at the University of Hawaii

In the third class I researched, students were learning Hawaiian, not English. Thirteen of the fourteen students in the class were of Native Hawaiian ancestry, though none grew up with anything more than a smattering

---

2 I have used the real name of the University of Hawaii throughout.

of Hawaiian. They were taking Hawaiian to fulfill the university language requirement and also to learn more about their own culture and language.

The faculty of the university's Hawaiian department consisted of politically aware Hawaiian educators and activists who were committed to revitalizing the language and securing more social, cultural, political, and economic rights for the Hawaiian people. Kapili Manaole, who taught the class I observed, was no exception. She had been involved in Hawaiian-language education for more than a decade, and her work as a language teacher was inseparable from her broader activism on behalf of Native Hawaiian rights. Kapili's political agenda extended to her use of new technologies as well. She hoped that students, by reading, writing, and communicating in Hawaiian on-line, would develop a sense that Hawaiian was a language of the future and not just of the past.

Students in the class carried out computer-assisted classroom discussion on a range of topics, some related to their personal lives and some related to cultural and political issues of importance to the Hawaiian community. They attempted an e-mail exchange with a Hawaiian class at another school in order to deepen the sense of Hawaiian community and solidarity on-line. Their final project was to carry out research reports on an aspect of Hawaiian culture and life, which they then developed into multimedia hypertexts and posted on the World Wide Web.

English at Bay College

As a large urban community college of ethnically diverse students (including a large number of immigrants), Bay College has a dual mission. On the one hand, it must prepare students of diverse academic backgrounds for transfer to the University of Hawaii; on the other hand, it must prepare large numbers of its students to enter directly into the workforce.

Joan Conners, an experienced English teacher at Bay College, used technology to try to achieve both these ends. Joan's English class included twelve immigrant or international students and six Americans (three ethnically Filipino students born in Hawaii and three white students from the U.S. mainland or Alaska). Joan believed that students' academic writing would improve through an immersion experience. In the first half of the semester, she used computer-assisted discussion almost exclusively – with very little face-to-face discussion, in order to give her students as much writing practice as possible. Students used these computer-assisted discussion sessions to tackle issues related to two academic essays that they wrote.

In the second half of the semester, the class took an even more practical turn, with students working in groups to create informational Web pages requested by community or campus organizations. Writing during this half of the semester focused to a large extent on the kind of short informational blurbs found on an organization's Web page; the purpose was not to write extended academic texts, but rather to gather information and express it in a communicative, brief style, surrounded by appropriate images and backgrounds, to effectively get across a multimedia message.

These four classes provided a powerful illustration to me that the Internet itself does not constitute a method, any more than books, or blackboards, or libraries constitute a method. Rather, each teacher shaped her teaching according to both her own beliefs *and* the more general sociocultural context. In this case, there was much overlap between the beliefs of individual teachers and the perspectives that seemed to be common in their departments and institutions. Mary Sanderson's structural approach was highly congruent with the outlook of her department, college, and church. Luz Santos's dialogical approach, which sought to involve students in critical reflection of new discourse communities, again reflected the values of the department in which she taught. Kapili Manaole's "language learning as sociopolitical act" view reflected the perspectives of her community and her department. And Joan Conners's practical approach – in which students learned to design the kinds of multimedia documents increasingly demanded in today's business world – was congruent with the vocational emphasis of the community college in which she taught.

One question that is sometimes raised is whether technology contributes to an empowering role for students or whether it serves to heighten aspects of social control (see the discussion in Warschauer & Lepeintre, 1997). This study suggests that technology can be bent to serve the particular purposes and beliefs of individual teachers and the contexts of their institutions. Critical, then, to thinking about how to use new technologies is not the particular techniques themselves, but rather the broader purposes to which they are put. A teacher who favors structuralism will use technology in a structural way. Teachers who favor constructivist or critical approaches will similarly find ways to use technology to further their ends.

Electronic literacy

In spite of the differences between the classes, there was also an important common thread: The students in these classes did not experience new technologies principally as an aid to second language learning; rather, they saw themselves as developing new literacy skills in a new medium of critical importance for their lives. The fact that they were learning these skills in a second language was to them either an expected outcome (for the ESL students, who tended to see English and computers as a natural combination) or a fortuitous turn of events (for students of Hawaiian, who had not previously learned to think of computers and Hawaiian as being linked but developed a new understanding of the relationship through the course).

In other words, students saw themselves as developing important new life skills that integrated technology and language. It was not as if "language" existed independently of the computer and the computer served as a vehicle to help them learn this autonomous language. Rather, learning to read, write, and communicate in the electronic medium was seen as valuable in its own right. I will illustrate this by looking at the three main groups of language learners in this study: international students, immigrant students, and Native Hawaiian students.

International students

Mary Sanderson's class at Miller College and Luz Santos's class at the University of Hawaii were made up of international students who were pursuing degrees in the United States but who were planning on returning to their countries. From my interviews with these students, I learned that they saw themselves as developing the skills to successfully compete in a world that they viewed as dominated by English and new technologies. These students saw technology as integral to their ability to compete in a U.S.-dominated high-tech global economy. As a female Korean student at Miller College told me, "I hated computers before, but it's either conquer or be conquered. So I wanna conquer computers rather than be conquered by them."

Prasit, a master's student from Cambodia, discussed how new technologies and English are intertwined in his country:

It's very important, because in Cambodia, if you to ask for a job at an NGO [nongovernmental organization] or somewhere else, the first thing they ask is computer skills and English speaking. They're very important for my career. . . . I like this class very much, because it use computer and make me very interested. Some time I sit in the class for one hour, and it feels like five minutes.

Prasit told me that he enjoyed the computer-based discussions in class, not so much because they improved his general language or writing skills, but rather because they helped him become more fluent in writing and communicating via computer. He said, for example, that he preferred computer-assisted discussion to oral discussion because it gave him more chances to practice and improve his typing.

Bagus, a middle-aged doctoral student from Indonesia, was similarly highly motivated to learn more about using computers. For a number of years, Bagus had worked as a professor of forestry in a small university in a provincial area of his country. He was sent to the United States by the Indonesian Ministry of Education with funding provided by the Asian Development Bank in order to assist in the development of young universities. Bagus explained to me why he felt that learning about computers was important to his task here.

We are a small university, far from Jakarta, we get very little funding from the department to attend outside seminars. Sometimes we can attend seminars in Jakarta, but only once could I attend outside the country, in the Philippines. We have a library but it needs to be improved. The computer right now is very important, you can get information from outside and I can also submit my findings or what I have done, because maybe I cannot attend seminars, because I cannot buy tickets, but by computer I can distribute the results of my research, so everybody else can know what I've done or find out.

Bagus devoted a great deal of time and energy to trying to learn about computers. He diligently copied down all computer-related instructions given in class, including those thrown out casually, and often asked that instructions be repeated. He sometimes came to my office for extra assistance or questions regarding using computers, related both to uses of the Internet and to formatting problems with his papers. He also used on-line discussion sessions to ask other students for computer-related tips, such as how to improve his typing. In spite of limited funding, he bought his own laptop computer during the semester, and by the end of the semester he was in regular e-mail contact with his colleagues in Jakarta.

Bagus and Prasit had very little previous experience with computers. Yet, even international students with more experience tended to similarly value new technology-based skills they were learning. Ping, a Chinese student majoring in political science, found and subscribed to an Internet service that sent out a weekly e-mail newsletter about events in China, which provided much more current political news than he could find in the library. Miyako, a Japanese student, subscribed to an e-mail list about Southeast Asian affairs and said that she benefited from newspaper articles from Southeast Asian countries that were regularly translated and posted there. Xiao Hui, a female graduate student in linguistics, became a real listserv enthusiast, subscribing to five lists related to her major. All these students told me in interviews of the value of learning these types of Internet-based research skills in class.

Zhong, a graduate student from China, had a lot of previous experience with both computers and the Internet, but had little knowledge of the genres of e-mail communication. During the semester, he had a major conflict when some colleagues in Sweden sent him an e-mail suggesting that they, not he, should be first author of a paper that they were writing. Zhong's first response to them was far too general and indirect for e-mail. Luz worked closely with him (via e-mail) to help him learn to write in an effective way in this medium. Zhong summarized what he learned from this intensive on-line exchange in an e-mail message to other students in the class:

1) When we communicate with somebody in English, as well as other languages, we have to understand the culture of whom you are communicating, and think according to this culture. Further, to familiar the culture other than you native culture may be more difficult than language learning itself.

2) Nowadays, INTERNET provide a great environment to communicate more frequent, wide and fast than before. During the disputation, I communicated with 14 persons, over 50 emails. Supposed without email, we would spend at least 2 months to discuss. During this two month period, both of us can complete one paper each.

Not all the international students felt unambiguously positive about the use of computers in their classes. Many of the students in Mary's class, and a couple of students in Luz's class, felt that too much time and effort was being put into technology at the expense of learning about English and writing. As a Korean student in Luz's class commented:

I think combining writing with computer is a very good idea because most papers are supposed to be written in computers, but the problem is how much emphasis is laid on the computer skills. We can learn computer skills at any time and from anyone who knows how to operate it skillfully. But not the writing skills. That's why I said to you that this class should concentrate more on the writing skills.

Just what factors seemed to contribute to positive and negative electronic literacy experiences will be discussed later on in this chapter in the section on the purpose of literacy activities.

Immigrant students

The other major group of nonnative English speakers were immigrant students, who had achieved permanent residency in the United States or were aspiring to it. These students, who in this study were all undergraduate community college students in Joan Conners's English class, were struggling with how to best work toward academic and vocational success in their adopted country. Students in this group also tended to value electronic literacies, though for somewhat different reasons.

A number of these students saw the opportunity to use and practice electronic literacy skills as a chance to overcome communication disadvantages that they might have in an English class. For example, a Chinese student named Weibing explained to me that she benefited from Joan's emphasis on computer-assisted discussion:

Last semester I took another English class with American students, and we did a lot of talk, but I didn't participate that much, because sometimes I want to say but I don't know how to say. When I talk I'm afraid that I'll make mistakes, so I don't like to talk in front of my class. I don't like that kind of pressure.

In [computer-assisted discussion], I do participate, I'm not shy about that. Sometime I just double-check before I send it. At least I have time, I can think before I write or when I write I can think, not like the way of talk, you just don't have time to think. In this class we do a lot of [computer-assisted discussion], and to help you to understand what we read, sometimes we have assignments, so it helps. Because you can get from other students, views or opinions from other students. Like when we read those textbooks, that essay is hard to read, I mean it's hard to understand so when we talk, I mean when we write, it helps to understand and get more. I like to sit there and write the opinion, not just talk, because I think that is easier for me to participate. I'm not afraid that I will make mistakes when I talk, that's the reason so I like this class.

I know American students like to participate, they like to ask questions, answer questions, but not for Chinese students, because we were trained differently, we were trained to listen, just listen.

Similarly, Japanese students working on a group project told me that they very much enjoyed being able to conduct interviews by e-mail as this helped make up for difficulties they have in listening comprehension.

Other students valued the opportunity to develop skills in nonverbal media to complement their developing skills in English. Two of the immigrant students in particular had a very strong interest in computer-assisted design and graphics, and thus relished the opportunity to be in an English class where they could learn to integrate writing and graphic work through the development of multimedia Web pages.

Native Hawaiian students

Most of the Native Hawaiian students in Kapili Manaole's class were from low socioeconomic backgrounds and similarly had little previous access to computers. A typical example is Kapua, a young woman from one of the poorer areas of the state. She had been admitted to the university through the College Opportunity Program for students from low-income areas. She had never previously used the Internet and did not have a computer at home. When I asked her if she had used a computer in high school, she took the opportunity to give me a broader view of what her high school experience was like:

In high school I don't remember even going on a computer. In elementary school, yes, but never in high school. High school was so easy, but it was like I wasn't learning anything, 'cause the teachers was like OK, do questions 1 through 10, and then turn it in at the end of the class, and that's the whole class period, you just answer questions from the book, and once a week we would do labs, but we didn't learn anything in the labs. Even English, we would just read paragraphs, like, the teacher would call like, OK Kerrie read the first paragraph, Makala read the second paragraph. And that's all we did. And we never had conversation, like OK, what'd you guys think about this? We just read. And then after we read that book, like Macbeth, we would watch the video. That's it.

She became quite excited about using new technologies in class, though, including computer-assisted discussion, e-mail, and, especially, making pages for the World Wide Web. She explained the impact that the class had on her knowledge and attitude toward using computers:

This class is very challenging, very interesting. It's really good. I think this is one of the best classes that I took, that really made me learn so much in a semester. Especially in computers. This is the first class where I used a lot of computers in the class, and I'm thinking of buying me one. I think it will be a good investment. A lot of things that it can do, like making a Web page, that was exciting, I didn't know you could take pictures with a digital camera, and e-mail, that was good too. I think it was really interesting. It just made me like the language more, using the computer you can see what other students have learned in the Hawaiian language, especially with the Web page.

I was either gonna use the rest of my money from my scholarship to fix my car or to buy a computer. And I think I would rather buy a computer, 'cause my sister and brother are in elementary and intermediate. And I think if I teach them things in the computer, 'cause right now they're just relaxing, they don't really care about school. They're not really studious in their classes, like my sister, she really doesn't care about school. I think computers can motivate them. So I think that that would be a good investment.

Next fall I'm gonna try to enter college of education. I'll try to use computers, I think it will be more exciting for kids, too, yeah, instead of those same old boring lectures and writing on the chalkboard kind of stuff. I'll teach science, I think it's interesting. Especially you find all kind of stuff to get the kids' attention, like projects and maps. Computers'll help too 'cause they'll see what other schools have done in that same project that we did.

Students had not been expecting to combine computers and Hawaiian, but all of them had been pleasantly surprised by the combination. As a male student named Kamahele told me:

It's like a double advantage for us, we're learning how to use new tools, like new technology and new tools, at the same time we're doing it in Hawaiian language, and so we get to learn two things at once. We learn new technology, and implementing it with Hawaiian language, which I think is really, really good. It looks almost as if it's a thing of the future for Hawaiian, because if you think about it, maybe there's [only] a few Hawaiian-language papers. But instead of maybe having a Hawaiian-language newspaper, you have something that might be just a little bit better, like the World Wide Web, it's like building things for all the kids who are now in immersion and even for us, someplace to go and get information, and so that's kind of neat, what we're doing, we're doing research and then finding out all that we can about a topic and then actually putting it on the World Wide Web, and then having that be useful to somebody else in the future.

The purpose of literacy activities

From the preceding discussion, we can see that students experienced the use of technologies in these classes, not as an aid for learning language or writing, but rather as an important new medium of literacy in its own right. In most cases, they saw a focus on new electronic literacies as complementing and contributing to their more general learning purposes. In other cases, they saw work on computers as taking away from the main purpose of the classes. What, then, seemed to help or hinder a positive integration of electronic literacies with the more general content material of the classes? Although there were many different contributing factors, I view them as all connected to a single overriding principle: the purpose of electronic literacy activities. In short, if students understood the purpose of the activities, found them culturally and socially relevant, and were able to use the new media in appropriate ways to strive to achieve the purpose, the activities were most successful. In situations where students did not understand the purpose, found the purpose culturally or socially irrelevant, or were instructed to use the new media in ways that were not appropriate for the purpose, the activities were less successful. A comparison of the features and results that describe the strong- and weak-purpose activities noted in this study is given in Table 1.

I will illustrate examples of these by revisiting each of the four classes. In Mary Sanderson's ESL writing class at Miller College, computer-based assignments included on-line grammar exercises, numerous typing drills (even for students who already knew how to type), small-group electronic exchange of paragraphs for correction, and submission of short e-mail letters to be corrected by the teacher before being sent to a number of different key pals. Students perceived most of this to be computer busywork with little or no relationship to their goal of becoming better writers, and they resented it. They felt overwhelmed with tedious tasks, especially during the first half of the semester. As Julie, a female student from Samoa, told me:

I think this class is called writing. Essay writing is what we should be doing, something that would help us learn how to write. Computer grammar exercises are a waste of time. The style of writing to key pals, just redoing the essays and sending them to the key pals, it's a waste of time. She doesn't see what's going on. On my essay, I always get 19 out of 20. But I fell behind because I couldn't do all those other assignments.

Students complained to me during interviews, and they resisted passively and actively in class. Facing a sullen group of students, Mary eventually put to a vote the question as to whether students even wanted to continue meeting in the computer lab. A narrow majority of students voted no. Mary moved many of the class sessions out of the computer lab

TABLE I. STRONG-PURPOSE VERSUS WEAK-PURPOSE ELECTRONIC
LITERACY ACTIVITIES

Strong-purpose activities	*Weak-purpose activities*
Conditions	
Students understand well the purpose of the activity.	Students have limited understanding of the activity's purpose.
Students find the purpose socially and culturally relevant.	Students find the purpose to have little social or cultural relevance.
Students find the electronic medium appropriate for fulfilling the purpose.	Students find the electronic medium inappropriate for fulfilling the purpose.
Students are encouraged and enabled to use the range of medium-appropriate rhetorical features to fulfill the purpose.	Students are not encouraged or enabled to use medium-appropriate rhetorical features to fulfill the purpose.
Results	
Students experience high motivation and engagement.	Students become bored or demotivated.
Students strive for excellence.	Students make minimal effort.
Students learn to communicate more effectively in a new medium.	Students learn little about the new medium.

and reorganized the class curriculum and assignments. In the second half of the semester, students were given more free rein to write to their key pals to gather information for their research papers (without being first corrected), and they were similarly taught and encouraged to use the Web for independent research. They were also allowed to develop a student-produced videotape to share with their partner class. Students' morale improved and, within certain limits, they seemed to gain more valuable research and writing skills. For example, in their last paper they integrated material from the interviews with their key pals and from the World Wide Web to compare aspects of their own and their key pal's culture. Although their papers were still somewhat stilted, the students at least had to engage in the process of gathering authentic information from different sources and attempting to put it together in a coherent framework.

In Luz's graduate ESL writing class at the University of Hawaii, students used computer-mediated communication for a number of authentic purposes. These included seeking information from listserv discussion groups and communicating by e-mail with the teacher regarding their questions and concerns about writing. Several of the students communicated quite regularly with Luz, and she was able to provide detailed feedback on their particular writings as well as on their questions about the writing process.

These computer-based activities worked well because they matched the purposes and goals of the students in the class, which were concentrated on improving their academic research and writing abilities so they could succeed in their graduate majors. However, when Luz gave computer-based assignments that did not match these goals, students similarly resisted. For example, Luz had students make their own homepages to put up on the World Wide Web. Her idea was that these could be linked to their curriculum vitae and perhaps to one or two of their writing samples, thus helping students achieve an academic presence on-line. The students were for the most part just beginning their master's studies, and they felt they had little academic profile to project. For most of the students, the assignment seemed like a detour from their academic goals, and they devoted little effort or attention to it. Here, for example, is the text of a not untypical page created by one of Luz's students:

Ping Chu Homepage

under constrcution

This forthcoming homepage is under construction. Come again. Well, I am still confused on what I can put on this homepage, and I am busy to make some changes as well, may you have any suggestions, please let me know. Any help from you would be much appreciated. E-mail address:ping@hawaii.edu

Kapili Manaole also had mixed results from her computer-mediated communication. She attempted to arrange an e-mail exchange with another class. However, the topics for the exchange, which were assigned on a weekly basis, lacked any strong focus and were not integrated with other class activities. In addition, the students at the other site seldom answered as they had little access to computer labs. As a result, for most of Kapili's students, the activity became an exercise in sending meaningless messages without much chance of response. Needless to say, they soon grew tired of it.

In contrast, Kapili developed a World Wide Web project that was thoroughly integrated into the course content and that matched well the students' overall goals for taking the class. The students, all but one of whom were Native Hawaiians, told me in their interviews that they wanted to take the class to learn about and promote their Hawaiian culture. When they started to explore the World Wide Web, they found little content about Hawaii, other than tourist sites, and virtually none of it in the Hawaiian language. They thus felt highly motivated to contribute to the development of Hawaiian-language cultural information on the Web.

In addition, Kapili encouraged students to take advantage of the full multimedia capacity of the Web in order to develop their sites. Some teachers might worry that this would detract from students' attention to texts, as they worry instead about background images and graphics. However, Kapili frequently checked the students' texts and encouraged them strongly to write to the best of their ability. Students thus devoted great amounts of attention to their texts and to the overall presentation. They spent long hours in the computer laboratory outside of class learning and practicing new skills such as photo editing and on-line layout. The students ended up producing sophisticated multimedia Web sites dealing with aspects of Hawaiian culture.

The Web assignment had an electrifying effect on the students. Almost all the students tried to take Kapili's class the following semester; several spoke of deciding to purchase computers or enroll in other computer courses. Others spoke of developing a better understanding of how Hawaiian could be connected to the present and the future, not just the past.

A 20-year-old student named Onaona provides a good example of how students responded to the assignment. Onaona had long had an interest in Hawaiian language and culture because of her family background but was having a hard time meshing her interest in Hawaiian with other interests, such as mass media. In the class, she produced an in-depth multimedia Web page about one of the last Hawaiian princesses. Through working on the project, she began to see new possibilities for combining her interests in Hawaiian and media. She decided to change her major to education so that she could become a teacher in the state's Hawaiian immersion program working with children on multimedia projects.

Finally, Joan Conners used service learning projects in order to promote an authentic purpose for students' computer-based writing. She had teams of students work with campus and community agencies to develop authentic brochures or Web pages requested by the organizations. As with the other classes, the success seemed to stem from the extent to which the students understood and internalized the purpose. For example, two students worked to develop a brochure for Bay College's Career Placement Center. However, they put very little effort into it and produced a mediocre piece of writing. When I asked one of the students about the assignment, she explained to me:

I didn't think this [brochure] is a real thing, because when I talked to [the Center director] and she said some students did a brochure before and we just leave it here and not use it, so that I realized, oh, it's not that important . . . I think because she knew that I'm a foreign student she probably didn't want to pressure me. It's like, just do your best, and no matter what kind of things will come out, we'll accept it. We will accept it, but it doesn't mean we'll use it. I don't know if they will use our brochure or not.

A contrasting situation was seen in a group of three students who developed a Web site for the Hawaii Writing Project. From the very beginning, they knew that the Web site they developed would be posted on-line, and they took their responsibility quite seriously. The group worked extremely hard to build an elaborate site with twelve separate pages. Some of the pages included material supplied by the Hawaii Writing Project director (such as the group's newsletter), and other pages were written by the students based on interviews they conducted and information they gathered. The students made a maximum effort to address the concerns and needs of the Writing Project's staff and participants as well as the interests of the readers of the Web site. For example, part of the Web site included profiles of the project's staff and board members. These profiles had been obtained through e-mail interviews. I observed the students while they were editing the profiles for the Web page. The issues they dealt with included:

- *Formality.* What level of formality was both appropriate for the Hawaii Writing Project and of interest to the readers?
- *Consistency.* How could they achieve a level of consistency among the individual profiles without straying too far from what individuals had stated in their interviews?
- *Organizational Integrity.* How could they organize and present the information so that it projected a coherent image of the organization overall and the proper relationship between its various constituents?
- *Readability.* How could they edit and present the information so that it was most accessible to the readers?

They worked closely with the director of the Hawaii Writing Project throughout this effort, showing him various drafts of the pages and making changes based on his suggestions. The end project was an attractive multipage Web site that included background information on the organization and its leaders, reports on upcoming conferences and events, an on-line copy of the group's newsletter, and links to affiliated organizations. One of the students, Anne, shared her comments with me about this service learning project:

I feel that's a great way to go, though I mean you're still learning how to write, but you're learning how to write like in the real world. You know when you go out in the business world or something, it's the same kind of thing, what we've been working on, for me anyway, making the pages and everything. Your audience is broad. You know what I mean. You have a broad audience, just like if you're working a job. You feel more responsibility than if it was just like a paper about John F. Kennedy or something [laughs]. Where's the responsibility in that? But for me I feel a responsibility to the Hawaii Writing Project, you know, 'cause that's a public service and if what I do doesn't look good then the Hawaii Writing Project doesn't look good. So it's a lot more responsibility than the regular English writing assignment. I think the responsibility of it makes you do even better work. Plus the fact that you're gonna have an audience. If you don't write well and clearly, you're gonna look like a fool, and you don't wanna look like a fool, so you're gonna do the best job you can, right?

Summary

The fact that having an authentic purpose is beneficial for learning is not a dramatic new insight. It certainly also applies to language and writing classes that are taught without computers. However, several additional twists on this point emerge from the observations above. First of all, research in both the classroom (Sandholtz, Ringstaff, & Dwyer, 1997) and the workplace (Zuboff, 1988) indicates that using computers seems to raise people's expectation that they can fully participate in and determine the shape of meaningful activity, so they are even more frustrated than usual when they are not given the opportunity. This might explain, for example, the resistance shown by students in Mary's class, who could sense the potential of computers for authentic communication but were at first denied opportunities to use them that way.

Second, it should be noted that authentic purpose generally coincides with rhetorical appropriateness. For example, many teachers enthusiastically view the Web as a chance to publish students' work but fail to give students the opportunity to develop their writings in ways appropriate for the Web medium. If this study is any indication, though, students view the Web not merely as a publishing vehicle but also as a rhetorical medium in its own right. They appropriated the task of writing for the Web best when they were encouraged and enabled to use a full range of medium-appropriate rhetorical styles incorporating texts and graphics. Similarly, e-mail has its own particular rhetorical features, and second language students can benefit from learning and practicing those features as well.

Third, although authentic communication is a necessary condition for purposeful electronic language use, it is not a sufficient condition. In this study, after some initial enthusiasm, students later tired of communicative on-line tasks that they perceived as meaningless; these tasks certainly did not bring forth the kind of effort and attention usually required for heightened learning. On the other hand, tasks that students perceived as being tied to larger, more important goals – developing academic research and writing skills, maintaining and promoting their language and culture, providing service to real organizations – did engender high motivation and serious engagement. Students paid closer attention to their language use during such tasks, and the extra effort resulted in more polished work and, one assumes, greater learning.

Fourth, the Internet appears to be a particularly important medium for fostering the exploration and expression of cultural and social identity. This has been pointed out earlier by Turkle (1995), based on her years of research on teenagers' on-line activity. Yet, although Turkle emphasized teenagers' use of anonymous chat lines to explore fantasy selves, students in these classes seemed to be developing their notion of their "real" selves (cf. Tobin & Tobin, 1997), in some cases making important life decisions based on their evolving identities. This was true in Kapili's class, where students used the World Wide Web to explore their sense of what it means to be Hawaiian, as well as in Luz's class, where several students used e-mail to explore their sense of what it means to be a graduate student.

In summary, then, for electronic learning activities to be most purposeful and effective, it would seem that they should (*a*) be learner-centered, with students having a fair amount of control over their planning and implementation, (*b*) be based on authentic communication in ways rhetorically appropriate for the medium, (*c*) be tied to making some real difference in the world or in the students' place in it, and (*d*) provide students an opportunity to explore and express their evolving identity.

Conclusion

Ethnographic research does not claim the generalizability that is often asserted of quantitative studies. Readers themselves must think about what other situation might be similar enough for some of the results of this study to be applicable. In particular, I should point out several constraints pertaining to this study. First, all the classes were of second language students, rather than foreign language students. Second, all the classes included an important focus on writing. Third, almost all the students were nonwhite language-minority students who faced some degree of marginalization from an on-line world that was launched and is still largely populated by middle-class white, native English speakers. A class, for example, of middle-class Americans studying German 1 in the U.S. Midwest, with an emphasis on oral communication skills, might face very different imperatives for on-line learning.

On the other hand, issues raised in this study – in particular the need for electronic literacy and the factors that help shape its development – will likely resonate with other classes of students confronting the power of global English, such as students in EFL, ESL, indigenous, or bilingual educational programs. By developing electronic literacy, students in these kinds of programs can learn to better participate in the English-language–dominated on-line world and also to carve out on-line space for their own language and culture. The Internet does not constitute or prescribe a particular teaching method; rather, it is an important new medium bringing together tens of millions of people throughout the world. The existence of the Internet provides the potential for purposeful, powerful use of on-line communication in language and writing classes. It is up to us to give life to that purpose and thus achieve the full potential of computer networks in second language teaching.

References

Chun, D. M. (1992). Beyond form-based drill and practice: Meaning-enhancing CALL on the Macintosh. *Foreign Language Annals, 25*(3), 255–267.

Erickson, F. (1986). Qualitative methods in research on teaching. In M. Wittrock (Ed.), *Handbook of research on teaching* (pp. 119–161). New York: Macmillan.

Kern, R. (1995). Restructuring classroom interaction with networked computers: Effects on quantity and quality of language production. *Modern Language Journal, 79,* 457–476.

Sandholtz, J. H., Ringstaff, C., & Dwyer, D. C. (1997). *Teaching with technology: Creating student-centered classrooms.* New York: Teachers College Press.

Tobin, J., & Tobin, L. (1997, July). Case studies of an adolescent girl's and an adolescent boy's lives on the Internet. Computers and Writing Conference, Honolulu.

Turkle, S. (1995). *Life on the screen: Identity in the age of the Internet.* New York: Simon & Schuster.

Warschauer, M. (1999). *Electronic literacies: Language, culture, and power in on-line education.* Mahwah, NJ: Lawrence Erlbaum Associates.

Warschauer, M., & Lepeintre, S. (1997). Freire's dream or Foucault's nightmare? Teacher-student relations on an international computer network. In R. Debski, J. Gassin, & M. Smith (Eds.), *Language learning through social computing.* Applied Linguistics of Australia Occasional Papers Number 16 (pp. 67–89). Parkville, Australia: Applied Linguistics Association of Australia.

Zuboff, S. (1988). *In the age of the smart machine: The future of work and power.* New York: Basic Books.

4 Negotiation in cyberspace

The role of chatting in the development of grammatical competence

Jill Pellettieri

Introduction

Recent technological advancements in network-based communication (NBC) hold special promise for second and foreign language teachers and learners, as they provide for connectivity between a wider range of speakers than previously believed possible. Particularly promising among the various forms of NBC are those that allow for synchronous, real-time communication, the obvious advantage being that messages are typed, sent, and received instantaneously, bringing the electronic communicative exchanges from the static to the more dynamic, and thus more closely resembling oral interaction. Communication through synchronous NBC has even been dubbed "chatting," further underscoring its resemblance to oral interaction. Because oral interaction is considered by many to be important for second language development, and because synchronous NBC, such as chatting, bears a striking resemblance to oral interaction, it seems logical to assume that language practice through NBC will reap some of the same benefits for second language development as practice through oral interaction. While interesting, this assumption is nevertheless one that has yet to be fully explored. Specifically, there is no published research that demonstrates that NBC chatting holds the same potential for the development of grammatical competence as does oral interaction. Grammatical competence is defined by Canale and Swain (1980) as the knowledge of the features and rules of the language, including the

I am extremely grateful to the following people for their assistance with this project: Adam Karp for his time and help with data collection and transcription; Cecilia Colombi and Mary Schleppegrell for their time and comments, which helped shape this chapter; Robert Blake for his help with data analysis; an anonymous reviewer for very detailed comments that also guided the focus of this chapter; Jeremy Smith for his technological assistance during the project; Janet Casaverde for useful editorial comments and suggestions on earlier versions of this chapter; and, finally, all the University of California at Davis students who generously donated their time to participate in this study. Needless to say, I alone am responsible for errors or oversights.

lexicon, the syntax, and the semantics.[1] The purpose of this chapter is therefore twofold: first, to present an analysis of nonnative speaker (NNS) discourse mediated by synchronous NBC software in an effort to specify the potential that this new form of communication holds for the development of grammatical competence in a second language; second, to demonstrate principled ways in which NBC chatting can be incorporated into the second language classroom so as to maximize this potential.

I will first examine ytalk, the particular software program used to mediate the NNS interaction; I will then review the research that motivates this investigation; finally, I will present the study along with a discussion of its findings.

Synchronous NBC through ytalk

Ytalk is a UNIX software program that allows for synchronous NBC. Unlike e-mail, where the entire discourse is composed and often edited before transmission of the message, ytalk chats occur "on the fly" and participants co-construct the discourse, much as in oral conversations. Topics can change rapidly and turn taking is not dependent on the computer processor; speakers can self-select or interrupt each other's message. This is possible because the ytalk software presents users with a split screen: In the top half they view their own messages as they type them and in the bottom half they view the replies from their interlocutors, letter by letter, as they are typed. This feature distinguishes ytalk from Daedalus InterChange, an NBC software program commonly used in language classrooms, because in InterChange users view only the final version of their partners' composed utterances. Because of these specific features of ytalk, it more closely resembles oral conversation than other NBC software programs and thus is an ideal tool to study synchronous NBC's potential role in the development of grammatical competence.

Research background

Oral interaction and the negotiation of meaning

One of the reasons that oral interaction is claimed to be beneficial to language development is that it fosters the negotiation of meaning. Through negotiation, interlocutors work cooperatively to zero in on and resolve problem spots in the discourse in order to successfully convey meaning. From this discourse objective of maintaining the flow of conversation

---

1 Canale (1983) notes that grammatical competence "focuses directly on the knowledge and skill required to understand and express accurately the literal meaning of utterances" (p. 7).

come dual benefits for the development of grammatical competence: Negotiation provides enhanced target-language (TL) input, as messages become more comprehensible, and perhaps equally as important, negotiation fosters modified TL output, as learners push their L2 abilities to their linguistic limits in trying to more precisely convey their messages.

With regard to input, numerous studies of nonnative speaker oral interaction have demonstrated that, through careful and often labored negotiation of meaning, learners have access to both linguistically modified input (including grammatical simplifications and repetition) and interactionally modified input (including comprehension checks, clarification requests, and recasts), both of which serve to make the TL input in conversation more comprehensible (Long, 1981, 1985; Varonis & Gass, 1985; Pica, Young, & Doughty, 1987). Comprehensible input has long been argued necessary for the development of grammatical competence, for some scholars (Krashen, 1985; Schwartz, 1993), because it triggers internal, perhaps innate, processes of language acquisition, and for others (Gass & Varonis, 1994; Pica, 1994; Long, 1996) because comprehensibility makes TL forms and structures more transparent, in which case learners' attention may be more easily drawn to them. Attention to L2 form, as I will discuss shortly, has been claimed to be necessary for the restructuring of the interlanguage grammar.

Turning to the issue of output, two aspects of interaction have been demonstrated to foster modified learner language, which in turn can be beneficial to grammatical development. First, there is form-focused negotiation work. Indeed, language production itself can push learners from the more semantic type of language processing required for comprehension to a more syntactic processing (Swain, 1985, 1995; Swain & Lapkin, 1995), but because through negotiation, interlocutors can zero in on the exact source of the communicative problem they are trying to resolve, and because often at the root of the problem is some aspect of the L2 form, be it lexical, syntactic, or semantic, L2 learners are even more likely to notice the problem and attend to these very aspects of form in their output while negotiating meaning (Varonis & Gass, 1985; Gass & Varonis, 1989; Pica, Kanagy, & Falodun, 1993; Call & Sotillo, 1995; Swain & Lapkin, 1995). This type of selective attention to form within the context of meaning creation has been claimed to be necessary for grammatical development in a second language (Schmidt, 1990; Spada & Lightbown, 1993; Gass & Varonis, 1994; Long, 1996).[2]

A second feature of interaction that leads to modified output is corrective feedback. Such feedback serves to temporarily shift attention to form by leading learners to carry out a cognitive comparison between

---

2 Long contrasts this notion, focus on form, with focus on forms, where attention is brought to numerous linguistic forms outside of a meaningful context, much like what might occur in the more traditional grammar-based language courses.

their interlanguage utterance and the L2 form offered (Tomasello & Herron, 1988, 1989). Corrective feedback can be explicit, where an overt indication of nontarget usage is made to the learner, but it can also be implicit, where, through negotiation strategies such as recasting, learners are offered a replay of their original utterance with the target form supplied in place of the original nontarget form. For example, if a learner of English says, "I live San Francisco," and the conversant responds, "No, you should say you live *in* San Francisco," that is explicit feedback. If the conversant instead responds, "Where do you live in San Francisco?" that is a recast and is an example of implicit feedback. Current research has shown that during negotiation learners are provided corrective feedback of both types and that both lead the L2 learners to incorporate TL forms into subsequent output (Gass & Varonis, 1989; Oliver, 1995).[3] Overwhelmingly, the research on NNS interaction suggests that, whether through interactional moves or more directly through corrective feedback, the negotiation of meaning pushes learners' L2 abilities and produces interactionally modified or "pushed" output. Modified output of this type is claimed not only to aid in the consolidation of existing linguistic knowledge, that is, increased control over a form or structure (Nobuyoshi & Ellis, 1993; Swain & Lapkin, 1995), but also to lead to the internalization of new linguistic forms and structures (Pica, Holliday, Lewis, & Morgenthaler, 1989; Gass & Varonis, 1994; Swain & Lapkin, 1995).

We therefore have the logical connection between the negotiation of meaning in oral interaction and the development of grammatical competence: Through the process of negotiation, learners are exposed to optimal input conditions (i.e., interactionally modified and comprehensible input) as well as optimal output conditions (i.e., modified or "pushed" output produced in the context of meaning construction). Both comprehensible input and pushed output have been claimed to be, at the very least, facilitative, if not necessary for the development of grammatical competence. This being the link between negotiation and the development of grammatical competence in oral interaction, it is indeed important to determine to what extent learners involved in NBC chats can negotiate meaning the way we know they do in oral communication.

NBC *chatting and virtual classroom language learners*

Overwhelmingly, classroom research on NBC chatting has demonstrated that learners accept this new medium as a valid means of communication. In fact, these studies show that, during NBC chats, learners report reduced anxiety about participating and increased motivation for using the target language, both of which result in greater quantities of target

---

3 The role of corrective feedback in language acquisition is a controversial one, but a discussion of this issue is beyond the scope of this paper. The interested reader is advised to see Schachter (1991) and Ellis (1994) for background.

language production (Bump, 1990; Beauvois, 1992; Chun, 1994; Kern, 1995; Oliva & Pollastrini, 1995). Current research also indicates that chatting can foster the development of sociolinguistic and interactive competence. For example, Chun (1994), investigating the language production of first- and second-semester learners of German during 15–20-minute chats about current topics of importance, found that learners produced a wide range of discourse structures and speech acts: Students greeted each other, asked and answered questions of each other, initiated topic changes, and expanded on topics. Chun also notes that students involved in electronic discussions took an active role in discourse management. Kern (1995) too reports that students in electronic discussions used a wide variety of discourse structures and notes that this variety was greater in the electronic discussions than in the oral discussions.

However, although many studies of synchronous NBC, such as those just mentioned, have offered valuable insight into how NBC chatting leads to quantitatively and qualitatively more target language production, few have addressed the issue of the role that this increased production might play in the development of grammatical competence. For example, Beauvois (1992), examining the production of Portuguese language learners in synchronous chats, reported that students were actively involved in the discussions and that their responses to each other "show that students understood what was said and [wanted] to reply" (p. 460). Nevertheless, she does not discuss or demonstrate how this understanding was brought about by learner interaction. In one of the transcripts she presents, a student emphatically asks for help with a phrase that had presumably been used in the previous discourse (Beauvois notes that her message was "sent in desperation after several attempts to get a response" [p. 458]), yet no one in the subsequent eight turns answers this call for help. Beauvois's paper does not include a transcript of the entire conversation, so we do not know if perhaps later this student's call for help was answered. Similarly, Chun (1994) offers a list of modificational interactions that learners produced during NBC chats, such as clarification and confirmation requests ("I don't understand," "Is that a question?" etc.); she also lists examples of what she terms "feedback," responses that learners used after receiving clarification ("thank you," "yes, you're right," etc.). Again, however, it is not clear how these discourse structures came together in interaction to facilitate mutual comprehension and foster modified output among the learners.

Kern (1995) is one of the few studies of NBC chatting that does address the issue of grammatical competence. In his comparison of target language produced by the same group of students during oral and electronic class discussions, he found that the increase in target language production during the electronic chats was accompanied by a greater number and wider variety of verb forms and clause types. However, he observes that this increase in language production might have come at the expense of grammatical accuracy. Kern states that "discourse mediated by networked computers bears linguistic consequences . . . details fall by the wayside: Orthographic accents are often missing, verb conjugations are simplified" (p. 459). Noting that, in NBC, learners are exposed to "defective" language, he suggests that "formal accuracy is not a goal well served by *InterChange* [the software for synchronous interaction used in his study]" (p. 470). I believe that this judgment is premature, especially because to my knowledge, no published research on synchronous NBC has yet focused on the role of the negotiation of meaning, in terms of either modified input or modified output.

The paucity of research on negotiated interaction in synchronous NBC is certainly *not* the result of a lack of potential for this kind of interaction to occur in NBC chats. If there has been a scarcity of negotiation work in electronic discussions, it is most likely because of other factors, such as the nature of the tasks in which language learners have been involved. Many of the studies of network-based interaction report on activities in which large groups of students discuss their opinions about current affairs, world politics, or even upcoming class assignments – in short, conversation-type activities. However, research by Crookes and Roulon (1985), Brock, Crookes, Day, and Long (1986); and Pica et al. (1989) has proven that the interactional structure of NNS conversations is both quantitatively and qualitatively affected by the type of task in which the learners are involved: the negotiation of meaning and the resultant learner modifications are much more prevalent in goal-oriented, task-based interaction than in casual conversation. Furthermore, current research suggests that negotiation will have a stronger effect on grammatical accuracy when the task demands rest crucially on the correct interpretation or usage of the target language (Loschky & Bley-Vroman, 1993).

Research questions

This chapter reports on a study of nonnative speaker chats mediated by ytalk designed to investigate the potential of task-based NBC to foster the negotiation of meaning and form-focused interaction and thus to be beneficial for the development of grammatical competence. The following research questions were asked: (*a*) Does the negotiation of meaning occur in task-based synchronous NBC as we know it does in oral interaction? (*b*) Do the negotiations facilitate mutual comprehension? (*c*) Do the negotiations push learners to output modifications that are both meaning- and form-focused? (*d*) Do the negotiated interactions foster the provision of corrective feedback and the incorporation of target-like forms into subsequent turns?

Methods

Subjects

Twenty students (eleven females and nine males) from the undergraduate Spanish program at the University of California at Davis volunteered to participate in this study in lieu of fulfilling their normal language lab requirement for the quarter. All participants were native speakers of American English and intermediate-level classroom learners of Spanish. Subjects were paired according to their schedule availability, which led to seven mixed dyads and three same-sex dyads (two female and one male). To ensure that all learners would feel comfortable using the computers, practice sessions were conducted before data collection began.

Tasks

During one university quarter, students participated in five communication tasks, which ranged in type from focused open conversation, in which students had a specific topic to discuss, to more closed tasks, such as jigsaw-type activities. Two of the tasks (3 and 5) included a subtask, in which learners were asked to jointly compose, on-line, a short piece of discourse based on the information they shared during the task. Table 1 presents a detailed description of each task.

PROCEDURES

Each dyad met once a week to complete a specific language task; dyad composition did not change throughout the study. Before beginning each session, instructions for that week's task were explained to help ensure clarity of the task directions. Additionally, students were reminded to use only Spanish in their chats. Participants were visually separated, and they carried out the language tasks using ytalk, a UNIX program that provides for synchronous computer interaction. The NCSA Telnet program was used to capture the transcripts of the language data produced during each task. This program records all keystrokes made by the participants including backspacing; the transcripts therefore display learner utterances as well as self-corrections.

Analysis

The purpose of this analysis of learner chats is mainly descriptive and concentrates on two general aspects: the nature of the negotiation routines themselves and linguistic modifications made during these negotiations. Based on the model for NNS negotiation established by Varonis and Gass

TABLE I. TASK DESCRIPTIONS

	Task instructions given to participants	*Outcome options*
Task 1	It is spring and you and your current roommate (your partner) are looking for a third roommate to share a place for next year. Which of the following list of characteristics do you consider important in your future roommate?	Multiple outcomes possible
	You have a list of three qualities, and your partner has a list of three different qualities. Your task is to share with your partner your list of characteristics and for your partner to do the same with his or her list. Together you will complete the following tasks: 1. Share and discuss each of your three qualities listed, in Spanish of course! 2. Together, decide which of these six qualities are the most important in your future roommate, and rank these qualities in order of their importance to you, from most important to least important. You may add additional qualities, but you may not omit any of the qualities on either of your lists. 3. Be sure to discuss why each of these qualities is more or less important in your search for the future roommate.	
	Average time on task: 20 minutes	
Task 2	Of the following eight pictures, your partner has five that are different from yours. These differences may be slight, or they may be more obvious. Describe your pictures with your partner and determine which are the same and which are different. For those that are different, determine what the difference is. Remember to discuss these pictures only in Spanish.	One outcome possible
	Average time on task: 30 minutes	
Task 3	In Task 1, you and your partner discussed finding a roommate for next year. Pretend now that it is well into the fall quarter and, in spite of your careful planning, you have ended up with the world's worst roommate. Both you and your partner have caught this roommate doing all kinds of horrible things, and now you want your roommate out of your house. This roommate is so horrible that you don't even want to talk to him, so you decide that you are going to leave him a note and tell him the reasons you want him to move out. You and your partner have exactly five pictures of horrible or intolerable things that you have caught this roommate	One outcome possible

TABLE I. (cont.)

	Task instructions given to participants	Outcome options
	doing. Of these five things, both of you have caught him doing exactly three. Describe each of your pictures to your partner so that you can figure out which three things you have both caught your roommate doing.	
Subtask	Once you agree on these three things, compose together on-line the note to your roommate telling him that you want him to move out and why. Of course, you will tell him the three things you both caught him doing.	Multiple outcomes possible
	Average time on task: 30 minutes	
Task 4	For each number, you have two pictures and your partner has two different pictures. Three of the pictures have something in common, and one of the pictures does not fit within that classification, category, or relation. Describe your pictures to your partner and try to figure out which of the four pictures does not fit with the rest and why.	Multiple outcomes possible
	Average time on task: 30 minutes	
Task 5	Calvin's mother asked you to baby-sit her precious son. You had an eventful day with Calvin, and now his mother has returned and wants to know what Calvin did today. You and your partner have different pictures depicting a story of what Calvin did while his mother was away. Discuss your pictures and determine what Calvin did.	Multiple outcomes possible
Subtask	Then, together with your on-line partner, compose the story that your collective set of pictures tells.	Multiple outcomes possible
	Average time on task: 20 minutes	

(1985), negotiation routines are defined as those exchanges that "push down" the participants from the main line of discourse and in which there is some overt indication of the need for negotiation (e.g., echo questions, clarification requests, explicit statements of misunderstanding, inappropriate responses). In accordance with this model, negotiation routines were identified by means of their four main components: *triggers,* which spur the negotiation routines; *signals,* the indicators of communication

Example 1. Negotiated modification (modification underlined)

1	L:	La semana pasada nosotros	L:	*Last week we started to notice*
2		empezamos a darse cuenta que		*that there are many things in*
3		hay muchas cosas en nuestra		*our house that are not there.*
4		casa que no estan alli.		
5	E:	umm ... uno minuto ... darse	E:	*umm . . . one minute . . . notice*
6		cuenta?		(inf + reflx pronoun 3rd person)?
7	L:	cuando nosotros descubrimos.	L:	*when we discover. realize*
8		realizar		
9	E:	bueno entiendo bien	E:	*good, I understand well*
10	L:	si pero la palabra no es realizar.	L:	*yes, but the word isn't realize.*
11		Y actualmente yo pienso que es		*And actually, I think it is* <u>notice</u>
12		<u>darnos cuenta</u>		(inf + reflx 1st person pl)
13	E:	bien	E:	*OK*

trouble or nonunderstanding; *responses,* which respond to the signals; and, optionally, a *reaction to the response.* This final component serves as a cue that participants are ready to "pop up" to the main line of discourse. To investigate the nature and range of linguistic problems that spurred the negotiations, *triggers* were classified according to their type. Three main categories were identified in the data: lexical and/or semantic triggers, morphosyntactic triggers, and content triggers. Routines with lexical/semantic or morphosyntactic triggers are those in which the communicative problem is directly attributable to a particular lexical or morphosyntactic item or items. In contrast, content triggers are those where a speaker's entire message is problematic.[4]

The analysis of output focuses on lexical, morphosyntactic, and semantic modifications and distinguishes between negotiated modifications and incorporations. Negotiated modifications, as Example 1 demonstrates, are those changes that learners make to their utterances in response to a partner's negotiation signal of communication trouble (echo question, clarification request, etc.).[5]

To investigate the effect that negotiated modifications had on the quality of the learner output, negotiation *triggers* containing nontarget forms were calculated. The *responses* of these routines were then analyzed, first with respect to whether a modification had been made, second for the

---

4 A second trained coder assisted in the identification of the negotiation routines and the coding of the trigger types; a 95% agreement rating was achieved for the identification of the routines themselves, and a 100% agreement rating was achieved for the coding of the trigger types.

5 Student transcripts are presented verbatim without any correction. Accents, tildes, and umlauts were not available with our ytalk software and are thus absent from these transcripts. Glosses are provided as a convenience to the reader but do not fully reflect the richness of the interlanguage.

Example 2. Explicit corrective feedback
A. (lexical)

1	A:	...tengo un tendron y un pez	A: . . . I have a "tendron" and a fish
2	G:	QUE (emphasis G's) es un	G: WHAT is a "tendron"?
3		tendron?	
4	A:	lo siento, es tendron, no?	A: I'm sorry, it's "tendron," isn't it?
5	G:	<u>El nombre es tiburon no?</u> Pero	G: <u>*The name is a shark, isn't it?*</u>
6		entonces los animales son el	*But then the animals are the*
7		caballo y el gato.	*horse and the cat.*
8	A:	Es posible que el tiburon no es	A: *It's possible that the shark isn't*
9		en el grupo, porque los otros	*in the group, because the others*
10		son cosas que pueden vivir en	*are things that can live in a*
11		una casa con gente, sabes?	*house with people, you know?*

B. (semantic)

1	M:	...Las otras cosas son cosas que	M: . . . The other things are things
2		puede usar en la clase. Si?	that can be used in the class. Right?
3	J:	si, <u>pero no puede usar la nina en</u>	J: yes, <u>*but you can't use the girl in*</u>
4		<u>una clase. todos son cosas que</u>	<u>*a class. they're all things that*</u>
5		<u>estan en la clase, si?</u>	<u>*are in the class, right?*</u>
6	M:	Si – es mejor.	M: Yes – that's better.

type of modification made (i.e., lexical, morphosyntactic, or semantic), and third for the direction of the modification (i.e., toward the target language or not).

In contrast to negotiated modifications, incorporation involves using a model form offered to the learner through corrective feedback from a partner. For the analysis of incorporations, corrective feedback was identified and classified as being either explicit or implicit. Explicit corrective feedback refers to those utterances in which a speaker overtly indicates a problem with a partner's utterance and offers a model form. Implicit corrective feedback, on the other hand, refers to those negotiation moves (i.e., recasts) that provide a model form for a partner's nontarget form in the previous utterance, without overtly indicating a problem. Examples 2 and 3 demonstrate the difference between these two types of feedback.

Instances of corrective feedback were tallied and evaluated for linguistic type (lexical, morphosyntactic, semantic) and for quality (target-like or not). Likewise, the total instances of incorporation of both target-like and nontarget-like feedback were tallied. However, following Oliver (1995), in calculating the incorporation rate, a consideration was made for whether or not the learner had the opportunity to incorporate the feedback. Often, feedback was given as only a part of the conversational turn, and after making the correction the speaker would continue with a

Example 3. Implicit corrective feedback

A. (syntactic)

1	E:	...si, yo pienso, cosas para ayudan	E:	. . . yes, I think, things for helping
2		el aprendier... yo no se.		the learning . . . I don't know.
3	L:	cosas que ayudan a aprender	L:	things that help you to learn
4	E:	si, lo siento.	E:	yes, I'm sorry.

B. (lexical)

1	C:	...tengo dos picturas de pies? los	C:	. . . I have two pictures of feet?
2		animales que son en el mar. uno		the animals that are in the sea.
3		es un pie que tu tienes a su casa y		one is a foot that you have at
4		el otro es un grande pie, uno		your house and the other is a big
5		como en el pelicula "jaws"		foot, one like in the movie "jaws"
6	G:	El caballo y el gato y la pez	G:	The horse and the cat and the
7		pequena son juntos porque son		little fish are together because
8		animales que son personas.		they are animals that are people.
9	C:	si, gracias para la palabra. no es	C:	yes, thanks for the word. it isn't
10		pie, es pez!		"foot," it's "fish"!

new discourse topic making incorporation difficult if not disruptive to conversation.[6]

Results and discussion

NBC *and the negotiation of meaning*

In response to the first research question, the language data generated across all five tasks confirm NBC's potential for fostering the negotiation of meaning in task-based interaction. When communication trouble arose, learners negotiated to resolve the problem, and their patterns of interaction look much like those seen in NNS oral conversation. Table 2 displays the variety of *trigger* types (in percentage) found per task, and demonstrates that learners negotiated over all aspects of the discourse, including both meaning and form.

These results corroborate the findings from studies of oral interaction, which report that a great majority of negotiations are triggered by lexical items and the overall content of utterances (Brock et al., 1986; Sato, 1986; Pica, 1994). Learners pop down from the main line of discourse to negotiate problem spots in the communication, and, as Brock et al. argue, the morphosyntax carries a relatively low communicative load and

---

6 A second person was trained and coded a 40% sample of the data. The following agreement percentages were achieved: (*a*) negotiated modifications versus incorporations, 96%; (*b*) explicit versus implicit corrective feedback, 100%; (*c*) linguistic type, 95%; (*d*) direction/quality of the modifications, 100%.

TABLE 2. PERCENTAGE OF TRIGGER TYPES PER TASK

Task	# of triggers per task	Lexical, %	Morphosyntactic, %	Content, %
1	21	71	5	24
2	41	46	0	54
3	18	61	22	17
4	23	57	4	39
5	19	63	16	21

thus understandably triggers fewer instances of negotiation. Interestingly however, in the present data, although overall the percentages of morphosyntactic triggers were low, Tasks 3 and 5 produced higher percentages of morphosyntactic negotiations than Tasks 1, 2, and 4. Current research indicates that task type can affect the amount of morphosyntactic negotiations produced in interaction (Loschky & Bley-Vroman, 1993), so this increase likely resulted from the fact that these tasks included a more form-focused subcomponent. In both tasks, learners were asked to first share information they each held, and then to jointly compose, on-line, a piece of discourse based on this shared information. In the case of Task 3, it was a short note for their roommate explaining why they want him to move out; in Task 5 it was the narration depicted in their respective comic frames. Transcripts of these tasks reveal that the majority of the morphosyntactic negotiation routines were in response to language produced during the composition of the on-line note and narrative, which suggests that the composed piece of discourse served as a product of language upon which the learners could then consciously reflect. Crucially, however, these negotiations over morphosyntactic form were not devoid of context; rather, they occurred as a natural part of the task context and served to assure learners that the form of the language produced would reflect what they meant to say. Learners were therefore focused on form in a meaningful context, something that has been claimed beneficial to interlanguage development (Long, 1996).

Moving from the types of communicative problems which triggered negotiation to the ways in which these problems were *signaled*, the data demonstrate that, just as in oral interaction, the need to negotiate was signaled in NBC chats by means of clarification requests, confirmation checks, echo questions, explicit statements of nonunderstanding, and even inappropriate responses. Example 4 displays some of the variety of *signals* found in the data.

In Examples 4a and b, L is trying talk about a cigarette, but because

Example 4. Types of negotiation signals (signals underlined)

a. explicit state- ment of non- understanding	1 2 3	L:	Si, la cosa que muchas personas tienen en sus bocas	L:	*Yes, the thing many* *people have in their* *mouths*
b. echo question	4 5 6	E:	<u>no entiendo.</u> <u>Una</u> <u>cosa que muchas</u> <u>personas tiene?</u>	E:	<u>*I don't understand.*</u> <u>*A*</u> <u>*thing many people*</u> <u>*have?*</u>
c. inappropriate response	1 2 3 4 5 6	R:	Creo que necesitamos cuatro relaciones distintos. Cada numero tiene un relacion diferente. Crees esto?	R:	*I think we need four* *different relations.* *Each number has a* *different relation. You* *think so?*
	7 8 9 10	G:	<u>Si, yo creo que mi</u> <u>segundo par de</u> <u>dibujos estan los</u> <u>animales.</u> Te acuerdas?	G:	<u>*Yes, I think my second*</u> <u>*pair of pictures are*</u> <u>*animals.*</u> *Do you* *agree?*
	11 12 13 14	R:	...Todos son animales, pero uno debe ser diferente. comprendes ahora?	R:	*...They're all animals,* *but one should be* *different. Do you* *you understand now?*

she does not know the word, she describes it (lines 1–3). The content of this description *triggers* the need for negotiation for E, who *signals* with an explicit statement of nonunderstanding (*no entiendo*) in line 4, followed by an echo question. Example 4c displays the second part of a negotiation over task directions, where G is uncertain about what to do. In lines 1– 6 of Example 4c, R again explains to G that they are to find one relationship among pictures in each set (see Table 1, Task 2 for task description). However, G responds by stating a relationship among just his two pictures, without considering R's pictures or which one is the odd one out (lines 7–10). R interprets G's inappropriate *response* as a *signal* for further negotiation, and in lines 11–14, she explains the task once again. As noted by Varonis and Gass (1985), in oral interaction the lack of a response can also serve as a *trigger*. In our data, a lack of a timely response prompted comments such as *hola* (hello), *estás?* (are you there?); it is unclear however whether the learners interpreted this short silence as an indication of nonunderstanding or as a technical problem.

Signals for negotiation brought about *responses* in which the original input was modified by repetition, paraphrase, and elaboration. Example 5 displays the variety of responses found in the data.

The final, and optional, component of the negotiation model is a *reaction to a response*. In the present data, this took the form of an indication of comprehension, such as *si entiendo* (yes, I understand), ok, *bien*

Example 5. Types of responses (responses underlined)

a. repetition	1	E:	quieres una companera	E:	*do you want a female*
	2		o un companero?		*roommate or a male roommate?*
	3	L:	que es companera?	L:	*what is "female*
	4		una persona en el		*roommate"? a person*
	5		mismo cuarto?		*in the same room?*
	6	E:	si una companera	E:	*yes a female roommate*

b. paraphrase	1	G:	...tengo una cosa poca	G:	*. . . I have a thing a little*
	2		similar. Es un circulo,		*similar. It's a circle,*
	3		con cinco circulos...		*with five circles . . .*
	4		entiendes?		*do you understand?*
	5	C:	los circulos, no entiendo	C:	*the circles, I don't understand*
	6	G:	es para como un juego,	G:	*it's for like a game, but*
	7		pero no exactamente		*not exactly a game.*
	8		un juego. La persona		*The person who*
	9		quien lanza un cosa		*throws a thing smaller*
	10		mas chica de un lapiz a		*than a pencil at a place*
	11		un sitia a otro lado del		*on the other side of the*
	12		cuarto gana.		*room wins.*

c. elaboration (lexical)	1	R:	Mi agua es en la (mano)	R:	*My water is in the right*
	2		derecha.		*(hand).*
	3	G:	yo me olvido mis	G:	*I forget my directions.*
	4		direcciones.		
	5	R:	La derecha es la mano	R:	*The right one is the*
	6		que muchas personas		*hand that many*
	7		usan para escribir.		*people use for writing.*

d. elaboration (morpho-syntactic)	1	E:	Creemos que necesitas	E:	*We think you need to*
	2		salir pronto. Miramos		*leave soon. We are*
	3		cosas que haces y no		*looking at things that*
	4		nos gusta		*you are doing and (the things) we don't like (3 sing.)*
	5	L:	gustan	L:	*like* (3 pl.)
	6	E:	que?	E:	*what?*
	7	L:	nos gustan	L:	*we like* (3 pl.)

(good), and so on, or, in a very small number of cases (3%, or 4 out of 122 routines), an overt indication of nonunderstanding such as *no comprendo, pero está bien* (I don't understand, but that's OK). Interestingly, only 7% (9 out of 122) of the routines did not include a reaction to a response. As Varonis and Gass (1985) note, this part of the negotiation serves to "tie up" the routine and signal readiness to pop up to the main line of conversation. I therefore speculate that this component of the

TABLE 3. ROUTINES PER TASK

	Number of negotiation routines				
Tasks	1	2	3	4	5
Number of negotiation routines	21	41	18	23	19

routine is even more necessary in NBC than in oral conversation, because NBC lacks all the visual cues available in oral conversation to signal readiness to pop up.

Turning to the issue of quantity, Table 3 displays the total number of negotiation routines generated during each task.

As Table 3 illustrates, these routines were not scarce. Interestingly, however, although all tasks produced negotiations, one particular task, Task 2, produced more negotiation routines than the others. This difference likely resulted from several aspects of the task itself. Pica et al. (1993) claim that closed tasks with convergent goals and only one outcome possible, where interactants each have different information that must be exchanged in order to complete the task, are expected to generate the largest degree of negotiation. Task 2 was just such a task, but it was not the only task that required infomation exchanged. The main component of Task 3 was very similar in that it also required that students find the pictures they had in common. The real difference with Task 2 was that, in addition to being a closed task with one outcome possible, it had a relatively high level of task difficulty, and this most likely affected the amount of negotiation produced (see Brown & Yule, 1983; Anderson & Lynch, 1988; Nunan, 1989; and Pica et al., 1993, for discussions of task difficulty). First, more than in the other tasks, in this task the naming of objects in the pictures required the use of nouns that were outside the vocabulary of most students, thus necessitating the use of circumlocution. For example, the lack of the vocabulary for the words "dartboard" and "darts" prompted one learner to the following description: *Es un circulo con cinco circulos, se tira cosa con pintas y con cosas de los pajaros a la cosa con los circulos* (it's a circle with five circles, you throw thing with points and with things birds have to the thing with circles). Second, in Task 2 many pictures included a collection of items that were not logically related (one picture, for example, displayed a man jumping up and down wearing party hats, and facing him was a bow and arrow), thereby reducing the possibility of learners' guessing based on "real-world" or contextual knowledge. The data from Task 2 therefore demonstrate the importance of task difficulty in designing interactive language tasks to foster the negotiation of meaning.

Example 6. Negotiation routine (from Task 2)

1	G:	...al lado derecho del sitia con	G:	*. . . on the right side of the place*
2		las dartas		*with the darts*
3	C:	el hombre, es al lado de las	C:	*the man, is at the right of the*
4		dartas? Y que es sitia?		*darts? And what is "place"?*
5	G:	sitia es como lugar, entiendes?	G:	*place is like location, do you understand?*
6	C:	no entiendo, lo siento	C:	*I don't, sorry*
7	G:	la palabra "sitia" o que es la	G:	*the word "place" or what is the*
8		sitia?		*place?*
9	C:	la palabra "sitia"	C:	*the word "place"*
10	G:	aqui es una frase: San Francisco	G:	*here is a phrase: San Francisco*
11		es la lugar donde estuve naciendo		*is the location where I was born*
12	C:	ok. sitia, como lugar. Si?	C:	*Ok. place, like location. Right?*
13	G:	si, y una otra. La mesa es la sitia	G:	*Yes, and one more. The table is*
14		donde comemos cena.		*the place where we eat dinner.*
15	C:	ok. el hombre esta al lado de la	C:	*Ok. the man is next to the place*
16		sitia de las dartas, si?		*where the darts are, right?*
17	G:	si, la sitia es una cosa con	G:	*yes, the place is a thing that has*
18		circulos. entiendes?		*circles. do you understand?*
19	C:	las dartas esta en la cosa con	C:	*the darts are on the thing with*
20		circulos?		*circles?*
21	G:	si, en el centro	G:	*yes, in the center*
22	C:	si. ENTIENDO!!! (emphasis	C:	*yes. I UNDERSTAND!!!!*
23		is C's)		

Negotiation, comprehension, and successful communication

In response to the second research question, the transcripts show that to ensure mutual comprehension, learners often went through labored negotiations before popping up to the main line of discourse. Consider the following example, taken from Task 2, in which students were trying to find the differences between their respective pictures. G is trying to describe her picture of a man who is next to a dartboard, but obviously does not know the term for dartboard.

In lines 2 and 3 of this transcript, we see that C pushes down the conversation in order to get confirmation that he understands G's description, and further to get a definition for the word "sitia."[7] He signals the need for negotiation by a confirmation check and a direct question about the word *sitia* (line 4). G, responding to C's signal, offers an explanation of the meaning of *sitia* by using the synonym "lugar" (line 5). Interestingly, when C indicates further nonunderstanding (*no entiendo, lo siento*), G attempts to zero in on the exact source of this nonunderstanding, and she asks C to clarify whether he does not understand the word or the

7 *Sitia* is not a target form; the correct form is *sitio*.

actual place she is trying to describe (lines 7–8). When C replies that it is the word that is causing him trouble (line 9), G offers an example of how the word (actually the synonym) can be used in context (lines 10–11). C signals his understanding in line 12 by offering a definition (one that G had originally offered) accompanied by a confirmation check. At this point, however, it appears that G is not ready to pop up without ensuring that C really does understand the word *sitia*, so she offers another example, this time with the word *sitia* in context (lines 13–14). C responds with a confirmation of his understanding and then takes the initiative to pop up to the conversation, from which point the two are able to continue and successfully determine the differences between their pictures.

Example 6 is representative of many of the routines found in the data. Similar to what was found in Varonis and Gass (1985) in oral interaction, we find numerous examples of embedded routines: those that lead to further push-downs in the conversation.[8] In fact, 31% of the total 122 routines found were embedded, further confirming the amount of work NBC participants will go through to ensure mutual understanding. Evidence that these routines are indeed making the language input produced in the tasks more comprehensible for the learners comes from two sources: the learners themselves and their level of successful task completion. In the overwhelming majority of cases (84% of all routines), learners did overtly express their understanding to their interlocutor by way of a reaction to a response, such as *entiendo, comprendo, ok,* and although one might argue that these reactions to responses could simply indicate the speaker's desire to return to the main line of discourse, the transcripts of the ensuing discourse also indicate that understanding of the message was indeed achieved.[9]

A further, albeit indirect, indication that these negotiation routines are leading to mutual comprehension comes from the learners' level of successful task completion. Each one of the language tasks had a specific goal, and in order for participants to achieve these goals, they had to successfully communicate with and comprehend each other. In Tasks 1, 4, and 5, where multiple outcomes were possible, all dyads were able to successfully complete the task by arriving at an appropriate possible outcome. In Task 3, where in the first component students had to identify the three pictures they had in common and then continue to compose a piece of discourse, all dyads also successfully achieved their goal. Task 2 was the only task in which there were differences with respect to successful task completion, most likely owing to its increased degree of difficulty. Nine

---

8 Often negotiation about a particular item triggered negotiation about a new item. In other cases, the same trigger occasioned multiple signals, which, in turn, brought about more responses until the misunderstanding was resolved.

9 Only those reactions to responses that overtly expressed understanding were counted here, thus the 84% out of 90% possible reactions.

of the ten dyads completed this task with between 63% and 88% accuracy (i.e., they correctly identified the differences), with the average accuracy rate being 84.5%. The tenth dyad, however, was the only one that did not negotiate at all during Task 2 and, interestingly, had an accuracy rate of only 50%, by far the lowest of all the dyads. Although there may be many reasons why this pair of learners did not negotiate during the task, this lack of negotiation was surely detrimental to their performance. These results thus indicate that in spite of the fact that negotiation routines push learners down (often far down) from the main line of discourse, they are ultimately bringing about mutual comprehension, facilitating communication, and allowing for successful task completion.

Having established that task-based NBC does foster the negotiation of meaning, and that this negotiation appears to facilitate comprehension and successful communication among the learners, it is now important to look in detail at the ways in which learners modify their output in response to these negotiations and the effect these modifications have on the overall quality of the learner output.

Negotiation, form-focused interaction, and modified output

The third research question sought to determine whether the negotiations pushed learners to produce modified output that was form-focused as well as meaning-focused. Transcripts of the interactions show that learners were indeed attending to form in their output and produced lexical, syntactic, and semantic output modifications in response to negotiations as well as corrective feedback. I will focus first on negotiated modifications.

The chatting data offer many instances where learners manipulated the linguistic form of their utterance (lexical, syntactic, or semantic) in order to more precisely convey meaning. Example 7 is an illustration of a syntactic modification produced during a meaning negotiation. Here two learners try to describe their pictures to each other (of a little man below the thumb of a large hand) in order to determine whether or not they have the same picture; they do, in fact, have the same picture.

S wants to confirm that their pictures are indeed alike, so in lines 3–5 he tells R that in his picture *el hombre pequeno solo estaba tocada con el dedo mas grande*. The meaning that S intends to convey is that the little man "is being touched" only by the thumb of the large hand; however, the form he uses (estaba tocada) is a nontarget form. There are actually two problems with S's utterance. First, the passive participle would be *tocado* and not *tocada*. Second, the passive in Spanish is formed with the verb *ser*. The closest possible target equivalent for S's utterance would be something like *está siendo tocado*, literally "is being touched." This triggers misunderstanding for R, who seems to interpret this form as the gerundive target form *está tocando* (line 6), which would mean that the

Example 7. Negotiated modifications

1 S: si creo que tenemos lo mismo	S: *yes I think we have the same but*
2 pero tengo una pregunta mas	*I have one more question*
3 porque en mi dibujo el hombre	*because in my picture the little*
4 pequeno solo estaba tocada con	*man is only being touched by*
5 el dedo mas grande eh?	*the big finger, huh?*
6 R: El estaba tocada con el dedo	R: *He is touched by the big finger*
7 mas grande en tu dibujo?	*in your picture?*
8 S: si y solo con el dedo mas grande.	S: *yes, and only with the big finger.*
9 R: Pues, creo que nuestros dibujos	R: *Well, I think our pictures are*
10 son diferentes porque mi dibujo	*different because in mine only*
11 esta solamente la cabeza del	*the head of the man is beneath*
12 hombre debajo del dedo mas	*the big finger. He's not touched*
13 grande. No esta tocada con el	*by the big finger?*
14 dedo?	
15 S: si solamente con el dedo mas	S: *yes only with the big finger on*
16 grande en su cabeza en mia.	*his head in mine. I think they're*
17 Creo que son lo mismo?	*the same?*
18 R: Yo no se porque tu dijiste que el	R: *I don't know because you said*
19 esta tocada con el dedo y mi	*that he's touched with the*
20 hombre no esta tocada con	*finger and my man isn't touched*
21 nada!	*with anything!*
22 S: ahora estoy confundido.	S: *now I'm confused.*
23 R: vale <u>mi dibujo tiene un hombre</u>	R: *Ok, <u>my picture has a man who</u>*
24 <u>que es pequeno y entonces una</u>	*<u>is small and then a big hand</u>*
25 <u>mano grande que su dedo mas</u>	*<u>whose biggest finger is on the</u>*
26 <u>grande es en la cabeza del</u>	*<u>head of the little man?</u>*
27 <u>hombre pequeno?</u>	
28 S: Si, tengo la misma.	S: *Yes, I have the same one.*

little man himself is touching something. In addition, interpreting the nontarget form as the gerundive allows R to interpret *el dedo* (the finger) in the remainder of S's phrase as meaning the little man's finger. In Spanish, body parts are identified generally by the definite article and not the possessive, so in fact the most logical owner of *el dedo* (when interpreting the sentence the way R has) is the little man. Further evidence that R is interpreting the verbal form as the gerundive is that two turns later (lines 19–21) she actually typed the gerundive form *mi hombre no esta tocando con nada* (my man isn't touching with anything), but then backspaced and changed the verbal form to *esta tocada*. In all three turns subsequent to the original trigger in lines 3–5, R intends to repeat that her man is not touching anything, but she continues to use S's nontarget form (lines 6, 13, 18–21). The fact that each has ascribed a different meaning to the same syntactic form leads to even more misunderstanding, and S finally indicates that he is confused. R then describes her picture once

Example 8. Negotiated modification

1	L:	La semana pasada nosotros	L: *Last week we started to notice*
2		empezamos a darse cuenta que	*that there are many things in*
3		hay muchas cosas en nuestra casa	*our house that are not there.*
4		que no estan alli.	
5	E:	umm... uno minuto... darse	E: *umm. . . one minute . . . notice*
6		cuenta?	(inf + reflx pronoun 3rd person)?
7	L:	cuando nosotros descubrimos.	L: *when we discover. realize*
8		realizar	
9	E:	bueno entiendo bien	E: *good, I understand well*
10	L:	si pero la palabra no es realizar.	L: *yes, but the word isn't realize.*
11		Y actualmente yo pinso que es	*And actually, I think it is <u>notice</u>*
12		<u>darnos cuenta</u>	(inf + reflx 1st person pl)
13	E:	bien	E: *Ok*

again; however, this time she uses relative clauses to be as specific as possible, and she avoids the troublesome verbal form altogether (lines 23–27). R first establishes that there are two items in her picture, a man and a hand. Then, by using relative clauses, she is able to clarify that it is the man who is little and the hand that is big. Further, she is able to specify that it is the big hand whose finger is on the head of the little man.

In many cases, by pushing learners to structural modifications to convey meaning, the negotiations were also pushing learners to more target-like forms. The analysis of the learner data across all tasks revealed 15 instances where an utterance that triggered negotiation had some sort of structural problem; 8 of these were lexical, 3 were morphosyntactic, 2 were both lexical and morphosyntactic, 1 was semantic, and 1 was orthographic. In 14 of the 15 instances, a modification of some sort was made to the original utterance. Some of these modifications were explanations or elaborations (lexical or syntactic) of the item or items in question, which thereby avoided the original nontarget form altogether (i.e., example 7). However, 8 of these utterances resulted in the original utterance being modified toward the TL, and only 1 led to a modification away from the TL. Example 1, repeated here as Example 8, illustrates a negotiation that brought about a syntactic modification in the direction of the target language.

In lines 5–6, E does not understand L's word *darse cuenta* (to realize or notice). This is a TL word, but in the context of L's utterance the reflexive pronoun should be *nos* (1st pl).[10] E does not understand the word and signals to L with a repetition of the word (lines 5–6). L explains the word using a synonym and then offering the false cognate *realizar* (to realize); in Spanish, this means to achieve. Once E expresses understanding, L tells her that *realizar* is not the correct word in Spanish, but it is here that L

---

10 Note that I am not claiming that the purpose of the negotiation was to indicate an error, but interestingly, the negotiation does cause L to focus on the form.

TABLE 4. CORRECTIVE FEEDBACK

| | | | | Feedback type | | |
| | | Explicit | | | Implicit | |
Direction	Target	Nontarget	Total	Target	Nontarget	Total
Lexical	9	3	12	8	0	8
Morphosyntactic	3	1	4	3	2	5
Semantic	2	0	2	0	0	0
Totals	14	4	18	11	2	13

also notices that she has used the wrong reflexive pronoun and offers E the TL form *darnos cuenta.*

Structural modifications were also made in response to corrective feedback offered during interaction, thus addressing the fourth research question. Table 4 summarizes the types of corrective feedback found in the data.

Table 4 indicates that corrective feedback was indeed offered on all aspects of the grammar, though a majority was focused on the lexicon. More important, Table 4 indicates that corrective feedback was present in almost equal amounts in both explicit and implicit forms, and that the quality of the feedback was quite good: Of the 31 total instances of corrective feedback, only 6 resulted in a nontarget form being offered as a model. In looking at how the learners used this feedback, some interesting patterns emerge. Table 5 displays the percentages of incorporation for the feedback, both in absolute terms and in terms of where incorporation was actually possible.

Table 5 indicates that learners incorporated 70% of the target-like explicit feedback and 75% of the target-like implicit feedback where incorporation was possible and conducive to conversation. These percentages are quite high and certainly indicate that the learners were making use of the feedback offered. Crucially, however, out of the total 31 cases of corrective feedback, only 2 nontarget forms were incorporated into subsequent conversational turns.[11] These results corroborate those found in Gass and Varonis (1989), which showed that the great majority of incorporations in NNS oral interaction were made toward the target language. Gass and Varonis note that "learners are able to recognize what

11 Whereas learners incorporated 66% of the nontarget feedback when it was delivered explicitly, they did not incorporate any nontarget feedback when it was delivered implicitly. Of course, the numbers we are dealing with here are too small to draw any conclusions; nevertheless, these results might hint at the benefit of recasts with respect to the usability of corrective feedback in NNS discourse. Long (1996) has suggested the superiority of recasts over other models in NNS oral interaction, and this seems an interesting hypothesis to pursue in NBC interaction as well.

TABLE 5. CORRECTIVE FEEDBACK AND INCORPORATION RATE

| | *Feedback type* | | | |
| | *Explicit* | | *Implicit* | |
	Target forms	*Nontarget forms*	*Target forms*	*Nontarget forms*
Total feedback forms	14	4	11	2
Incorporations	7 (50%)	2 (50%)	6 (55%)	0 (0%)
Total forms possible for incorporation	10	3	8	2
Incorporations	7 (70%)	2 (66%)	6 (75%)	0 (0%)

is correct and what is incorrect even in the absence of a native speaker and even when their own forms are not in conformity with the target language" (p. 82). Of course, those learners who come to the language task with a high level of metalinguistic awareness might well be better equipped to gauge the quality of the corrective feedback than those who do not; however, there are features of the interaction itself that can facilitate this awareness, even for the less metalinguistically aware. For example, Long (1996), addressing the usability of corrective recasts, notes that because they are a reformulation of the speaker's utterance, the model form is contextualized in a message whose content is already more or less clear, and thus allows more processing resources to be directed to the form of this utterance. In NBC chats, the learners have the added advantage of the visual saliency of the model form, whether delivered explicitly or implicitly, which can allow even greater opportunities for a cognitive comparison of the new form against the speaker's original utterance, which is also visible on the screen. It is therefore possible that extra processing time and resources allow learners to better discriminate between the target and nontarget-like forms. This is an interesting hypothesis that certainly merits further investigation.

Before concluding the discussion of learner output, some interesting observations made while analyzing the learner language data deserve comment. The transcripts indicate that in addition to monitoring partner utterances, learners were doing a good deal of self-monitoring, as evidenced by their same-turn self-repair. Before giving up a conversational turn, learners would often backspace to repair typographical and/or spelling errors, and also to repair errors involving morphological agreement, as shown in Example 9 (lines 1–4).

Perhaps even more interesting is that our learners backspaced to make syntactic elaborations, thus pushing their utterances to a more advanced syntax. For instance, in Example 10, line 3, R backspaced to add a clitic pronoun to the verb phrase.

Example 9. Self-repair (morphological agreement, spelling)
L = start of back spacing; bold indicates items erased; [] = repaired part of utterance

1	M:	...El hombre tambien tiene un	M: *. . . The man also has a necktie,*
2		**corbata**L[a corbata], **lo**L[as]	*the glasses, the white shirt,*
3		gafas, el camiso blanco,	*black pants.*
4		**pantolone**L[alones] negros.	

Example 10. Self-repair (syntax)
L = start of back spacing; bold indicates items erased; [] = repaired part of utterance

1	G:	Es tu hombre tiene una corbata	G: *Does your man have a tie and*
2		y los anteojos?	*the glasses?*
3	R:	Si, el **tiene.**L[los tiene]. Mi dibujo	R: *Yes, he has them. My picture*
4		numero 5 es un mano que	*number 5 is a hand that is*
5		**tiene**L[esta haciendo] el	*making the number three with*
6		**nuim**L[mero] tres con sus dedos.	*his fingers.*

As teachers of Spanish to English speakers well know, the use of clitics in the speech of beginning and intermediate learners is uncommon. At least for the intermediate learners, this is most likely *not* because of unfamiliarity with the structure, but rather because of the increased demands on cognitive processing that the production of clitics can require.[12] In synchronous NBC, however, learners have additional time to think about their language use, as well as a visual display of their utterances. Perhaps these very features of chatting allow students to practice and gain control over more cognitively demanding aspects of grammar that otherwise might not be so frequently practiced in classroom oral interaction.

Thus, the results of the analysis on learner output are indeed meaningful, especially in view of the fact that the formal quality of language produced during NBC chats has been called into question (Beauvois, 1992; Kern, 1995). Clearly, what we are dealing with in NBC chats among nonnative speakers is interlanguage; however, this interlanguage is no *more* "defective" simply because it is mediated by a computer processor. Developmental errors should be expected in any interlanguage because part of successful language learning involves formulating and testing hypotheses about the target language. Therefore, we cannot expect the exposure to interlanguage in NBC to be any more detrimental to language development than it would be in the classroom. To the contrary, our data suggest that because in NBC students have more time to process language than in oral conversations, and because they can view their language as they produce it, they are more likely to focus on language form and

12 See Van Patten and Cadierno (1993) for a discussion of these processing constraints.

"monitor" their messages, all of which can result in even more "quality" interlanguage than there would be in a nonelectronic environment.

Conclusion

The results of this study demonstrate that task-based synchronous NBC, such as chatting, can indeed foster the negotiation of meaning. Learners involved in NBC chats negotiate over all aspects of the discourse, which in turn pushes learners to form-focused linguistic modifications. Additionally, learners provide and are provided corrective feedback, which was demonstrated to result in the incorporation of target-language forms into subsequent turns. Furthermore, this study indicates that although these routines might temporarily push learners down from the main line of discourse, ultimately they are facilitating mutual comprehension and thus successful communication. Because synchronous NBC fosters the negotiation of meaning and form-focused interaction, and because students communicating through this medium have more time to process and monitor the interlanguage, I believe, contrary to what has been suggested in the recent literature, that NBC chatting can play a significant role in the development of grammatical competence among classroom language learners.

This study also demonstrates the importance of the language task for the quantity and type of negotiation produced. Synchronous NBC language tasks should be goal-oriented, with a minimum of possible outcomes, and they should be designed in such a way that all participants are required to request and obtain information from one another for successful task completion. Task difficulty is also an important factor in task design. The data presented would suggest that those tasks that involve vocabulary beyond the repertoire of the learners, and that involve ideas, concepts, or items outside of their real-world expectations, can increase the quantity of negotiation produced. Furthermore, this study suggests that if the language goal is to promote an even higher level of learner focus on grammatical form, those tasks that require learners to produce and then reflect on the language produced might be fruitful avenues to pursue.

Of course, because of the descriptive nature of this study, generalizations of these results to other populations should be made cautiously. Future research of a more experimental nature is needed to better compare the differential effect of task types and use of corrective feedback, as well as to elucidate individual differences that could affect negotiation routines. Such research should also consider the advantages of the ytalk software for the investigation of issues such as self-repair and monitoring during chatting. Finally, further classroom research should consider the role that synchronous NBC can play in the development of grammatical competence, especially over a period of time. Because NBC chats can be captured and automatically displayed in a typed format, transcription preparation time is relatively short, which can allow researchers to consider larger amounts of data, such as would be generated by a long-term study. Studies such as these will continue to fuel the increasing need to integrate technology into the classroom in a principled manner.

References

Anderson, A., & Lynch, T. (1988). *Listening*. Oxford: Oxford University Press.

Beauvois, M. H. (1992). Computer-assisted classroom discussion in the foreign language classroom: Conversation in slow motion. *Foreign Language Annals, 25*(5), 455–464.

Brock, C., Crookes, G., Day, R., & Long, M. (1986). The differential effects of corrective feedback in native speaker conversation. In R. Day (Ed.), *Talking to learn: Conversation in second language acquisition* (pp. 229–236). Rowley, MA: Newbury House.

Brown, G., & Yule, G. (1983). *Teaching the spoken language*. Cambridge: Cambridge University Press.

Bump, J. (1990). Radical changes in class discussion using networked computers. *Computers and the Humanities, 24,* 49–65.

Call, M. E., & Sotillo, S. M. (1995). Is talk cheap? The role of conversation in the acquisition of language. *Hispania, 78*(1), 114–121.

Canale, M. (1983). From communicative competence to communicative language pedagogy. In J. Richards & R. Schmidt (Eds.), *Language and communication* (pp. 2–27). London: Longman.

Canale, M., & Swain, M. (1980). Theoretical bases of communicative approaches to second language teaching and research. *Applied Linguistics, 1*(1), 1–47.

Chun, D. M. (1994). Using computer networking to facilitate the acquisition of interactive competence. *System, 22*(1), 17–31.

Crookes, G., & Roulon, K. (1985). Incorporation of corrective feedback in native speaker non-native speaker conversation. (Technical Report 3). University of Hawaii, Manca: The Center for Second Language Classroom Research/Social Science Research Institute.

Ellis, R. (1994). *The study of second language acquisition*. Oxford: Oxford University Press.

Gass, S., & Varonis, E. (1989). Incorporated repairs in nonnative discourse. In M. Eisenstein (Ed.), *The dynamic interlanguage: Empirical studies in second language variation* (pp. 71–86). New York: Plenum Press.

Gass, S., & Varonis, E. (1994). Input, interaction and second language production. *Studies in Second Language Acquisition, 16,* 283–302.

Kern, R. (1995). Restructuring classroom interaction with networked computers: Effects on quantity and characteristics of language production. *Modern Language Journal, 79,* 457–476.

Krashen, S. (1985). *The input hypothesis: Issues and implications*. London: Longman.

Long, M. (1981). Input, interaction and second language acquisition. In H. Winitz (Ed.), *Annals of the New York Academy of Science, 379,* 259–278.

Long, M. (1985). Input and second language acquisition theory. In S. M. Gass & C. G. Madden (Eds.), *Input in second language acquisition* (pp. 377–393). Rowley, MA: Newbury House.

Long, M. (1996). The role of the linguistic environment in second language acquisition. In W. Ritchie & T. Bhatia (Eds.), *Handbook of second language acquisition* (pp. 413–468). New York: Academic Press.

Loschky, L., & Bley-Vroman, R. (1993). Grammar and task-based methodology. In G. Crookes & S. Gass (Eds.), *Tasks and language learning: Integrating theory and practice* (pp. 123–167). Clevedon, UK: Multilingual Matters.

Nobuyoshi, J., & Ellis, R. (1993). Focused communication tasks and second language acquisition. *ELT Journal, 47,* 203–210.

Nunan, D. (1989). *Designing tasks for the communicative classroom.* Cambridge: Cambridge University Press.

Oliva, M., & Pollastrini, Y. (1995). Internet resources and second language acquisition: An evaluation of virtual immersion. *Foreign Language Annals, 28*(4), 551–563.

Oliver, R. (1995). Negative feedback in child NS–NNS conversation. *Studies in Second Language Acquisition, 17,* 459–481.

Pica, T. (1994). Research on negotiation: What does it reveal about second-language learning conditions, processes, and outcomes? *Language Learning, 44,* 493–527.

Pica, T., Holliday, L., Lewis, N., & Morgenthaler, L. (1989). Comprehensible output as an outcome of linguistic demands on the learner. *Studies in Second Language Acquisition, 11,* 63–90.

Pica, T., Kanagy, R., & Falodun, J. (1993). Choosing and using communication tasks for second language instruction. In G. Crookes & S. Gass (Eds.), *Tasks and language learning: Integrating theory and practice* (pp. 9–34). Clevedon, UK: Multilingual Matters.

Pica, T., Young, R., & Doughty, C. (1987). The impact of interaction on comprehension. *TESOL Quarterly, 21,* 737–758.

Sato, C. (1986). Conversation and interlanguage development: Rethinking the connection. In R. Day (Ed.), *Talking to learn: Conversation in second language acquisition* (pp. 23–45). Rowley, MA: Newbury House.

Schachter, J. (1991). Corrective feedback in historical perspective. *Second Language Research, 7*(2), 89–102.

Schmidt, R. (1990). The role of consciousness in second language acquisition. *Applied Linguistics, 11,* 219–258.

Schwartz, B. (1993). On explicit and negative data affecting competence and linguistic behavior. *Studies in Second Language Acquisition, 15,* 147–163.

Spada, N., & Lightbown, P. (1993). Instruction and the development of questions in L2 classrooms. *Studies in Second Language Acquisition, 15,* 205–224.

Swain, M. (1985). Communicative competence: Some roles of comprehensible input and comprehensible output in its development. In S. M. Gass & C. G. Madden (Eds.), *Input in second language acquisition* (pp. 235–245). Rowley, MA: Newbury House.

Swain, M. (1995). Three functions of output in second language learning. In G. Cook & B. Seidlhofer (Eds.), *Principle and practice in applied linguistics:*

Studies in honor of H. G. Widdowson (pp. 125–144). Oxford: Oxford University Press.

Swain, M., & Lapkin, S. (1995). Problems in output and the cognitive processes they generate – a step towards second language learning. *Applied Linguistics, 16*(3), 371–391.

Tomasello, M., & Herron, C. (1988). Down the garden path: Inducing and correcting overgeneralization errors in the foreign language classroom. *Applied Psycholinguistics, 9,* 237–246.

Tomasello, M., & Herron, C. (1989). Feedback for language transfer errors. *Studies in Second Language Acquisition, 11,* 385–395.

Van Patten, B., & Cadierno, T. (1993). Explicit instruction and input processing. *Studies in Second Language Acquisition, 15,* 225–243.

Varonis, E., & Gass, S. (1985). Non-native/non-native conversations: A model for negotiation. *Applied Linguistics, 6,* 71–90.

5 Writing into change
Style shifting in asynchronous electronic discourse

Boyd Davis
Ralf Thiede

Asynchronous electronic discourse presents researchers with a way to look at how writers accommodate to each other in a medium that is new to them. Even when the asynchronous exchange is relatively brief, as in monthlong asynchronous computer conferences, one can spot some aspects of style shifting in extemporaneously composed on-line replies to other writers' postings. Style shifting in response to each other's texts takes place in the writings of both L1 and L2 writers and, like conversation, is keyed to the preferences of the individual. For L2 writers, newly plummeted into an L1 environment, such style shifting can be a signal that they have become aware of a range of discourse conventions in the L1 and are beginning to imitate or accommodate to these conventions. That is what student writers told us in their reflections on participating in a pair of asynchronous conferences, and it is what we think their writing substantiates.

This study examines what happens to different features of discourse when EFL learners must move to function in an ESL situation, as shown by changes in their writing in asynchronous, or delayed-time, mainframe conferences. Specifically, we examine style-shifting patterns in rapidly keyboarded writings by three newly arrived Chinese and Japanese graduate students as they participated with thirty-one other graduate and advanced undergraduate students from Asia, the United States and Canada, France, Egypt, and the United Arab Emirates (UAE) in a sequenced pair of asynchronous mainframe conferences. This pair of conferences was one of the requirements for a semester-long course in linguistics that all thirty-four students took together at the University of North Carolina-Charlotte, a public urban university in the upper South.

Our research examines participant accommodation to the experience of creating a learning community on-line, as suggested by two kinds of student reactions to the conference: L1 English writers predominantly wrote in their final reflections about the experience of learning to write for a community, whereas L2 (NNS) writers commented on how they noticed discourse patterns and modified their own writing. In this chapter, we look first at conference discourse conventions of approbation, agreement, and alignment and their appropriation. An examination of changes in one student's compliments and summary patterns allows us to propose the extension of Wolfson's (1989) "bulge hypothesis" to electronic discourse, and suggests how electronic discourse offers opportunities for reflective inquiry and metacognition to its participants. Next, we look at lexical and syntactic indications of style shift and accommodation to identify where the forum of electronic conferences might create opportunities for accommodation and learning. Here, we hope to suggest how a corpus of electronic discourse can offer opportunities to researchers. By describing particular usage patterns that developed as the participants evolved their own conventions for discourse routines in the electronic conferences, we hope to contribute to the emerging discussion of characteristics and features of electronic discourse (Ferrara, Brunner, & Whittemore, 1991; Murray, 1991; Herring, 1993, Warschauer, 1995; Davis & Brewer, 1997) and suggest its benefits for both participants and researchers.

Background: The pedagogical rationale for the conferences

Computer conferencing differs from other asynchronous, or time-delayed, exchange of information via networked computers, such as e-mail lists or news groups, in that conferencing software archives and threads all writings so that participants can access, select, and retrieve at any time any written message in the conference, regardless of topic or time written, as long as the conference is stored on its host. All messages from all participants are equally and imminently available, with their storage topically, as opposed to chronologically, arranged.

The mainframe conferencing software program that we used, VAX-Notes, has an additional feature. Instead of presenting writers with a subject line in memo format typical of e-mail messages, it initially splits the screen between the message being read and the one to be composed, and, when the writer uses keyboard commands to save and post a written reply, VAXNotes prompts the writer to add a title. This title can serve as a signpost (Davis & Brewer, 1997) to some aspect of the writing and may even signal some aspect of the writer's purpose. The title is filed in the conference directory under the topic holding the original message that stimulated the reply. Storage requirements can be higher than those for the average e-mail list or news group, which may be why conferences are often of short duration and specific focus. However, because all messages are always available, letting participants track and interact with a discussion at any time, they are useful for collaborative work, which, say Sussex and White (1996), fosters "new patterns of intellectual activity" (p. 207; cf. Bibliography, pp. 215–219); that is, "networked learning provides not only a medium but also a stimulus . . . [with a] new emphasis on discovery-based learning and an interest in student-driven learning in a wider sense" (p. 204; cf. Warschauer, 1995).

We chose to develop a pair of asynchronous conferences for two reasons. First, the focus of the course was to introduce key concepts about language acquisition: It seemed desirable for the students to participate directly in some sort of learning or acquisition process, regardless of how rudimentary or how limited. None of the thirty-six students had had any prior experience with mainframe conferencing, and only a handful (four) had learned to send and receive e-mail, though slightly more (eleven) had some facility with CD-ROM bibliographic searching. This was, after all, 1993: The World Wide Web was only beginning to inch onto campus horizons, and word processing was the only computer-supported activity with which all of the students had some familiarity. Learning the routines and formulas involved with locating terminals, accessing and logging on to the correct mainframe, calling up the conferencing software, and entering the conference with ease would, we thought, provide both challenge and a relatively brief learning curve.

Second, we wanted to build communications in the sense of learning partnerships within the class, because its constituency was disparate in terms of dominant language, class standing, and prior experience with linguistic content. Half of the students were speakers of American Englishes; the other half had, as their dominant languages, Mandarin (Taiwan), French (Paris, Montreal), Guatemalan Spanish, Japanese, Standard classical Arabic, and Egyptian Cairene. Two-thirds of the students were junior and senior undergraduates, who were primarily taking the course to fulfill a requirement of a language course in their major or minor concentrations and who had had no prior course in linguistics. One-third of the students were graduate students with at least one undergraduate course in linguistics. All but one were in their first semester of a master's degree in TESOL, and six had just arrived in the United States from Taiwan and Japan.

If the class were to adequately prepare the graduate students to pursue the next courses in their sequence without disenfranchising or abandoning the undergraduates, some sort of community would, we thought, need to be established, particularly because we wanted to foster discovery-based, student-driven learning (Warschauer, 1995) through enabling their collaboration in a variety of ways. According to Scardamalia and Bereiter (1996), computer-supported collaborative learning can provide what they call a knowledge-building discourse, which is characterized by "focus on problems and depth of understanding; decentralized, open knowledge environments for collective understanding; and productive interaction within broadly conceived knowledge-building communities" (p. 258). In order to support collaborative work among the students, two kinds of communities were constructed as part of the course, each of which had a specific task whose product was to be presented to the full class. The first was the development of small groups constructed by numbering off: These groups met occasionally in the class, and more usually outside it, to prepare their oral presentations on group-specific chapters in the second course textbook. The second community was virtual; intended to include each member of the class, it developed in two stages, each stage being a separate conference involving different approaches to interpreting and producing text. The interactions can be schematized as follows:

Week	Face-to-face groups	Virtual
1–3 (primary text)	initial in-class meetings	brief training in log-on routines
4–7 (primary text)	out-of-class meetings begin single in-class meeting	Conference 1: classic studies entries posted by individuals summary/paraphrase (1) reply to peers (2)
8 (midterm exam)		
9–12 (primary text)	oral presentations begin (out-of-class meetings; single in-class meeting)	Conference 2: debate positions entries planned by dyads, posted in tandem: pro/con argument (1); by individuals, replies to peers (2)
13–15 (primary text)	oral presentations conclude	
reflective paper on conferencing		[additional 9 replies posted by Wang after conference ended]

Overview of the conferences

Each of the mainframe VAXNotes conferences was designed to last about 3 weeks. Individual computer accounts were given to each student; after initial instruction in how to access the mainframe and the conference, and the basic commands required by the conferencing software, a student intern offered additional support and training for an hour each day. The instructor never wrote anything in any of the conferences, to avoid privileging any particular reply or style of writing, though students knew that she, like them, would read the conference postings. In Bell's terms, she was an auditor (Bell, 1984, p. 159). Students could print any posting at any time; the full set of postings was printed at the end of each conference and placed in the library for student use.

Each conference had a slightly different set of purposes and a slightly different task, and intended thereby to elicit different patterns of discourse. The goal for the first conference ("Classics") was to initiate student interaction, and through it to establish a student-generated body of shared knowledge. Students chose one of forty articles or chapters from a list of "classics" from 1960 to 1990 that represented disciplinary perspectives on the study of language acquisition and language learning, including linguistics, psycholinguistics, psychology, and education. Students were required to post a summary of their chosen article or chapter in Conference 1 and, at a later date, to post responses to any two other student summaries.

The second conference ("Debate") required pairs of students to jointly read and post analyses of a current article from a professional journal, with one person presenting an analysis supporting the article's findings and the other presenting a rebuttal of some kind; each pair of students worked with a different article. At a later date, students were again required to post two responses, this time to any single student-generated text. The purposes here were to extend the previous student interaction by asking the students to stage a debate, to familiarize themselves with professional journals, to become conversant with ways to handle dissent, and to practice identifying the four moves noted by Swales for initiating scientific or professional writing: Establish the field, summarize relevant research, find the gap in that research into which the researcher-writer can enter, and outline the purpose of the new study (Swales, 1990; cf. Connor, 1996, p. 41).

We think that the use of the computer conferences was not the innovation in and of itself; it was instead that the "functional writing environments they [the students] created using computers as tools involved new participation structures . . . and affected the length and quality of student writing" (Johnson, 1991, p. 76; from Mehan, Moll, & Riel 1985). The conferences provided student readers with a variety of text types and styles, from which they could identify and incorporate into their own writing those features that seemed effective, useful, or attractive. Those features could replicate the involvement of multiparty conversation or the informational density of academic prose; the latter terms here are from Biber (1988). The students found electronic discourse surrounding them with multiple models for emulation, both in their carefully composed summaries and critiques of the texts and in the more casual responses they wrote to each other.

The student reflections: In their ending is our beginning

The mainframe conferences were constructed in order to promote student interaction (Johnson, 1991), to introduce or reinforce patterns of sanctioned disagreement (Mathison, 1996), to present a variety of voices (Elbow, 1994) as models for emulation, and to create a rough-and-ready scaffolding for sharing new information. As such, they presented a stilted but available, and malleable, conversational opening that was extended and reconstructed by participants. The conferences provided sustained and topically threaded exposure to a variety of discourse models within a sequenced set of writing prompts. This exposure and participation was, both first and second language writers wrote in their end-of-term reflections on the conferences, a major reason for their perceived changes in writing. Interestingly, whereas L1 students more often focused their comments on changes to their notion of writing in and to a community, or on the role of the conferences themselves, L2 students saw their changes in general as reflecting their composing and revising in a second language within the conference.

Comments by native English speakers Bonita and Patty in their reflections suggest initial discomfort and eventual resolution. Bonita was beginning to find herself drawn to writing as a profession; initially, she had been resistant to the public nature of conference writing:

The difference here has not been in how I approach the machine, but in thinking about the implications of what I have just written as part of a conversation with at least forty other people. . . . Community is not a thing that comes easily to me. I found that I really enjoyed reading other people's entries, that I couldn't wait to find out if someone had responded to something I had written, that there were a lot of ideas floating around in our class that I seldom heard expressed on Monday or Wednesday mornings. . . . It seems only fitting that I should come full circle by putting this summary in the conference as well. More and more I am writing for an audience – I am writing to be read. (Bonita)

Patty found herself reflecting on her experience with linguistic terminology, computer commands, and a variety of conversations:

Throughout the past three months, I have truly sensed myself to be a traveler in a strange land, a land whose inhabitants used not one, but three unfamiliar languages. . . . The variation of audience from the impersonal, to a dialogue, to a conversation among all thirty-some class members as we replied to one another's writing, elicited different voices in our written language. At no other time have I been so almost palpably aware of choices I make when I speak and when I write, and of the effects of those choices. (Patty)

Comments by Mick (also a native speaker of English) summarized what he thought the conferences provided the class and how he had approached the task of writing in them; having taught ESL in Latin America, he was particularly interested in issues of competence:

The conferences provided us with three different windows through which we could look at language acquisition and communicative competence: (1) the content of the conferences, (2) the changing discourse between conference participants, (3) the individual participant's learning to communicate with the computer. . . . I read the previous entries and asked myself if I felt they were appropriate formats. I tried to emulate things that helped me understand other compositions and tried to avoid what I saw as their flaws. (Mick)

In contrast, the L2 students reflected on their reactions to their peers' writing and their awareness of their own changes, as illustrated by Monique, Wang, and Yoshi. Monique's new interest in cohesion, from her small-group report, carried over into her reflection:

My first writing, a summary of Roger Brown's article, displays many features of the typical, common essay, usually handed back to the teacher. Lots of linking words or expressions articulate and unify the whole piece, expressing a deduction or a consequence [or] introducing an opposition. . . . some basic features seem to emerge from my electronic writings: a generally informal style, an important use of direct speech, a vocabulary and tone typical of an oral register. Gradually, as the conferences went on, my writings were developing into very interactive pieces, in total contrast with the plain common paper that only the teacher can read. (Monique)

Wang's reflection recorded her surprise at finding different rhetorical patterns used for a single task; perhaps this awareness grounded her own variations of pattern in the additional replies she posted at the end of the conference (which we analyze later):

After writing my own summary for conference #1 on the mainframe, I read other peoples' summaries and I discovered that even though we were all supposed to summarize what we had read, there could be so many different ways to present a summary. For instance, some people gave specific statements and marked numbers for those statements, some people gave examples to explain and support what he/she had read, some people gave their own opinions about the article they had read, some people simply condensed the original article. (Wang)

Yoshi's first summary and his subsequent debate position had elicited a number of responses to the question he (indirectly) posed in each, about the impact of culturally preferred discourse styles. Later, we discuss his summary and his personal responses to peers; in this clip from his final reflection, we see him looking at his own discourse:

From another point of view, there seems to exist a "logical writing" in common. I am not good at writing "logically," as my concept of logic is culturally different from others. However, I could get some points of this [new] logic by reading others' essays.

When it comes to responding to others, I found a very interesting feature in my writings. I unconsciously copied or mirrored some sentence structures, idioms, expressions, or vocabulary of the original writing. To read good sentences helps me to write good sentences. (Yoshi).

The clips from Bonita, Patty, and Monique point to one crucial aspect of conference discourse: It provides participants with an audience beyond the teacher through interaction with peers. Extemporaneous asynchronous conference composition, like e-mail exchanges (Kern, 1996), provides a way for researchers to elicit interactive discourse, a way more limited of course than natural observation of conversation, because the discourse is written, required for class, and initiated with the teacher's prompt. However, the discourse elicited is probably fuller than responses to survey, questionnaire, or rating scales, and is directed by the individual participant. The discourse resulting from asynchronous interaction differs again from papers written for the teacher's eyes because the participants, in the absence of teacher participation or a model, themselves establish and maintain conventions for both genre of writing (here, summary versus debate) and sanctioned interactions, such as ways for agreeing or disagreeing with another writer.

Identifying social practices

The investigation of politeness, authority, status, or distance is not always simple in electronic discourse; indeed, the investigator of any kind of computer-mediated communication (CMC) must often work with subtleties in order to reconstruct or infer social practice. Herring claims that "text-based CMC makes transparent as never before the role of language in the presentation of self, and in the genesis and organization of social practices" (1996, p. i). We share her conviction that computer-mediated communication is a "boon to the study of language-in-use" (p. 1); we also find that investigating social practices and identifying what people may have learned can be rather tricky.

For example, students participating in asynchronous conferences can very easily present themselves exclusively in a positive, polite manner that seems to cut across issues of power, status, or distance. They can enter the conference at any point; they can read as little or as much as they wish; they can choose the writing to which they want to reply. If one disagrees with another's posting, if that posting offends or bores, one's personal reaction will never be seen unless two choices are made. One must choose first to reply in writing and then to save that reply to a conference where it can be read by all of one's peers who, because the VAXNotes software logs the date, time, and user ID of the writer at the head of each saved reply, can identify the writer should one forget to sign a personal name. Students may have been particularly careful not to offend because they would see their peers in class, possibly even in their small groups. In terms of status, all of the participants in the two conferences were students, with less power than the teacher, who, for that reason, never wrote in the conference to avoid privileging any summary, debate-position statement, or individual reply to a peer. Nonetheless, some signals of social practice including status or distance can be detected.

One convention, or practice, for conference interaction must have been something like this: Be more than usually polite; that is, do not, in your replies to your peers, make any other writers look dumb or wrong or feel bad by appearing to dismiss, disregard, or disparage any statements – or the shape and form of any statements – they have written. The felicity of the students' interaction, then, was heavily dependent on manner. We infer this convention because signals for approbation, agreement, and alignment were prevalent in the extemporaneous replies, whereas dissent was both infrequent and usually indirect.

By *approbation,* we mean some signal of approval: in conference discourse, this was most usually signaled by a compliment. Compliments in this tiny corpus of electronic conference discourse were *one-way;* that is, they were proffered, but they were not answered in a subsequent posting by the recipient. (Agreement was also one-way; dissent can be joined but seldom attracts the rejoinder of the person disagreed with. We reviewed four additional conferences staged from 1993–97 for other courses, and found the same situation to hold.) In both conferences, the compliments usually initiated the reply and were directed toward the person's performance in writing a summary or taking a position vis-à-vis a professional article or chapter: "Your summary was excellent. . . . Your writing is very clear when you . . ." Only one person named the recipient of the compliment ("Great job, Nora! I really liked how you . . .") Although compliments projected approval, suggesting a move toward involvement and an affirmation of solidarity (cf. Scollon & Scollon, 1995, pp. 44–45), they did not always preface *agreement* or a statement of partisanship with a position, which was a form of *alignment.*

If the compliment was immediately followed by a new topic that differed from that complimented in the peer's statement, we saw this as approbation alone. If the compliment was immediately followed by information or opinion that controverted or contradicted the peer's statement, we read this as indirect dissent, because the writer provided no verb or phrase that would signal alternative illocutionary force. Dissent that was direct ("I don't agree with you.") was as unmistakable as it was infrequent. Like dissent, agreement could be direct or indirect. With direct agreement, the writer used a verb such as "agree" ("I agree with you when you . . .") or a modifying phrase ("You are certainly right when you point out that . . . "). Indirect agreement was signaled by the writer's repeating, quoting, or paraphrasing some part of the peer's statement, without presenting contradictory information or introducing a new topic in the immediately following sentence, and often with additional, confirmatory opinion, information, or anecdote.

Tina, for example, followed her opening statement of agreement with a compliment:

I agree that more studies and subjects are needed. Like everyone who takes Psychology 1101, you learn that randomization and a good number of subjects are necessary for a good study. It was very interesting how you used real life examples to prove your point.

Della's first reply aligned her with one group – "you guys" – that was concerned with color naming:

I certainly agree with what you guys have been saying about the study not being fair with the terminology of "gender differences." Just because a woman uses mauve and a guy uses pink does not mean anything.

This clip from Marji's reply shows her moving into indirect dissent:

Perhaps this is what makes critical analysis of literary works so tricky. The work literally takes shape as the reader responds to it. Thus the poem or story is a DIFFERENT literary piece for each individual reader.

Kirk's reply, on the other hand, presents overt dissent:

I understand your side of the debate – it's true – standard English is taught but not spoken. We all have our own subcultures, from the language of a teenager, a black person, Italian, English, American to people simply within different majors. But I do not agree with the statement by either yourself or the article's author.

Approbation and agreement in the debate conference

So far, the examples of assent and approbation have been from L1 writers; there is a reason for this. When we looked more closely at these features in the 41 replies of the debate conference, we found the recently arrived L2 writers (Chinese and Japanese) handling compliments differently. Compliments in the replies fell into two categories: 2, written by a single (L1) person, that directly addressed a fellow student ("Great job, Micky!") and 15 that indirectly addressed a fellow student by proffering a compliment about some aspect of that student's writing ("I like how you summarized the first part"). Seven were written by the 3 female Chinese graduate students. Compliments prefaced or "staged" passages of support and agreement; however, student writers were able to signal agreement in additional ways. Of the 17 replies using verbs and modifiers ("I agree with your point that. . . . You are certainly right when you . . .") to signal support or agreement, only 2 uses were by the recently arrived Asian students; of the 7 additional postings presenting indirect agreement, by paraphrasing or repeating words and phrases, or emulating the order of topics in a posting, only 1 was by an Asian student. A total of 7 replies presented no compliments, no signals of agreement; 3 of them presented disagreement with an immediately preceding reply by another student, but no student presented outright disagreement with another student's debate position. A brief tabulation may be useful:

Compliment/agreement	Combinations for L1 Students	Combinations for recently arrived L2 students
Compliment + new data	4	3
Compliment + direct agreement	0	2
Compliment + indirect agreement	6	2
Direct agreement, no compliment	10	0
Indirect agreement, no compliment	5	0
Overt dissent	9	0

This small sample suggests that some kind of compliment was assumed as obligatory by recently arrived L2 Chinese and Japanese writers (in their first semester in the Unites States) when replying to other students in a public conference. Although L1 writers often presented replies containing direct or indirect agreement without including a compliment to the writer or on the writer's performance, only one L2 writer, a male with more prior experience with both English speakers and extemporaneous writing, did this. L1 writers, then, apparently brought a repertoire for the structure "Reply-to-peer" that included compliments followed by the introduction of new topics, compliments followed by direct or indirect agreement, direct or indirect agreement with no prefatory or included compliment, and overt dissent; L2 newcomers may have had fewer templates in their repertoire, but they began to vary features within these templates in their conference replies. Wang's additional set of nine replies, which she added to the conference after it officially closed, show her gradual modifications of her basic pattern keyed, we think, to social practice within the conference and her assessment of distance and involvement.

Wang's modifications

Wang wrote a third set of replies in the conferences as a way of practicing keyboarding and extemporaneous writing. These replies are listed in Appendix A; the times noted for each posting make it apparent that she was, indeed, composing at the keyboard before and after her 12:30 class.

She added her nine extra replies (March replies) to the summary conference several weeks after that conference had ended, writing them on the day she also wrote her final reply in the debate conference.

In Wang's March replies, we glimpse her expanding range of strategies. Type-token ratios of successive fifty-word chunks indicated that Wang presented less repetition (and more variation) when summarizing salient features of the student-written text to which she was responding than when she was either writing her own reaction to that text or offering a compliment or suggestion to its writer. We found especially interesting the distribution of variations within Wang's pervasive pattern that in general typified the structure of replies written by all Chinese students in the conference: compliment (*qi*) – expansion (*cheng*) – summary (*zhuan*) – and final compliment or suggestion to the writer (*he*). That her preferred pattern as well as her predilection for compliments is well established and highly valued in Chinese rhetoric has been amply explained by Kirkpatrick (1995) among others (Purves, 1986; Wu, 1990; Leki, 1991; Takano, 1993; Ye, 1995; Connor, 1996); commentators generally note that the *zhuan* section may involve several different kinds of changes, such as changes in mood, tense, point of view, topic, or grammatical subject. We think, however, that something else was at work as well, that her use of compliments indexed the ways she was beginning to expand her construction of social identity in conference discourse.

Henderson (1996) reminds us that although complimenting does reinforce solidarity, it goes beyond that; she claims that complimenting "performs social negotiation." This discussion is intended to contribute to the description of acts of social negotiation through language in the context and medium of electronic discourse. Given the absence of prosodic cues in written text, it is hard to discern when a compliment as delivered is unambiguously intended as a compliment and only as a compliment. And although electronic discourse presents a conversational flavor for several good reasons, it is always a possibility in electronic discourse that the recipient of the compliment may not have an opportunity for either an immediate or a direct reply. If one is to envision a response, the response must be inferred as having been projected by the person proffering the compliment, which brings us to the issue of what Bell (1984) calls audience design (cf. Zuengler, 1993).

The force of a compliment is often interpreted by the response of the recipient (Wolfson, 1989; Bergman & Kasper, 1993; Chen, 1993; Ye, 1995); it must, then, be contextualized in terms of cultural behavior. In the electronic conferences, an additional cultural overlay evolved: the norms for interaction and social practice for group discourse during the conference. The de facto official language of the conferences was English. The conference – in terms of its host mainframe and its accessing terminals – was literally physically situated in the United States. Because the participants were native English speakers (NESs) and learners of English as a foreign language (EFL), we might assume that the EFL speakers would accommodate to American English conventions in terms of social interaction. But in the conference, the social interaction was emergent: The EFL speakers were, though they might not have realized this at the outset, as powerful as the native English speakers and – because almost all the EFL speakers were graduate students – were part of a power bloc in which graduate students outranked undergraduates. Within that power bloc, things were probably a bit more complex, involving issues of gender, age, nationality, and perceived intelligence.

A compliment in electronic discourse may cause readers to back away. In the two conferences we study here, we noted that direct personal compliments offered to a named person were seldom used. In fact, only one person presented these in either conference, and their use was not emulated. His responses attracted little affirmation in the sense of eliciting a reply: In addition, he received no replies to his summary and but two replies to his debate, both from close friends who acknowledged their connection in their replies. His compliments may have perplexed his peers about either his intent or his status, according to Wolfson's (1983) account of the directionality of compliments.

Henderson (1996), citing Wolfson's study, claims that "compliments tend to flow from high status" and that "the compliment topic tends to be the ability of the complimented person in this context" (p. 196; on the impact of topics in general, see Zuengler, 1993). Perhaps this explains why nobody emulated Rick's use of direct address coupled with personal compliments: The direct address in a response (as opposed to a title) may distance everyone else in the conference, placing other readers in the status of eavesdroppers, and may have the impact on the addressee of shouting (similar to the use of all capitals in e-mail).

The emulation of a style or a rhetorical feature adds the function of agreement to that sincerest of flatteries. With emulation as a sign of approbation in electronic discourse, audience design and accommodation theory converge. By the time Wang added her final group of replies, she was working with a different notion of social distance because she now knew the writers from face-to-face involvement in this and in other courses. In two entries (108, 110), Wang emulated the organization of the NES writer to whose text she was responding; beginning with entry 110, her *zhuan* section focused on selected concepts presented by her peer's text rather than summarizing the key points in the order established by the peer. In the regular conferences, her replies presented the pattern shown in the first two of her March replies.

For Wang's March replies, she browsed the conference sequentially to find postings she could reply to. She wrote some replies to undergraduates with whom she did not have other courses, and here her pattern of replies suggests that she held higher status. She wrote other replies to graduate students whom by then she knew fairly well, and there her reply pattern varies with the degree to which she knew the person. The significant issue is that she seems to have changed her style or general pattern relative to her perception of the status, here defined as possession of knowledge base, or friendship tie with the peer. She had evidently decided not only to be a more facile keyboard composer, but also to become effective in using "linguistic resources in ways that are socially appropriate among speakers of the target language" (Wolfson, 1989, p. 219). Table 1 outlines key features in the March replies.

Wang's compliments and the bulge hypothesis

Would Wang's use of compliments in electronic discourse fit Wolfson's (1989) "bulge hypothesis"? In this hypothesis, which Wolfson and a number of other researchers have corroborated for speech situations, we find "the minimum and maximum degrees of social distance showing very similar patterns as opposed to the middle section (consisting of status equals) which displays a characteristic bulge. . . . the more status and social distance are seen as fixed, the easier it is for speakers to know what to expect of one another" (ibid., 223). At the beginning of the first electronic conference, the participants were status equals in that all of them were students; none of them had taken a course in this particular area of language study; none of them had ever done computer conferencing; all of them were apprehensive to some degree about composing on terminals. They began as strangers and moved quickly to knowing something about one another – and formed, via the first conference, a shared and jointly created knowledge base, accessible to everyone. By the time the first conference ended, the students had begun meeting in small groups within the class, and the graduate students had taken a month of additional classes in a special program with one another. Although the graduate students were not necessarily all intimates by the time of the second conference, they were certainly status equals with one another and had as a group a sequence of professionalizing routines as pre-TESOL teachers, which divided them from the undergraduates.

What we found, as we examined features in Wang's March replies, was a series of pragmatically interesting patterns. Replies to status equals, or fellow graduate students, had two forms: those to acquaintances in her program began and ended with strong compliments; those to students with whom she was good friends began with compliments and ended with solidarity building in the form of a joke or a surmise alluding to and extending the comments of the friend. Wang's replies to undergraduates, who held slightly lower status, also had two forms. These replies began

TABLE I. WANG'S ADDITIONAL MARCH REPLIES

	Orientation qi "opening"	Complication cheng "continuing"	Text summary zhuan "turning"	Coda he "concluding"	Immediate audience (peer) characteristics
Reply					
105	compliment	expanded compliment	summary	compliment	male grad student
106	compliment	expanded compliment	summary	request (directive)	female undergraduate
107	compliment	expanded compliment	summary	compliment	female grad student
108	personal insight	expansion, peer's insight	selected point "I agree"	compliment	male undergraduate
109	context (information)	expanded context, mild dissent	summary	compliment	male undergraduate
110	personal insight	expanded insight	selected point allusion to text (indirect agreement)	compliment	female undergraduate
111	compliment	expanded rationale	selected point allusion to text (indirect agreement)	surmise	male grad student
112	compliment	expanded rationale	selected point "I agree"	allusion/joke	female grad student & close friend
113	compliment	expanded rationale	question linked to example	question (directive)	female undergraduate

with contextualizing statements and moved to compliments if Wang thought the undergraduate's information had been correct, appropriate, or sufficient (or, in other words, had met the conditions of quantity, quality, and relevance). If Wang found the information incorrect, inappropriate in form, or insufficient in detail, the reply began with a mild compliment and ended with a request or question that, had a classroom teacher spoken it, would actually constitute a mild directive to refocus and present an adjusted answer.

Although this sample is too small for conclusive comments, we suggest that the bulge hypothesis could account for most of the giving of compliments in electronic conference interaction, but that the nature of conference discourse, being one-way and written, means that additional signals of agreement as approbation must be taken into account. The fewest number of strong or multiple compliments was proffered to intimates and lower-status strangers; the greater amount of compliments and compliments plus signals of assent were proffered to status equals or those with the propensity for becoming equal.

Lexicosyntactic indicators of stylistic emulation

In order to test our discourse-based hypothesis that the second language students were indeed recognizing different styles and shifting between them, we used several measures designed to let us compare their varying performances, particularly in terms of syntactic complexity and lexical density. In what follows, we identify some patterns and tendencies that we saw emerging as the second language students attempted to control the professional style of the summary and to separate it from the intimate style of responding to peers. Here, we discuss our findings from examining writings by two recently arrived Asian students, Chang (Taiwan) and Yoshi (Japan). We selected them because each of their final reflections on the conferencing experience had suggested heightened awareness of their composing processes, and we hoped to confirm or disconfirm their implicit claims. In his reflection, cited earlier, Yoshi had described his emulation of new patterns; Chang's reflection had focused on her awareness of the importance of word choice, ending with a comment on the impact of the computer itself:

There are some differences between learning a new language and learning to use a new computer system. . . . the computer system does not have other channels, such as nonverbal, to help convey meanings. It has only one sensor, operating. So it has to be very strict. It is not fuzzy and is really picky. If you mispronounce one word, people may still understand you. If you mistype one word, the computer will never take it. (Chang)

The two different writing tasks of the electronic conferences had invited the participants to adopt two different writing styles. *Summarizing* – the task of prioritizing and assimilating someone else's ideas and representing them in a condensed form – invited the writer to adopt a professional persona and voice, which could also carry over into a critique or position taken about the material. *Responding* to a fellow participant in the electronic conference, however, required shifting into a different style. The professional voice that in a summary could establish trust by representing the source's authority could, if it appeared in a reply, be taken as a signal of distancing from or exclusion of peer readers through assuming authority unlicensed by a task. Writing within the knowledge community that we hoped the conferences would establish brought with it two demands on the ability of its participants: that they have or develop a sensitivity to both styles and enough linguistic ability to switch between them to be perceived as doing so. This ability to perform, to recognize styles and to shift into them as part of group social practices, comes at a higher linguistic cost for nonnative speakers.

In a summary, a student must negotiate between capturing the source's professional voice and writing "in your own words," between appropriating and emulating. In a response, the student must find the balance between being personable to peers while being faithful to the academic subject. Linguistic restrictions surely complicate both tasks. Among the pitfalls of overcompensation facing second language learners is one described in Pennycook's (1996) article "Borrowing Others' Words: Text, Ownership, Memory, and Plagiarism."

Kirkland and Saunders (1991) have reviewed studies of constraints that might affect L2 students' performance with summaries. The factors include the source's length, complexity (information density, degree of abstractness), and familiarity, or "the degree to which the information or genre is related to individual schemata" that the reader already possesses (ibid., p. 107; see also Bouldin & Odell, 1993). Surely the student's own linguistic ability is also a factor. To summarize means first and foremost to capture the "gist" of the source, a "mentalese" representation of propositions in the conceptual-intentional system (Pinker, 1994, pp. 57–58; cf. Chomsky, 1992, p. 3). To do that while at the same time spending conscious effort in decoding the foreign language taxes the short-term memory work space. A compensatory strategy would be to rehearse verbatim strings of text in memory or to use the printed page of the original source as "virtual memory" while working out its content. Either way, summarizing a text in a second or foreign language would automatically focus learners' attention on the original author's wording, syntax, and style (see, for example, the review of empirical studies of second language reading during the 1970s–1980s in Carrell, 1988).

Syntactic complexity: Identifying two trends

We anticipated a difference between the professional style of the summary and the personal style of a response keyed to variation in syntactic
complexity. To measure the amount of syntactic complexity across the two
styles, we adopted an "acquisition scale" originally described in Rosenberg
and Abbeduto, with seven developmental levels (Rosenberg & Abbeduto,
1987, p. 26), here reproduced in an abbreviated form:

Level 1   embedded infinitival complement with subject identical to that
           of the matrix clause
Level 2   *wh*-infinitive clause; conjunction within or between clauses
Level 3   object noun phrase with relative clause; nominal clause as object
Level 4   gerundive complement; comparative
Level 5   subject noun phrase with relative clause; nominal clause as
           subject; nominalization
Level 6   subordinate clause with subordinating conjunction
Level 7   more than one use of clause combining within a sentence

Although these are developmental levels, they can also be used to measure syntactic complexity. (See, for example, the "Nun Study" by Snowdon, Kemper, Mortimer, Greiner, Wekstein, & Markesbery [1996], which
used such measures to track signals of Alzheimer's disease in nuns' di-
aries written over time.) We chose passages of summary and of response
to peers written by Chang and Yoshi, and analyzed the sentences according to which features they presented. Sentences not showing any of
the characteristics above received a rating of "0." The syntactic complexity of a text can then be expressed as the average of the ratings of all
of its sentences. Using this as a measure, we attempted to find syntactic
indications of style shift. No "neat" patterns emerged, as they rarely do
in linguistics, but we identified and can illustrate some trends.

Chang's contributions to the conference typically ranged at Level 4,
except for two postings that were at the Level 2 range. What is interesting about Chang's summary for the "Classics" conference, which summarized a selection by M. A. K. Halliday (1978) is that Chang's summary
was at her mean, the Level 4 range (4.4), even though the source she
worked from was much higher in syntactic complexity (6.4). One might
conclude from those numbers that Chang either refused or was unable
to align with the syntactic patterns of the professional source, possibly
intimidated by their complexity. But a sentence-by-sentence study comparing how she represented her source, with a similar analysis of that
source, suggests otherwise, indicating not only her awareness of the stylistic profile of the published text but also her attempt to control it.

For example, in one part of the passages we selected, Halliday, the original author, uncharacteristically dips to the low end of the spectrum, with a sentence scoring a "0" preceding a typically complex Level 7 sentence:

The work of Basil Bernstein has sometimes been referred to as a 'theory of educational failure' [Level 0]. Less, because Bernstein does not claim to be providing a total explanation of the causes of educational failure; he is offering an interpretation of one aspect of it, the fact that the distribution of failure is not random but follows certain known and sadly predictable patterns – by and large, it is a problem which faces children of the lower working class in large urban areas. [Level 7; both sentences combined average 3.5]. (1978, p. 101)

It appears that Chang perceived the zero-level sentence as an anomaly. In her "summary," she worked the two sentences into one combined sentence. Thereby, she raised the combined profile of those two original sentences from 3.5 (Halliday) to 7.0:

This article discusses the theory of educational failure which according to Bernstein the distribution of failure is not random but follows certain known and sadly predictable patterns – by and large, it is a problem which faces children of the lower working class in large urban areas [Level 7]. (Chang)

The resulting sentence was more consistent with Halliday's overall level of syntactic complexity.

Combining the two sentences involved a linguistic effort for Chang, so we can assume that it was not done for convenience. To combine the two sentences, Chang used what originally appears to be a relative pronoun, "which," as a subordinating conjunction. This was a creative solution for what presented itself to her as a syntactic problem, not ignorance of the proper use of relative pronouns. One paragraph later in the same sample, Chang used "which" productively and correctly as a theta-role-bearing relative pronoun: "it is . . . society's attitude to language and to dialect which put them at a disadvantage." One way to read Chang's motive in combining those sentences into one, if it is not linguistic convenience, is sensitivity to what she perceived was the typical style of Halliday.

Let us assume that Chang's sentence combining shows awareness of the original author's typical syntactic profile. But let us also keep in mind that Chang's summary is *not* out of line with her other postings in syntactic complexity (4.4 versus 4.0, 2.2, 2.5, and 4.0). It would appear that although Chang may well have appropriated Halliday's *words,* she did not appropriate Halliday's *syntax.* But it is not an outright rejection. Chang's postings *throughout* have some of the authoritative tone of the professional. It may be that Chang "scaled down" the syntactic profile she found typical in Halliday to a complexity level that she found comfortable for herself, as a participant of the conference. Chang clearly demonstrated that she is capable of Level 7 sentences in her postings. She also demonstrated that she can analyze complexity levels in the writings of others, as when she took control of her source (Halliday) by raising its complexity level when the original was uncharacteristically low. Given those indications of her demonstrated syntactic and stylistic sophistication, we must conclude that her own syntactic profile overall reflects a stylistic decision not to emulate her source syntactically.

A different trend emerged when we studied Yoshi's contributions, in particular three passages: the beginning of his summary, which followed the original very closely; the end of his summary, where he paraphrased more and breaks away from the syntactic constructions of the original; and a response to a fellow conference participant. (We include these three passages as Appendix B.) Yoshi's original source (Obler, 1989) was not quite as complex syntactically as Chang's source. The material corresponding to his opening paragraph scores at 4.8, which Yoshi nearly matched with a 3.6, the lower number indicating omissions. What is interesting is that when Yoshi broke away from the verbatim wording and started to insert his own paraphrases at the end of the summary, his syntactic complexity *increased* to match the original more closely (4.6 compared to Obler's 5.0 during this stretch of her chapter). He clearly attempted to present a style different from that of his responses to course members, where his syntactic complexity level dropped to a low 1.8 and 2.2. The following two sentences may serve as representative samples:

That is, there are some possibilities that older adult, as well as younger adult, can develop their language, by using proper strategies for language processing. [Level 4] (From summary)

Japanese farmers use KAKASHI to protect their crops from birds, monkeys, and sometimes a human. [Level 2] (From response)

Yoshi's self-evaluation at the end of the conference had professed conscious awareness of differences in style, and of his attempts to emulate them. The stylistic choices of the two passages represented by the quotes above reflected different purposes. In the summary, Yoshi represented the content and authority of the Obler article. In the response, Yoshi diplomatically attempted to differ with the content summarized by a previous poster; he kept the tone very amiable and personal and opened with a humorous observation about the computer-generated user ID of that poster, KAKASHI, which reminded Yoshi of the Japanese word for "scarecrow." Lowering syntactic complexity appears to have been one way for Yoshi to disassociate his posting from the authoritative style of the professional voice, making his observations acceptable not only to the fellow Japanese graduate student, but also to the other conference participants who, he anticipates, will read his response as well (note that he explains his pun for the non-Japanese reader).

Lexical inventory

The two quotes from Yoshi above suggest that one of the ways in which he observed himself as emulating a Western style of writing is by his lexical selections. The introductory "That is" echoes the same phrase in a preceding passage and different context in the original source. Its word choice appears to correspond more to an academic, or lecturing, style. The second sentence illustrates a more conversational style. Both would, of course, be appropriate choices to make, given the task of each posting.

To explore whether Yoshi's lexical inventory was an indicator of stylistic change or accommodation, we computed an index of "lexical density" as defined by Michael Stubbs, in which lexical density equals $100 \times L/N$ (L being the lexical words and N the total number of words) (Stubbs, 1996, p. 72). The percentages for the two passages in Yoshi's summary were consistent, both 62% (compared to 60% and 58.6% in the original by Obler). The percentage of lexical words dropped considerably, however, in his more personal reply to KAKASHI, to 49%. Such a relative increase in function words over lexical words has been taken to indicate a different style of discourse. Stubbs summarizes surveys by Ure (1971), according to which written texts tend to have a lexical density in the range of 36% to 57%, whereas spoken texts typically range from 24% to 43% (Stubbs, 1996, p. 72). On the basis of Stubbs's own surveys, the density index of Yoshi's summary would pattern with written non-fiction in the Lancaster-Oslo Bergen (LOB) corpus, whereas the lexical density of his personal response would pattern either with written fiction from that same corpus or with spoken "public speeches" or "answer-phone" messages in the Lund corpus, right on the border (45%–50%) between spoken language with and without feedback from other speakers (p. 74). If large-corpus surveys have established typical ranges of lexical density for different language tasks, there is a possibility that Yoshi's self-reported awareness of stylistic differences extended to their lexical inventories.

It should be noted that Yoshi's consistency in lexical density for both samples from his summary and his remarkable closeness in this feature to Obler's original source are not simply the result of copying. Yoshi's clause length is slightly different from Obler's in both samples: 10.3 words per clause compared to Obler's 10.7 in "Yoshi 1," 8.1 words per clause compared to Obler's 9.5 in "Yoshi 2" ("Yoshi 3" drops to 7.3 words per clause).

Figures 1 and 2 show that Yoshi matched Obler's lexical density *proportionately*, not merely by appropriation of text. We believe this to be another indication of Yoshi's sensitivity to stylistic patterns. Achieving the same ratio of function words to lexical words with different clause length appears to be a sign of emulation.

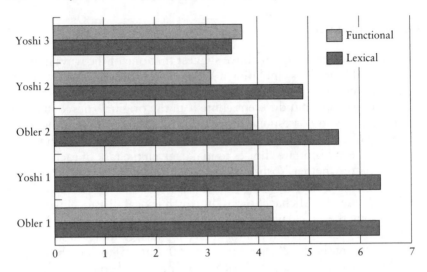

Figure 1   Average numbers of function words versus lexical words per clause. "Yoshi 1" is a close copy of "Obler 1," whereas "Yoshi 2" contains considerably more paraphrase of "Obler 2." "Yoshi 3" is not a summary but a personal response to a fellow conference participant.

To find more indications of stylistic choice, we compiled a detailed inventory of which kinds of words Yoshi used in the first passage of his summary ("Yoshi 1" in Figure 1), the final passage of his summary (with the paraphrases: equals "Yoshi 2"), and the response to KAKASHI ("Yoshi 3"). We also compared them to the corresponding passages in Obler, his source. In particular, we looked at the average occurrence of certain parts of speech per clause: nouns [N], main verbs [V], adjectives/adverbs [A], lexical prepositions such as "in" and "under" [P(lex.)], functional prepositions that are inserted to indicate syntactic functions, such as possessive "of" and passive "by" [P(funct.)], auxiliaries [Aux], modals [M], copulas [COP], coordinating conjunctions [C-CONJ], subordinating conjunctions [S-CONJ], determiners [D], including possessive determiners "my," "your," etc. (cf. Thiede, 1996), and all "pronouns" [PN], (here understood as only those proforms that stand for entire noun phrases, i.e., "pro-NP." Overall, the proportions are fairly consistent.

The clearest *differences* showed up in the use of nouns, lexical prepositions, and pronouns. The farther Yoshi is removed from Obler, the lower his count drops for nouns per clause. But only in his personal response did we see a proportionate increase in his use of pronouns per clause. When Yoshi paraphrased and assumed a professional style, the use of pronouns actually drops. It appears that Yoshi must have associated the use of pronouns as more informal, or maybe less informational. The

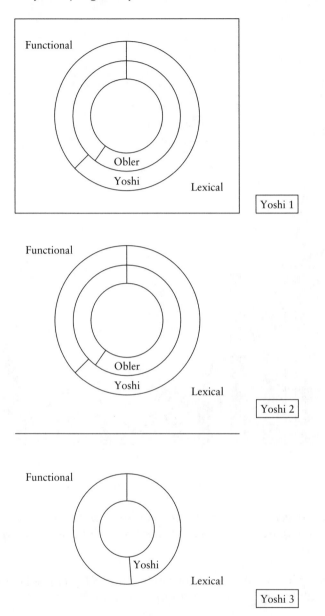

Figure 2   Relative proportions of lexical to functional words in the three samples from Yoshi, as compared to Obler.

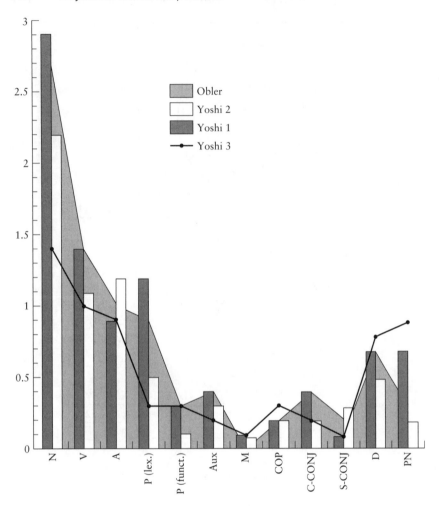

Figure 3   Selected average lexical inventory per clause in three passages by Yoshi, compared against the source text of his summary, Obler.

overall drop in lexical prepositions may reflect a lower need to elaborate, possibly indicating a lower assumption of authority.

What do these trends suggest about learning?

All the information we have on the students' *prior* experience in electronic conferencing and in their ability to select styles appropriate to different tasks is self-reported and anecdotal, so this part of our observation is uncontrolled. Electronic conferencing was a new forum for everyone. This is why we have focused on indications of accommodation *within* the conference. But can such a short time span yield indications of linguistic learning?

Learning (unlike acquisition) requires *awareness* of what is to be learned. Where learners fail to have awareness of a difference between the target language and their own language variety, they have a "matching problem" (Klein, 1986, p. 62). We have presented some indications of such awareness: Chang's instance of sentence combining to maintain syntactic complexity, even at the cost of having to create a linguistic solution for doing so; her choice not to emulate Halliday's level of syntactic complexity; Yoshi's strict separation of styles to signal authority versus comity, and his self-reported awareness of how he emulated the "logical" writing style of academe, are surely indicative of conscious efforts rather than accidental effects. Such conscious awareness would at least imply that the conferencing provided an atmosphere conducive to learning.

Although we believe that we have seen indications of conscious awareness and attempts at accommodation in syntax, lexicon, and style, we cannot rule out the possibility that other factors may have contributed to the trends we observed. To test for the possibility that, in summaries, emulation of patterns in syntactic complexity and lexical inventories in smaller clauses were simply the result of omission, we computed a factor for the average number of propositions per every ten words, a technique we adapted from Snowdon et al. (1996). We did that for all three Asian students whose writings we had specifically examined: Chang, Yoshi, and Wang. For the first ten sentences of a number of contributions by foreign participants (or for as many sentences as there were, if the posting was shorter), we wrote out the propositions contained in each sentence, then computed the propositional density index for each sentence (propositional density $= P/N \times 10$, with P the number of propositions and N the number of words per sentence). A typical entry would look like this:

Note 2.71-1. I think you did a great job of summarizing Krashen's Input Hypothesis. (12 words)	1 (DO, YOU, 2)
	2 (GREAT, 3)
	3 (JOB, 4)
	4 (SUMMARIZE, 5)
	5 (INPUT HYPOTHESIS, KRASHEN, 6)
	6 (THINK, I, 1)
	6 propositions / 12 words $\times$ 10 = 5

We then averaged the indexes for each posting. It turned out that the propositional density, as we measured it, was quite consistent, not only between source and summary, but *across a writer's postings*. Yoshi's samples ranged from 3.25 to 3.8 (the author of the source of his summary, Obler, scored at 3.75). Wang's samples ranged from 3.1 to 4.1.

Chang varied from 2.7 to 3.8; her summary is actually slightly denser in propositions than her source (3.6, comparing to Halliday's 3.2). Even an increase in the ratio of function words over lexical words, as observed in Yoshi's lexical profile ("Yoshi 3," Figure 1), does not significantly affect propositional density (compare 3.25 in the "Yoshi 1" sample from the beginning of the summary to 3.7 in "Yoshi 3," the personal response). Such consistency in the density of information would seem to indicate that the students were in control of their information management and seems to speak against the possibility that similarities in lexicosyntactic profiles between original source and summaries can be attributed to accident, or simply to the fact that material was copied and simplified.

We believe that more was at work here, and that, like Wang's discourse-level shifting, the syntactic and lexical performance of Yoshi and Chang is suggestive of some consciously motivated choices of style, of lexico-syntactic accommodation, and of linguistic awareness that is the prerequisite to learning.

Concluding remarks

An asynchronous electronic conference has a number of learning curves associated with it, for its sponsors as well as its participants. Its utility for researchers is that it stores all contributions, preserves the dynamics of responses, and provides a window into the group mechanisms of how a knowledge community forms, even with subgroups. Thus, a completed conference becomes a document – and a data collection. A number of questions and investigation techniques could be brought to bear on such a collection. Here we worked mainly with discourse and corpus linguistic issues and limited the scope mainly to how three Asian graduate students accommodated to styles they perceived in the conference interaction, particularly those of native speakers.

The final self-reports of the second language students were more reflective of their realization that they had adjusted their discourse patterns, whereas the native English students wrote more about their awareness of writing in and for a community. The conferences seem to have had a netiquette of their own, such as adhering to a rule like "be more than usually polite." At the same time, politeness indicators such as compliments also reflected social negotiation, especially assumptions of authority, for instance, in how they signaled approbation alone without bestowing explicit agreement or alignment. The Chinese and Japanese participants showed a trend of cultural adjustment here, which we illustrated with the changing contributions by Wang. Compliments also reflected the fact that the second language graduate students had more authority in the classroom than the primarily NES undergraduates in the same course. Status and distance dynamics among the participants suggested that compliments (including compliments plus agreement) were more likely to be offered to current or prospective status equals. This is, we think, an apparent confirmation for electronic conference interaction of Wolfson's bulge hypothesis: that minimum, or, in this case, maximum, degrees of status and social distance among intimates on the one hand, and "strangers" on the other, foster very similar patterns, as opposed to the greater variation in the middle section.

Although the data suggest awareness of, and accommodation to, social status and discourse conventions, looking at syntactic and lexical profiles in two of the Asian graduate students' postings suggested further signs of student awareness and, possibly, learning. We found indications that both Chang and Yoshi were aware of syntactic complexity in the sources they summarized and that they probably anticipated that a different syntactic complexity was expected in responses to other postings. Yoshi's syntactic patterns showed alignment to the authority of the published source he summarized, and a clear separation of the professional style of the summary from the personable style of his responses. Chang, on the other hand, assumed more control over syntax by scaling down her original source's syntactic complexity and by extending her voice of authority, and its syntactic profile, to her other postings. Lexical and propositional profiles for density show an amount of linguistic control and stylistic awareness that indicates active accommodation beyond mere appropriation: Indications are that we identified their awareness as a stage prerequisite for learning.

We set up the electronic conferences as a forum for discovery-based, collaborative learning. It appears that this learning, for the EFL students we examined, included linguistic learning. We learned, too, by identifying sociostylistic and lexicosyntactic patterns of adjustment in our students. All in all, the extra effort of setting up the conferences, and of requiring the students to do the additional writing and adjusting, profited both sides.

Appendix A: Wang's additional replies

Note 2.105   1-MAR-1993 11:24
•   <REPLY TO Note 2.5 ADULT ACQUISITION OF LANGUAGE>-
You did a great job in summarizing this particular classic study. You made very clear statements about what language skills are possessed by adults and how those language skills are processed by adults. You also gave a lot of examples to interpret your statements.
Based on you summary, I realize that
1) males and females use different language forms,

2) language forms may vary based on the interactants' relationship,
3) different social classes use distinctly different languages,
4) it's not impossible for adults to acquire a new language, but, they need to practice more
5) older people might not performe worse in identifying the lexical features except they might use some obsolete words.
Furthermore, I want to tell you again that I really enjoy reading your summary.
==
Note 2.106   1-MAR-1993 11:34
• < REPLY TO Note 2.7 THEORY OF SIGNS >-
I like that you state the purpose of this article you read at the very beginning of your summary. It provides me a very clearpicture about your summary.
Based on reading your summary, I realize that there are three types of signs: indexical, iconic, and symbolic signs and each of those signs has three elements (the sign vehicle, the interpretant, and the object) which tie together and make the sign meaningful. Furthermore, you made a diagram to interpret the three types of signs.
Because, I've never study any theory that are directly related to the article you summarized. I do have problems to understand how people choose a particular type of signs instead of the other. I hope you can give me some examples to help my understanding. Thank you.
==
Note 2.107   1-MAR-1993 11:41
• < REPLY TO Note 2.16 TALKING TO CHILDREN >-
I enjoy reading your summary very much. Especially, in addition to summarizing the article you read, you gave your personal ideas about this article. I feel that you did interact with the author even though you think this article is quite boring.
Based on reading your summary, I think there are a lot of characteristics about communicating to young children could also be easily found in my country- Taiwan. I saw a lot of parents talk to their children exactly the same way you described, even a child talk to the younger one will employ this kind of method. It's quite amazing, isn't it?
Again, I want to tell you that you did a wonderful job and I wish I could be a reader like you.
==
Note 2.108   1-MAR-1993 12:01
• < REPLY TO Note 2.21 CULTURE AND PERSONALITY>-
As a foreign student in UNCC, I always have problems to explain and classify my behaviors to American friends. Because I really don't that some of my behaviors are either influenced by my culture or by my own personality.
I agree that cultural behaviors are learned and personality contivues to

add to itself and grow. But, how can I determine the language spoken by any individual is the result of the culture or the personality, or perhaps both. I think it's quite difficult to make a distinction, isn't it?

Anyway, I think yu did a good job on making your summary short and clear and I really appreciate your work.

===

Note 2.109   1-MAR-1993 12:12

• 	< REPLY TO Note 2.26 SPEECH PROCESSES >-

When people speak they are usually not aware of the cognitive process. Especially, when we talk in our first language we often think that we just speak spontaneously without passing through any mental cognitive processes.

Your summary was divided into two parts. In the first part, you describe the four problems faced in oral description (level, content, order, and rela-tion). In the second part, you gave a very brief and clear interpretation about the three categories of a sentence (prepositional content, illocu-tionary content, and thematic structure). I think it's really interesting that when we utter one particular sentence we have already examined so many things in our mind.

I always feel that psychology is a very difficult subject to study, but now I realize that's because human being's cognitive processes couldn't be more complex.

I think you did make a clear interpretation about the article you read and I really enjoy reading your summary.

===

Note 2.110   1-MAR-1993 12:22

• 	< REPLY TO Note2.33 THE MAN WITH THE SHATTERED WORLD

I really feel sorry for those terrible things he went through and I also feel proud of his spirit of continuous learning after his brain injury.

One of the learning methods he used to overcome the difficulty of re-membering the individual letters is to draw upon associations form things he already know. I think this method is also valuable for all the language learners. Because, when we can make the language becomes more meaningful for ourself then we will become more capable of memorizing or using the language.

Your summary gives me the will to read the entire story about the person who suffered a horrible brain injury. I also want to say that how lucky we are to be healthy.

===

Note 2.111   1-MAR-1993 13:48

• 	< REPLY TO Note 2.39 CHOMSKY ON LENNEBERG >-

Your summary gave me a very clear concepts about how Chomsky's idea is related to Lenneberg's idea and how Chomsky's idea is different from Lenneberg's endogenous paradigm of linguistic competence.

I think that studying language performance should consider both the internal variables and the external variables in order to have better understanding about individual's language performance.

Although, experts in human and language study field have already provided some insight of the language performance, it seems to me that it's still not enough. Maybe, that's the reason why we still can't answer how people acquire a language without any doubt.

```
=========================================================
```

Note 2.112   1-MAR-1993 13:56
• < REPLY TO Note 2.57 A NEW PARADIGM OF REFERENCE>-
Your summary gave me a very clear picture about why communication is a fuzzy concept. Besides, you gave a lot of examples to clarify the fuzziness, prototypicality and the concepts of basic object level.

I agree that all this classification is very subjective and influenced by different point of views. For instance, I could never classify a tomato into a certain category. Because, my mother thinks it's a kind of vegetables and my brother thinks it's a kind of fruits. Well, which kind of categories do you think tomatoes will fit into.

```
=========================================================
```

Note 2.113   1-MAR-1993 14:05
• < REPLY TO Note 2.58 SUMMARY OF GEORGE MILLER
Your summary is very thoughtful and clear. Based on reading your summary, I realize that a child first use gestures to communicate, then utter a single sound, naming manipulated objects, utter two word sentences, use tag questions, and then use the irregular verbal forms.

However, I feel confused about the stage of using the irregular verbal form. Because, according to my understanding, there's no irregular forms of verb or noun in Chinese. I wonder, what really happens to those children's language acquisition at the time when American children are at the stage of using the irregular verbal form. Do they skip this stage and go to next stage or do they simply remain at the prior stage.

Appendix B: Passages by Yoshi

SUMMARY OF A CLASSIC (Obler, 1989) [opening and final passages]
Adult language acquisition is not formally learned but is acquired in context. There are registers or styles of speech we need to acquire in our work and in our relationship. This book helps us consider what these adult language skills are and the process of it.
1. Language in Adolescence and Adulthood
Special registers are mastered starting in childhood, exploited in adolescence, and refined in adulthood for special activities and for many aspects of interpersonal relationships. . . .

. . . given certain sorts of lexical tasks, in particular confrontation-naming tasks, the 30-year-olds performed somewhat worse than the 50-year-olds. And when older adults are asked to define words, they perform as well as younger adults. Thus, lexical items are not actually being lost in older adults. Older subjects may fail to name a picture because they use a word that is no longer common.

However, the older adults recognized the items as well as the young subjects. That is, there are some possibilities that older adult, as well as younger adult, can develop their language, by using proper strategies for language processing.

11-FEB-1993 11:27   -< A REPLY TO: CULTURE & PERSONALITY >-

The topic of the relationship of the individual to society, and of personality to culture is very interesting but somewhat confusing for me to understand. I was born and brought up in Japan. I had lived in the Japanese cultural contexts for thirty years. I believe that Japanese culture has had a great influence to some parts of my personality to be made. But I can't analize my bihavior whether it is cultural or not.

It might be a person-defining behavior. In your summary, you noted that "personality contains a combination of elements of experience, and continues to add to itself and grow." I do agree to this opinion.

Because my personality is changing, especially since I came to America. I will bring new culture back to Japan which might influence the Japanese culture. That is, individual can make new culture.

Individual can influence his/her society, and cultures in the society will influence individual personalities. Next time when you write, I would like to know how culture influence his/her native language.

11-FEB-1993 11:50 -< A REPLY TO "KAKASHI" >-

First of all, how did you get a great name "KAKASHI"? I just love it, it's a Japanese name. Japanese farmers use KAKASHI to protect their crops from birds, monkeys, and sometimes a human.

Your topic interested me very much, because I am one of the people who is trying to master English. I am thirty, so I would like to know how adult can acquire a second language. According to your writing, you mainly noted two important conceptions of acquiring language. I don't think I am a 'self-confident' learner, but 'flexible'. I am a kind of 'take-it-easy' man. As you said, personality is one of the main factors to learn a new language fast.

Talking about child's acquisition of a second language, I do agree with your opinion. "Children under ten might acquire the phonological system of a new language more successfully than adults might do." I have a difficulty in producing the English sounds. I wish I were under ten. . . . So teach me how to make the English sounds, OK?

References

Bell, A. (1984). Language style as audience design. *Language in Society, 13,* 145–204.

Bergman, M. L., & Kasper, G. (1993). Perception and performance in native and nonnative apology. In G. Kasper & S. Blum-Kulka (Eds.), *Interlanguage pragmatics* (pp. 82–106). New York: Oxford University Press.

Biber, D. (1988). *Variation across speech and writing.* Cambridge: Cambridge University Press.

Bouldin, T., & Odell, L. (1993). Surveying the field and looking ahead: A systems theory perspective on research on writing in the workplace. In R. Spilka (Ed.), *Writing in the workplace: New research perspectives* (pp. 268–284). Carbondale: Southern Illinois University Press.

Carrell, P. L. (1988). SLA and classroom instruction: Reading. *Annual Review of Applied Linguistics, 9,* 223–242.

Chen, R. (1993). Responding to compliments: A contrastive study of politeness strategies between American English and Chinese speakers. *Journal of Pragmatics, 20,* 49–75.

Chomsky, N. (1992). *A minimalist program for linguistic theory.* MIT Occasional Papers in Linguistics, no. 1.

Connor, U. (1996). *Contrastive rhetoric: Cross-cultural aspects of second-language writing.* Cambridge: Cambridge University Press.

Davis, B., & Brewer, J. (1997). *Electronic discourse: Linguistic individuals in cyberspace.* Albany: State University of New York Press.

Elbow, P. (1994). What do we mean when we talk about voice in texts? In K. Yancey (Ed.), *Voices on voice: Perspectives, definitions, inquiry* (pp. 1–35). Urbana, IL: National Council of Teachers of English.

Ferrara, K., Brunner, H., & Whittemore, G. (1991). Interactive written discourse as an emergent register. *Written Communication, 8,* 8–34.

Halliday, M. A. K. (1978). The significance of Bernstein's work for sociolinguistic theory. In *Language as social semiotic* (pp. 101–107). Baltimore: University Park Press.

Henderson, A. (1996). Compliments, compliment responses, and politeness in an African-American community. In J. Arnold, R. Blake, B. Davidson, S. Schwenter, & J. Solomon (Eds.), *Sociolinguistic variation: Data, theory, and analysis* (pp. 195–208). Stanford, CA: Center for the Study of Language and Information.

Herring, S. C. (Ed.). (1996). *Computer-mediated communication: Linguistic, social and cross-cultural perspectives.* Amsterdam: John Benjamins

Herring, S. (1993). Gender and democracy in computer-mediated communication. *Electronic Journal of Communication, 3*(2), n.p.

Johnson, D. (1991). Second language and content learning with computers: Research in the role of social factors. In P. Dunkel (Ed.), *Computer-assisted language learning and testing: Research issues and practice* (pp. 61–83). New York: Newbury House.

Kern, R. (1996). Computer-mediated communication: Using e-mail exchanges to explore personal histories in two cultures. In M. Warschauer (Ed.), *Telecollaboration in foreign language learning* (pp. 105–119). Honolulu: Second Language Teaching and Curriculum Center, University of Hawaii.

Kirkland, M., & Saunders, M. (1991). Maximizing student performance in summary writing: Managing cognitive load. *TESOL Quarterly, 25*, 105–122.

Kirkpatrick, A. (1995). Chinese rhetoric, methods of argument. *Multilingua, 14*, 271–295.

Klein, W. (1986). *Second language aquisition.* Cambridge: Cambridge University Press.

Leki, I. (1991). Twenty-five years of contrastive rhetoric: Text analysis and writing pedagogies. *TESOL Quarterly, 25*, 123–143.

Obler, L. K. (1989). Language beyond childhood. In J. B. Gleason (Ed.), *The development of language* (pp. 275–301). Boston: Merrill.

Mathison, M. A. (1996). Writing the critique, a text about a text. *Written Communication, 13*, 14–35.

Mehan, H., Moll, L., & Riel, M. (1985). *Computers in classrooms: A quasi-experiment in guided change. Final Report.* ERIC Microfiche No. ED292460.

Murray, D. (1991). *Conversation for action: The computer terminal as a medium of communication.* Philadelphia: John Benjamins.

Pennycook, A. (1996). Borrowing others' words: Text, ownership, memory, and plagiarism. *TESOL Quarterly, 30*, 201–230.

Pinker, S. (1994). *The language instinct: How the mind creates language.* New York: William Morrow.

Purves, A. (1986). Rhetorical communities, the international student, and basic writing. *Journal of Basic Writing, 5*, 38–51.

Rosenberg, S., & Abbeduto, L. (1987). Indicators of linguistic competence in the peer group conversational behavior of mildly retarded adults. *Applied Psycholinguistics, 8*, 19–32.

Scardamalia, M., & Bereiter, C. (1996). Computer support for knowledge-building communities. In T. Koschmann (Ed.), *CSCL: Theory and practice of an emerging paradigm* (pp. 249–268). Mahwah, NJ: Lawrence Erlbaum Associates.

Scollon, R., & Scollon, S. (1995). *Intercultural communication.* Cambridge, MA: Basil Blackwell.

Snowdon, D. A., Kemper, S. J., Mortimer, J. A., Greiner, L. H., Wekstein, D. R., & Markesbery, W. R. (1996). Linguistic ability in early life and cognitive function and Alzheimer's disease in late life: Findings from the Nun Study. *JAMA, 275*, 528–532.

Stubbs, M. (1996). *Text and corpus analysis.* Cambridge, MA: Basil Blackwell.

Sussex, R., & White, P. (1996). Electronic networking. *Annual Review of Applied Linguistics, 16*, 200–225.

Swales, J. (1990). *Genre analysis: English in academic and research settings.* New York: Cambridge University Press.

Takano, S. (1993). The transfer of L1 rhetoric in L2 texts and its implications for second language teaching. *Journal of Intensive English Studies, 7*, 43–83.

Thiede, R. (1996). The "possessive case" in English: A postmortem. *SECOL Review.*

Ure, J. (1971). Lexical density and register differentiation. In G. Perren & J. L. M. Trim (Eds.), *Applications of linguistics* (pp. 443–452). London: Cambridge University Press.

Warschauer, M. (Ed.) (1995). *Virtual connections: On-line activities and projects for networking language learners.* Honolulu: Second Language Teaching and Curriculum Center, University of Hawaii.

Wolfson, N. (1983). An empirically based analysis of complimenting in American English. In N. Wolfson & E. Judd (Eds.), *Sociolinguistics and language acquisition* (pp. 82–95). Rowley, MA: Newbury House.

Wolfson, N. (1989). The social dynamics of native and nonnative variation in complimenting behavior. In M. Eisenstein (Ed.), *The dynamic interlanguage: Empirical studies in second language variation* (pp. 219–236). New York: Plenum Press.

Wu, D-Y. (1990). Chinese/English biliteracy, a study of written codeswitching behavior among the Chinese community in U.S. universities. *Florida Journal of Anthropology, 15,* 5–15.

Ye, L. (1995). Complimenting in Mandarin Chinese. In G. Kasper (Ed.), *Pragmatics of Chinese as native and target language* (pp. 127–154). Honolulu: Second Language Teaching and Curriculum Center, University of Hawaii.

Zuengler, J. 1993. Explaining NNS interactional behavior: The effect of conversational topic. In G. Kasper & S. Blum-Kulka (Eds.), *Interlanguage pragmatics* (pp. 184–194). New York: Oxford University Press.

6 Computers and collaborative writing in the foreign language curriculum

Jean Marie Schultz

Not long ago, as the technological revolution began accelerating at an astounding rate, a number of humanists admonished their more reticent colleagues to put aside their misgivings about the educational potential of the computer and to begin integrating technology into their approaches to teaching. Some scholars argued that the humanities, by not implementing new technologies, ran the risk of increasing obsolescence (see Herron & Moos, 1993, p. 479). Partially on this basis, Richard Lanham (1993) argues strenuously for the integration of computers into the humanities, and particularly into the writing curriculum, noting that "The students we teach are going to do most of their writing and much of their reading on an electronic screen. They are going to live – they live now – in a world of electronic text" (p. 121).

As Lanham suggests, one of the most compelling areas of exploration for computer use is in the field of foreign language writing. Part of this attention derives quite naturally from the English composition curricula from which the teaching of foreign language writing takes its cue. With the advent of the word processor, the teaching of writing has drastically changed, making the radical revision of a text possible with a few keystrokes. This technological ease of revision has in turn served to bolster the parallel shift in the teaching of writing from an end-product approach, where the teacher alone reads and comments on papers students have written without the benefit of feedback on a rough draft, to a process approach, where students work in small groups of peers for suggestions for multiple drafts, subsequently revising their papers before finally handing them in to the teacher. In foreign language as well, process writing has become the accepted approach not only because it has been shown to improve students' writing significantly, but also in part because it necessitates verbal communication in small groups on an authentic task, thus articulating particularly well with the communicative goals of the foreign language classroom (Gaudiani, 1981; Barnett, 1989; Schultz, 1991b). Textbooks overtly implementing a process approach now occupy a significant place in the field of foreign language composition, with the most recent composition textbooks advocating the use of computers in their writing programs (see Garrard, Rusterholz, & Long, 1993; Siskin, Krueger, & Fauvel, 1996).

Despite the increasing push to use computers in the foreign language curriculum, the effect of computer use on actual writing skills is in need of more rigorous investigation. Articles advocating the use of various computer programs have yet to offer concrete studies of these programs' actual benefits for writing. Most are satisfied to claim that student writing is simply "improved." For instance, in an article on the possibilities for using computer technology in the foreign language classroom, Armstrong and Yetter-Vassot (1994) advocate the direct use of computers in the process-approach peer-review process (pp. 479–480). They propose that students begin writing their papers during class time on computers in a lab setting. During the activity, students are encouraged to discuss their work with each other; and the teacher also makes an effort to visit each student, offering suggestions for improvement. During the next session, students bring their completed drafts to class on diskette and work in small groups on computer terminals for peer review. Armstrong and Yetter-Vassot (1994) remark at the end of the "Process Writing with Computers" section of their article that student writing improves and that "students are willing to take more risks, that is, experiment with unfamiliar vocabulary or difficult grammatical structures, because they have the opportunity to preview them with the instructor" (ibid.).

Their article raises some interesting issues in terms of student writing improvement and computers: It suggests that a qualitative difference in papers exists, depending on mode of production. The first question to be asked in an attempt to evaluate computer efficacy is: To what writing format is computer writing to be compared? What approach to writing had been used prior to the incorporation of computers? Also, could factors other than computer use be responsible for improvement in writing, particularly in light of the fact that the authors cite instructor previewing as a significant element of their approach? The authors note that the writing activity requires two full class periods and assert that the time trade-off is worthwhile in terms of the improvement in writing. However, given the lack of comparative evaluative basis, is this expenditure of time justified? Might there be other more efficient formats, computer or noncomputer, that would improve writing? The notion of writing improvement is itself a vague, catchall term. What exactly constitutes improvement? How is improvement defined? And for what types of improvement is the computer responsible? Additional questions have to do with group interaction during face-to-face and computer response-group work. How do students interact in each format? Do they respond to their classmates' writing differently? Do they offer different types of advice, depending on response-group format? Does the discourse community change? How?

Rationale of the study

It was with these questions in mind that the present study was consti-tuted, to compare the effects of two distinct process-approach formats, one computer-based and one face-to-face, on intermediate-level French students' writing. Since 1986, the writing component of the second-year (intermediate-level) French program at the University of California at Berkeley has involved peer editing. Students bring two copies of the rough draft of their compositions to class, where they exchange them with two other classmates. As homework, students are asked to analyze the com-positions for content, organization, and style, to comment on the com-position drafts in the margins, and to write an evaluation offering sug-gestions for improvement at the end, an evaluation modeled on the ones teachers provide on the final drafts of compositions. The next day in class, students meet in their small groups and go over their comments, discussing ways to improve the compositions and addressing issues of interpretation. The in-class small-group discussions take approximately 20 minutes of class time. Working from their commented rough drafts, students then write the final draft of their papers, which they then turn in to their instructors (see Schultz, 1991b).

In 1992, the Language Media Center at Berkeley acquired the Daedalus Integrated Writing Environment package, whose "InterChange" com-ponent allows students to communicate with one another via networked computer stations in real time. The program had been used successfully in Berkeley's French 2 courses (second semester of first-year French). In a French 2 study comparing language produced via computer with that produced during in-class discussion, Kern (1995) found that students using InterChange took from two to three-and-a-half times more turns in discussion than students not using InterChange (p. 465). He also found that the length of utterances increased for the InterChange stu-dents. Moreover, according to the attitude questionnaire distributed to the students in the study, 93% responded favorably and considered InterChange to be a positive addition to the French 2 curriculum (ibid., p. 469).

The results of the French 2 InterChange study seemed to hold prom-ise for the second-year (French 3 and 4) response group formats. Instead of discussing rough drafts orally and face-to-face, InterChange students would each have a computer terminal networked with the terminals of the two other students in their response-group. In addition to the posi-tive effects detailed in the Kern study, InterChange potentially offered to overcome three problematic areas of traditional response-group work for intermediate program students. In principle, students would be able to "talk" all at the same time instead of waiting their turn as in the face-to-face format, and therefore they would be able to produce more extensive feedback on peers' compositions. Students would receive a written transcript of their response-group session, helping them to remember the points of discussion and consequently to act on peers' suggestions. Finally, students who were more reticent to participate in face-to-face response-group discussion might be more encouraged to respond to compositions via computer-mediated discussions.

With these possibilities in mind, InterChange was piloted in one section of French 3 in fall 1994 with positive preliminary results in student writing and in student attitude toward the activity. Based on these findings, all French 3 and 4 sections began using InterChange for response-group work during the spring semester. The current comparative study was undertaken in the spring semester of 1996. The purpose of the study was, first, to analyze concretely and quantifiably some of the issues raised when students moved from the traditional face-to-face format of process writing to networked computer communication, which many researchers see as the ultimate future for teaching composition (e.g., Holdstein, 1987; Lanham, 1993; Armstrong & Yetter-Vassot, 1994), and, second, to determine the efficacy of computers as a vehicle for response-group work. The study sought to answer four major questions:

1. Did students respond differently to each other's work in each format?
2. Did they take the work produced in one format more seriously than in the other?
3. How useful did students find the computer response-group format compared to the face-to-face response-group format?
4. Did student group interactions change depending on the type of response-group format?

In order to answer these questions, the study was organized as described below.

Method

Subjects and treatment

Subjects were drawn from a pool of 108 students enrolled in eight sections of French 3 and 4 at Berkeley. Not all of these students participated in all aspects of the study, however. Each of the eight course sections had from two to four small groups of three students involved in the study, and these groupings remained constant throughout the study. A total of 54 students participated in the essay analysis portion of the study, and 106 students participated in the attitude questionnaire portion of the study.

Within each course level there were two control and two experimental sections.[1] For both French 3 and 4, the control groups engaged in the traditional, noncomputerized, in-class, face-to-face response-group format described earlier. The two experimental sections in French 3 used only the InterChange program for their response-group work, except for the first composition, which incorporated face-to-face oral peer editing to provide students practice in responding to drafts. In French 4, students in the two experimental sections alternated between the face-to-face and computer formats for their response-group work. Alternating the experimental French 4 groups' formats allowed for a comparative analysis of work done by the same student using different formats and a comparative attitudinal assessment. In the French 3 program, students write a total of nine different one- to three-page compositions over the course of the 15-week semester. French 4 students write a total of ten one-and-a-half- to three-page compositions. Because they may not have previous experience in process writing, French 3 students begin response-group work with the fourth composition of the semester. French 4 students begin the process approach with the third composition. Therefore, students in the French 3 experimental sections used InterChange in the peer editing of five compositions, while students in the French 4 experimental sections peer edited four compositions using InterChange and another four compositions using face-to-face discussion.

Data collected

Ninety-three of the total number of essays that students wrote were considered ratable and therefore included in the study. There were several reasons for not including all essays. First, because students may not have had experience using the process approach, the first composition written using this format was not included in the study. Because of data-collection logistics, the final composition of the semester likewise could not be used. Second, as is always the case in a real classroom situation, not all students consistently turned in their rough drafts, drafts that were crucial for carrying out this analysis, as will be described later. Moreover, a significant number of rough drafts simply were not ratable for a variety of reasons. After receiving feedback from peers, some students changed their papers so radically that they were unrecognizable from the first version. This was a very positive effect of the response-group process; such students obviously think very deeply about their writing and are concerned about the validity of their interpretations. However, such compositions were impossible to tabulate in terms of numbers of changes from rough

1 Twenty-seven students from each level participated in the essay analysis portion of the study. In French 3 there were 13 experimental group students and 14 control group students. In French 4 there were 15 experimental group students and 12 control group students.

drafts.[2] Another significant number of students turned in outlines or semantic maps of their essays rather than full rough drafts (see Schultz, 1991a). These also were impossible to tabulate accurately. Finally, on one of the initial InterChange sessions, the program developed a bug, which made the transcripts unavailable for use in the revision process. Included in this study are two sets of French 3 compositions, one on Maupassant's "Le Horla" and one on Camus's "L'Hôte," for a total of 42 compositions. In French 4, composition sets on women authors (Yourcenar, Sarraute, Colette), on poetry, on Chateaubriand's *René*, and on Flaubert's *Un Cœur simple* were originally considered, but the composition set on women authors was ultimately rejected for problems of colinearity in the statistical analysis. A total of 51 French 4 essays were included in the current study.

In addition to the compositions and rough drafts, all InterChange transcripts were collected, all students filled out an attitude questionnaire adapted to whether they were in an experimental or a control section (see Appendix A), and tape recordings were made of face-to-face response group work in two groups per class, both in the pure face-to-face control sections and in the French 4 experimental sections, where editing was done by both face-to-face and computer-mediated communication.

Composition assessment

Assessment of compositions is a very difficult endeavor. Evaluative criteria are, of course, crucial, as are anchor compositions to determine the appropriate grade. In Berkeley's Intermediate French program, compositions are assessed according to the four classic writing categories used in many composition programs: content, organization, style, and grammar (see Gaudiani, 1981). These four categories were maintained in this study. However, no holistic assessment of compositions was carried out. This had already been done by the instructors teaching in the program in the grading process.[3] Moreover, for this study, a holistic assessment would reveal nothing as to the efficacy of the computer versus face-to-face formats, because individual writing styles and skill levels would confound the results. Instead, the number of changes students made between rough drafts and final papers was used as the assessment indicator, with a higher

2 There was a total of ten such compositions, the majority from the face-to-face and French 4 groups. Only three radically changed compositions came from the computer groups, and only one of these was from French 3. The remaining seven compositions were written by French 4 students in face-to-face formats.

3 Instructors receive a great deal of training in grading compositions. They receive a packet of anchor compositions illustrating grade levels for student work at different points in the program. They practice grading compositions collectively in their pedagogical seminars three times during the 15-week semester. Also, three times during the semester, they turn in to the intermediate program coordinator samples of their own graded and commented compositions.

TABLE I. SAMPLE SUMMARY FEATURES OF TWO FRENCH 3 ESSAYS ON "LE HORLA"

	C	O	S	G	*No. of pages*
Student A	4	1	4	1	2.5
Student B	11	0	1	2	2.5

number of changes indicating a positive result. The underlying assumption for this assessment method was that the number of changes correlates with a positive effort on the part of the students both to take seriously their peers' suggestions and to try to improve their compositions.

Analysis was carried out essentially by comparing rough and final drafts of papers. Each change students made from rough draft to final composition was coded "C" for "content," "O" for "organization," "S" for "style," and "G" for "grammar." The changes in each category were then tabulated and calculated on a changes per page basis. Table 1 summarizes two French 3 students' revisions. Student A made four content changes, one organizational change, four style changes, and one grammar change. Student B, on the same composition, made eleven content changes, zero organizational changes, one style change, and two grammar changes. Both students wrote compositions two-and-a-half pages in length.

There were a number of particularities within each assessment category. The grammar category was the most straightforward. Each time a student corrected a mistake in grammatical structure, it was counted as one change. However, incorrect "corrections" were also counted. These were included as indicative of a conscientious effort on the part of the students to improve their work, even though the result was ultimately incorrect. Spelling corrections were included in the grammar category.

The style category encompassed changes in vocabulary, transition usage, sentence structure, clause combining and creation of complex sentences, and changes in wording that had no impact on the content. As an example, we can see a fairly sophisticated style change in the following passage from a French 4 student's composition comparing Ponge's poem "Pluie" to Claudel's "La Pluie." In the rough draft, the student writes:

Bien que Ponge aborde la pluie comme quelque chose structurée et presque scientifique tandis que Claudel décrit la pluie dans une manière plus spirituelle et mystique, tous les deux poètes montrent par leurs examinations minutieuses un profond respet et vénération pour la pluie au même temps qu'ils font référence à l'acte d'écrire le poesie.[4]

---

4 All passages quoted from students' work are exactly as the student wrote them, with only minor grammar mistakes corrected. Translations do not reflect minor surface errors, including missing accents, but try to capture the stylistic effect.

[Although Ponge approaches the rain as something structured and almost scientific, whereas Claudel describes the rain in a more spiritual and mystical way, both poets show by their minute examinations a profound respect and veneration for the rain at the same time that they refer to the act of writing poetry.]

In the final composition, the sentence becomes:

Bien que Ponge aborde la pluie comme une chose structurée et presque scientifique tandis que Claudel décrit la pluie dans une manière plus spirituelle, tous le deux poètes montrent une vénération pour la pluie et au même temps révèlent un lien existe entre l'acte d'écrire la poèsie et la pluie.

[Although Ponge approaches the rain as a structured and almost scientific thing, whereas Claudel describes the rain in a more spiritual way, both poets show a veneration for the rain and at the same time reveal a link exists between the act of writing poetry and the rain.]

All the ideas of the original passage are maintained in the final rendition, with nothing new added. The wording in the last clause has changed, however.

The following excerpt from a French 3 student's composition on "Le Horla" represents a much less sophisticated style change. On the rough draft, the student writes, *Pourquoi est-ce que le horla choit hanter le narrateur et comment est-ce qu'il fait peur le narrateur?* (Why does the horla choose to haunt the narrator and how does he scare the narrator?). On the final composition, she writes, *Mais, si le horla existe, pourquoi est-ce que le horla choit hanter le narrateur et comment est-ce qu'il fait peur le narrateur?* (But, if the horla exists, why does the horla choose to haunt the narrator and how does he scare the narrator?)

Organizational changes fell into three broad categories. The most common was elimination of what the student evidently considered extraneous material. For example, a sentence might be deleted from the middle of a paragraph. This was the most frequent and simplest type of change. Students also revised their paragraphing, most often in an equally simple manner by breaking up a long paragraph. The most interesting types of organizational changes were made by moving whole paragraphs to a different position in the paper. This type of reorganization was almost always accompanied by massive content changes in which students added entire paragraphs to their compositions.

Content was the most problematic area to tabulate and is the area in need of the most intense examination in future studies. As mentioned earlier, compositions evidencing radical changes in interpretation throughout had to be eliminated from the study. Virtually all remaining content changes fell into the category of elaboration. Here, however, there was wide variation in terms of length. The least striking changes involved the addition of a brief phrase further refining an idea in a specific sentence.

For example, in the same "Le Horla" composition already mentioned, the student writes in the rough draft, *Il y a beaucoup de preuve que le horla existe. Le horla ne tortue pas le narrateur physiquement* (There is a lot of proof that the horla exists. The horla does not physically torture the narrator). In the final copy, the student writes, *L'auteur pense que le horla existe parce que beaucoup d'éventments étrange arrivent dans sa maison. Il est clair que le horla ne tortue pas le narrateur physiquement* (The author thinks that the horla exists because lots of strange events happen in his house. It is clear that the horla does not physically torture the narrator). Although the passage is still somewhat vague, the student here has become more specific in her analysis, evoking events that she will then treat in greater depth later in the paper. We find a more massive content change in the following passage taken from the Ponge/Claudel composition. In the rough draft, the student writes:

...la pluie... est liée diretement à l'acte d'écrire. Dans le dernier vers du poème Claudel, une ses trois idées principaux du poème: la pluie, la religion, et l'acte d'écrire le poesie. Il dit simplement, "Je fais aux tempêtes la libation de cette goutte d'encre." La libation – quand on verse le vin comme une collecte à Dieu – est ce que Claudel fait avec sa goutte d'encre, l'encre qu'il utilise pour écrire ce poème, quand il pleut. Toutes ses idées centraux – sa vénération pour la pluie présentée comme une expérience religieuse liée à son existence comme poète – sont succintement présentées dans le dernier vers de "La Pluie."

[. . . the rain . . . is linked directly to the act of writing. In the last verse of the Claudel poem, one of his three main ideas of the poem: the rain, religion, and the act of writing poetry. He says simply, "I offer the libation of this drop of ink to the tempest." The libation – when one pours wine as an offering to God – is what Claudel is doing with his drop of ink, ink that he uses to write this poem, when it is raining. All of his main ideas – his veneration for the rain presented as a religious experience linked to his existence as a poet – are succinctly presented in the last verse of "The Rain."]

This long passage reads as follows in the final version of the paper.

...la pluie... est liée diretement à l'acte d'écrire. La fluide symbolise la progression de pensées. Les formes divers de l'eau symbolise les idées du poète. "Je fais au tempêtes la libation de cette goutte d'encre." La libation – quand on verse le vin comme une collecte à Dieu – est ce que Claudel fait avec sa goutte d'encre. Il emploie l'encre pour écrire ce poème quand il pleut, quand une terrentielle existe dans son âme. La vénération religieuse avec lequel Claudel regarde la pluie réfléchissit son attitude vers son existence comme poète.

[. . . the rain . . . is linked directly to the act of writing. The fluid symbolizes the progression of thoughts. The diverse forms of water symbolize the ideas of the poet. "I offer the libation of this drop of ink to the tempests." The libation – when one pours wine as an offering to God – is what Claudel is doing with his drop of ink. He uses the ink to write this poem when it is raining, when a torrential rain exists in his soul. The religious veneration with which Claudel looks at the rain reflects his attitude toward his existence as a poet.]

Here ideas are synthesized and interpreted symbolically, with the connection between liquid, writing, and thought made more explicit.

As can be seen from this comparison of two content blocks, length varied greatly in the student writing samples. For the purposes of this study, all changes involving interpretation and refinement of original ideas were tabulated the same, regardless of length; that is, each new idea, along with the complete development of that idea, either in a new paragraph or embedded in the paragraph, was counted as one content change. The measure thus marks each new direction in students' thought processes as they refine their ideas and revise their papers, and is adequate for the purposes of this study where the concern is the effects of response-group format on revision. However, it is obvious that a short phrase added to the final composition represents much less profound thought than an entire interpretative block. A future, much finer, analysis of length and elaboration of content changes should prove fruitful for understanding more intimately the cognitive processes involved in foreign language writing.

Statistical analysis of data

Statistical analysis was carried out using multivariate regression analysis. This allowed for the combination of all data (increasing degrees of freedom), while controlling for variation in average numbers of changes owing to differences in assignments, class level (French 3 versus French 4), venue, and multiple observations provided by individual students. The regression analysis provided a broad perspective on the benefits of the computer versus face-to-face venue. The unit of analysis for the statistical inquiry was the assignment (e.g., individual essay). Of the 54 students who turned in usable assignments, 24 students turned in two or more usable assignments.

Regression analysis seeks to explain variation in a dependent variable given changes in a set of related independent variables. In this research, there were four dependent variables of interest: average number of changes per page in content, organization, style, and grammar. This required the estimation of four separate regression models.

Several independent variables were thought to influence the average number of changes per page that students made. Of greatest interest was the role that venue played in influencing how intensively students edited their papers. Thus, the first independent variable was *Venue,* which was coded 0 if the communication was face-to-face, and 1 if communication was via computer. A positive regression coefficient would indicate that the computer venue was associated with more changes than the face-to-face venue. In order to account for a unique effect for the mixed venue, a second variable was created, *Mixed* (*Mixed* = 0 if venue was pure, and 1 if venue alternated the face-to-face and computer formats). Again, a pos-

TABLE 2. ABRIDGED REGRESSION RESULTS* (STANDARD ERRORS
IN PARENTHESES)

Independent variables	Dependent variables – differences in average number of changes for:			
	Content	Organization	Style	Grammar
Venue	−0.52	−0.20	−1.22[†]	0.69
	(0.53)	(0.17)	(0.59)	(0.67)
Mixed	4.03[†]	0.14	1.94[†]	0.69
	(0.83)	(0.27)	(0.92)	(1.06)
Course	−1.00	0.02	−1.88[†]	−1.17
	(0.55)	(0.18)	(0.61)	(0.70)
R^2	0.55	0.38	0.44	0.32
F value	2.31[†]	1.15	1.51	0.89

* For expositional clarity, regression coefficients and associated standard errors for specific assignments and students have not been presented. These are available from the author upon request.
[†] $p \leq .05$

itive regression coefficient would indicate that the mixed venue led to more changes. A *Course* variable was created to control for level of training students had already received (*Course* = 0 if the student was in French 3, and 1 if the student was in French 4). One series of dummy (0, 1) coded variables was created to control for differences in assignments, and another to control for students providing data on multiple assignments. Because 24 of the 54 students provided data on multiple assignments, 24 associated dummy variables were created. With the exception of the Flaubert assignment for organization changes, assignments did not explain a significant portion of the variation in the dependent variables. Thus, specific assignment results will not be presented or discussed. Some students exhibited more (or less) intense editing behavior. However, a detailed discussion of individual students' results is outside the scope of this investigation, and individual student effects will thus not be discussed.

Results

Regression analysis

By combining all student subgroups, the regression analysis presented in Table 2 provides a broad perspective on communication venue. Overall, communication venue had its clearest impact on composition changes in the content and style categories. The content regression equation was statistically significant, explaining 55% of the variation in average number of content changes per page. French 4 students tended to make fewer content changes than did French 3 students, although the effect was not statistically significant at the .05 level.[5] Qualitatively, however, the French 4 students' content changes were more massive than those of the French 3 students, who tended to make changes at the sentence level.

The style regression equation was not statistically significant at the .05 level, but the R^2 value of .44 indicates that 44% of the variation in the average number of changes per page was nevertheless explained by the style regression. Looking at the independent variables, we see statistically significant effects for *Venue, Mixed venue,* and *Course.* The face-to-face venue led to more changes than the computer venue (the negative regression coefficient indicates fewer stylistic changes in the computer venue relative to the face-to-face venue). This result was counterbalanced by the benefit of the mixed venue (computer-mediated *and* face-to-face communication), which led to more changes than either pure format. Within the course variable, we see that the French 4 students made fewer style-related changes overall than did the French 3 students.

Neither the organization nor the grammar regression equations were statistically significant. No independent variables in these two regressions reached statistical significance, although the *Course* variable might have reached statistical significance at the .05 level had the number of subjects been higher, because overall the French 4 students made fewer grammar changes than did the French 3 students. Response-group format therefore played no role in organizational or grammatical improvement in this particular study.

The most interesting area for future investigation is the mixed venue group. The *Mixed* venue led to higher average numbers of content and style changes than did either the pure face-to-face or the pure computer venues.

Pairwise comparison analysis

Table 3 and Figures 1, 2, and 3 present a summary of the average number of content, organization, style, and grammar revisions made per page, broken down by level and experimental/control condition.

Table 3 shows three statistically significant differences (as determined by t-tests). First, in French 3, students in the control (face-to-face) group averaged 2.56 content changes per page, compared to students in the experimental (InterChange) group, who made an average of 1.61 content changes. In French 4, on the other hand, we see a dramatic positive difference between the experimental and control groups in terms of content

---

5 With a larger total number of subjects it is quite likely that statistically significant differences would have been found.

TABLE 3. SUBGROUP COMPARISONS OF AVERAGE NUMBER OF CHANGES PER PAGE (STANDARD ERRORS IN PARENTHESES)

	Content	Organization	Style	Grammar
French 3, control and experimental groups				
Face-to-face (control) (N = 20 essays)	2.56 (0.31)	0.26 (0.10)	2.15 (0.39)	1.11 (0.32)
Computer (experimental) (N = 21 essays)	1.61* (0.27)	0.07 (0.03)	1.44 (0.25)	1.82 (0.56)
French 4, control and experimental groups				
Face-to-face (control) (N = 17 essays)	1.32 (0.34)	0.34 (0.14)	1.00 (0.29)	0.28 (0.12)
Mixed (experimental) (N = 36 essays)	2.56* (0.29)	0.29 (0.07)	1.63 (0.29)	0.68 (0.19)
French 4, within mixed group only (experimental)				
Face-to-face (N = 23 essays)	2.80 (0.38)	0.19 (0.09)	2.00 (0.42)	0.83 (0.28)
Computer use (N = 13 essays)	2.12 (0.41)	0.48 (0.12)	0.98* (0.26)	0.39 (0.18)

* $p \leq .05$ (t-test comparisons)

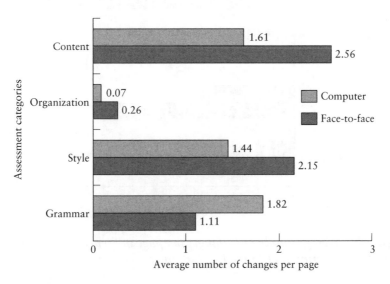

Figure 1   Average number of changes per page in French 3 students' compositions in four assessment categories.

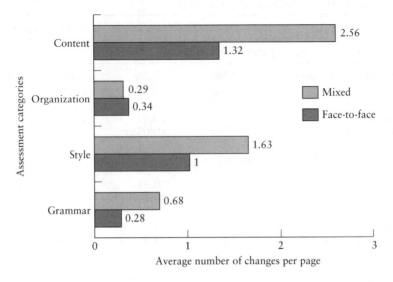

Figure 2   Average number of changes per page in French 4 student compositions: control (face-to-face) and experimental (computer and face-to-face mixed).

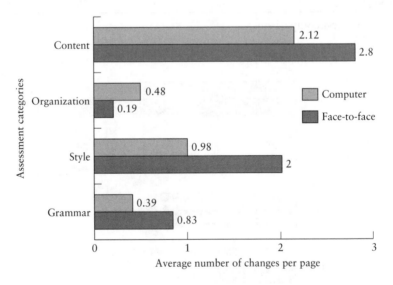

Figure 3   Average number of changes per page in French 4 students' compositions: experimental (mixed) group only.

changes. Presenting almost a mirror image of the French 3 data, the French 4 experimental group (which alternated face-to-face and computer peer-editing formats) made an average of 2.56 content changes per page versus the control group's average of 1.32 content changes per page. Finally, within the French 4 experimental group we see that students averaged half as many style changes in the computer-mediated peer-editing as in the face-to-face peer-editing.

Qualitative analysis of face-to-face and computer transcripts

An examination of the tape and computer transcripts of response-group sessions reveals a number of characteristics that might explain the differences produced by each format (see Appendices B and C for sample InterChange and face-to-face peer-editing exchanges). In the transcripts of face-to-face peer-editing, students at both course levels generally concentrated on content alone, making suggestions to their peers for elaboration and clarification of ideas. In the InterChange transcripts, on the other hand, students elaborated on both content and organization, offering suggestions for improved argumentation. In the computer format, however, the French 3 students tended to veer off the topic to discuss personal subjects irrelevant to the task, once they had written an evaluation (frequently modeled on the written evaluations they received from their instructors on their compositions). Thus, although students carried on conversations via computer, they did not necessarily stick to the business at hand. By contrast, in none of the French 3 face-to-face discussion tapescripts did any of the groups get off the topic. All discussion concerned compositions and interpretation of the works under consideration. This difference in student interaction dynamics might help explain the fewer organizational changes made by the French 3 experimental group students. Basically, French 3 students seemed to take InterChange less seriously than face-to-face peer-editing, and considered their work completed as soon as they had written their assessment in one single InterChange turn.

Both tape and computer transcripts of French 4 students evidenced significantly greater intellectual maturity than did those of French 3 students. These students did not get offtrack to discuss irrelevant subjects in either format, and in InterChange they concentrated on both organization and interpretation. Their ideas were decidedly better developed and more profound than in the French 3 groups (see Appendix B for sample InterChange transcripts). This difference would explain the statistical results obtained within the French 4 experimental group, which indicated no statistically significant difference in content changes due to venue (Table 3).

Style is a particularly important variable in the qualitative analysis. As mentioned earlier, although the French 3 students produced quantitatively more style-related changes than the French 4 students, their changes were qualitatively much less substantial, often limited to rewording of individual sentences. The French 4 students' style-related changes, on the other hand, tended to be both more massive and more sophisticated. The relative paucity of sophisticated style changes among the French 3 students in both face-to-face and computer formats can be traced, first, to the relative lack of writing maturity in this group and, second, to the French 3 curriculum itself, which does not aggressively target style (see Hunt, 1970; Kern & Schultz, 1992). In French 4, on the other hand, style is an important area of concern, with students engaging in a variety of exercises to improve their sentence structure (Schultz, 1994). Interestingly, however, the tape and InterChange transcripts revealed that students did not target style as a category for criticism in either the face-to-face or computer formats. The more striking effect on style of the mixed and face-to-face formats over the pure computer format is thus most likely related to the intertwining of the cognitive processes involved in reflection on interpretation. Results in both the grammar and style categories would thus seem to call into question the findings of Armstrong and Yetter-Vassot (1994) that computer use contributes to improvement in these areas.

Attitude questionnaire

The attitude questionnaires (see Appendix A) help explain the effects of face-to-face, computer, and mixed formats. When students were asked to evaluate the face-to-face response-group format alone, the vast majority found peer editing helpful for improving their writing. Students in the experimental computer groups were much more ambivalent in their assessments, with comments ranging from the very positive to the extremely negative. When asked if they found the face-to-face format helpful, 91% of the 106 students from whom questionnaires were collected responded favorably. When polled as to the benefits of InterChange, 65% of the sixty-eight people responded that they found InterChange effective for improving the overall quality of the final draft of their compositions. The following excerpts from student questionnaires illustrate the range of assessments for the computer groups. One French 3 student writes, "Having a concrete document of peer suggestions is very helpful. The experience of spontaneous writing has also been a great asset." Another student from the same class, however, states that "I actually think it [InterChange] is detrimental to the discussion necessary between peers when editing. Oral discussion allows for much more to be said much more quickly and facilitates more in-depth conversation concerning the essays." This second assessment is characteristic of those who saw peer editing via computer as a misguided use of technology.

When the mixed venue French 4 students were asked to assess both formats, they tended to find both formats helpful, although they over-whelmingly found face-to-face work more helpful. Of the twenty-two students who expressed a preference, seventeen stated that they found face-to-face response-group work more helpful. Unlike the more polar-ized opinions of the pure groups, when expressing a preference for face-to-face peer editing, the mixed groups' attitudes toward the InterChange format were nevertheless much milder than those of the pure groups. The following two mixed-mode students' assessments summarize the attitudes toward each format. When asked only about the in-class response group work, the first student writes: "Basically, I find the response groups highly effective because of the difficulty of evaluating one's own work objec-tively. In the response group a student has the opportunity to receive feedback on what *works* and what *doesn't work* and what needs to be clarified, elaborated, or deleted from his/her composition." About Inter-Change he writes, "I find the InterChange conferencing highly effective because there is adequate time to think out a response and to respond articulately and yet it is still a dialogue." When asked to compare the relative benefits of both modes, he writes, "If there could be one, it would have to be the in-class response group because students should have the opportunity to have a conversation. However, the InterChange is a highly valuable form of responding. In combination, the two are ex-tremely helpful." When asked to compare, a woman from the same class writes: "Nothing like a spirited debate and personal context when giv-ing comments. InterChange takes from that – but does have its good points, that is – practice in spelling, grammar with exactly what comes to mind, and ability to talk extensively about one or two points without interruption."

Conclusion

This study holds a number of practical implications for the implementa-tion of computer-assisted instruction in the foreign language classroom. The analyses revealed that the course level of students is of primary con-cern. Although students benefited from either format of response-group work, face-to-face interaction produced quantitatively more changes and qualitatively more extensive changes in the content category than did InterChange among the less advanced (French 3) students. This is a very important finding, because a student's interpretative abilities are crucial for improving content and producing a compelling composition at any level. For French 3 students, content modification seems to have a re-verberative effect on organization and style as well. Fundamentally, the three other assessment areas of grammar, organization, and style can be more easily relegated to the editing process after the ideas have been gen-erated. This finding must also be evaluated against time factors and other language acquisition goals. The InterChange sessions required an entire 50-minute class period, as opposed to the face-to-face sessions, which required only 20 minutes. This study thus calls into question the ultimate efficiency of synchronous conferencing as a tool for fostering writing improvement. Although the possible impact of InterChange on speaking skills was not part of this study (cf. Kern, 1995), the students' attitude questionnaires not surprisingly pointed to a decided preference for face-to-face work in order to practice their spoken French.

We get a very different picture of the role of computers from the more advanced students. When computer and face-to-face formats are assessed separately, differences in mode are unimpressive. However, when students alternate formats, they make dramatically more interpretative-level content changes than in either pure mode. Moreover, according to the regression analysis, the mixed venue students also make more style changes. This study suggests, then, that it is important for students to participate in both experiences in order to achieve optimum results in writing skill development.

These findings are particularly significant for better understanding the writing process itself. Despite frequent recommendations from both English composition and foreign language specialists to move response-group work to computer formats (Herron & Moos, 1993; Lanham, 1993), the findings of this study do not support an exclusively computer-based implementation of the activity. Different cognitive processes are involved in the computer and face-to-face response-group formats. Essentially, the face-to-face format, which is a predominantly verbal mode, is nonlinear in nature, being characterized by digressions and departures from the topic (Williams & Holt, 1989, pp. 26–27). This was clearly the case of the tape transcripts where, as described earlier, students would shift focus from a specific paper to discussion of tangential issues of interpretation (although always remaining on task). Thus, in the face-to-face format students generated many different interconnected ideas about the text under consideration. This interactive process directly feeds into the networking cognitive processes essential for formulating interpretations (Flower, 1988; Hayes & Flower, 1980; Schultz, 1991a, 1991b). Our knowledge of cognitive processes in writing and the results of this study in terms of InterChange's relatively negative effects on content point to the importance of the unconstrained digressive and recursive characteristics of speech for the idea-generating process (Flower & Hayes, 1980) that forms the foundation for writing.

Although the InterChange transcripts had some characteristics of speech, as a vehicle for composition assessment, students' utterances were modeled predominantly on the written comments of their instructors. This was particularly true for French 3 students, but for French 4 students as well. Despite efforts to transpose the more fluid characteristics of speech into a written mode, according to Williams and Holt (1989, p. 27), the computer fosters essentially linear forms of discourse. This was borne out in the computer transcripts, which overwhelmingly evidenced more features of writing than speech. As indicated in one of the student attitudinal questionnaires, the computer allowed students to target one or two ideas, but without the digressions that seem to feed positively into idea generation. Moreover, research by Holdstein and Selfe (1990, pp. 37–38) suggests that seeing writing on a computer screen has a decided impact on the composing process, affecting differently the way in which one reads a text, to both positive and negative ends.

As mentioned, the mixed-mode students, however, made the most changes in content and style of any group. We can understand these dramatic gains in terms of the interactive nature of different cognitive processes. In *Interfaces of the Word*, Walter Ong (1977) discusses the differences of the visual and the verbal as they pertain to noetic activity. According to Ong, sound, which is fleeting but more tactile and corporeally internalized, allows for a more generic understanding (p. 139). Ong elaborates as follows:

Sound . . . reveals the interior without the necessity of physical invasion. Thus we tap a wall to discover where it is hollow inside, or we ring a silver-colored coin to discover whether it is perhaps lead inside. To discover such things by sight, we would have to open what we examine, making the inside the outside, destroying its interiority as such. Sound reveals interiors because its nature is determined by interior relationships. (Ibid., p. 140)

Ong's point is pertinent to this study where, in fact, relatively few specific ideas generated in the face-to-face mode actually found their way into students' compositions, and yet students made more content changes when in this format. There seems to have been a vaguer, more generalized, and nevertheless more profound effect of speech and discussion on writing. On the other hand, the visual, according to Ong, provides a more immediate comprehension of the specific. It is both fragmenting and distancing (ibid., p. 138). It is through sight that we come to understand the surface of things. Ultimately, it is the fusion of these two senses, the visual and the vocal, that allows us to make tremendous intellectual strides:

What is distinctive of the visualist development leading to our modern technological culture is that it learns to vocalize visual observation far more accurately and elaborately than primitive man, by vocalizing it manages to intellectualize it, and by intellectualizing it comes to generate further specific visual observation, and so on. The visualism we are talking of is thus a visualism strengthened by intimate association with voice, directly in speech or indirectly through script. This association is capital. For if vision is the most tempting symbol for knowing, noetic activity itself is rooted directly or indirectly in the world of sound, through vocalization and hearing. In order to make what we see scientifically usable, we have to be able to verbalize it, and that in elaborately controlled ways. For man there is no understanding without some involvement in words. (Ibid., pp. 129–130)

In this study we see directly manifested in the writing of foreign language students the interaction of two different cognitive processes for ultimately superior benefits. When response-group formats are considered separately, this study speaks for the crucial nature of the verbal in an interactive personalized context for a positive impact on generating processes that in turn have a reverberative effect on organization and style. However, the verbal characteristics of the face-to-face formats in tandem with the visual characteristics of the computer format bring to bear different cognitive processes, which interact to produce superior results in writing development.

Appendix A: Attitude questionnaires for control and experimental students, respectively

Questionnaire for in-class response-group work (control sections)

Please comment on the following questions:
1. In what ways do you find response-group work on rough drafts to be effective for improving the overall quality of the final draft of your compositions?
2. How much time do you spend analyzing your peers' composition rough drafts the night before?
3. What types of written feedback do you provide?
4. What types of oral feedback do you provide in the in-class small group?
5. How much overlap is there between the written and oral feedback? How are the types of feedback the same? If not, how are they different?
6. What types of revisions do you make in your own rough drafts?
7. To what extent do you take your peers' comments into account in revising your work?
8. In which area do you make the most extensive revision? Content? Organization? Style? Grammar?
9. In which of the above areas is peer commentary most useful?
10. Compare the feedback you get from your teacher and the feedback you get from your peers.
11. Please rank the following in terms of usefulness for improving your overall writing skills. Use a scale of 1 to 9, 1 being most useful. If

features are of equal importance, use the same number to show equivalent value.

    a) class discussion of texts
    b) response-group discussion
    c) individual lessons on composition principles
    d) grammar instruction
    e) analyzing examples of good writing
    f) analyzing examples of weak writing
    g) teacher comments on papers
    h) the revision process itself
    i) personal consultation with teacher

12. Is peer response-group work useful for enhancing your speaking ability? Explain.
13. What are the positive aspects of peer response-group work?
14. What are the negative aspects of peer response-group work?
15. Please comment on your overall experience using peer response-group work in your second-year French courses.

InterChange composition response-group questionnaire (experimental sections)

1. Do you find InterChange conferencing on rough drafts effective for improving the overall quality of the final draft of your compositions? Please explain why or why not.
2. How much time do you spend analyzing your peers' composition rough drafts the night before? Do you spend more, less, or the same amount of time as in the in-class format?
3. Do you analyze differently than in the in-class format?
4. Compare the quantity of feedback you provide using InterChange and the in-class format. (Take into account both oral feedback and written feedback in the in-class format.)
5. What types of revisions do you make in your own rough drafts?
6. To what extent do you take peers' comments via InterChange into account in revising your work?
7. Discuss the extent to which you take peers' comments into account in the revision process using InterChange and the in-class format.
8. In which areas do you make the most extensive revision? Content? Organization? Style? Grammar?
9. In which of the above areas are peers' commentaries the most helpful using InterChange?
10. Compare teacher response in general and peer response using InterChange.

11. [Same as item 11 in the questionnaire for in-class response-group work.]
12. Does InterChange have an impact on your speaking ability? If so, how?
13. What are the positive aspects of using InterChange?
14. What are the negative aspects of using InterChange?
15. Please comment on your overall experience using InterChange in your second-year French courses.
16. Compare the relative benefits of in-class peer response-group activities and InterChange response-group activities.

Appendix B. InterChange transcript excerpts

French 3 (week 11; names have been replaced by letters)

G: Ou est-ce que tu a fini le lycee.
N: Que-est-ce "lampe"?
N: Je ne pense pas de l'ote... (he, He)
G: Vraiment? Tu penses de quoi alors?
V: J'ai fini le lycee en Garden Grove, CA (c'est dans Californie de Sud), mais je suis ne dans Virginia. Et "lampe" est "a lamp".
G: Quand as-tu demenage en Californie?
N: Je me sens stupide... pardon oi la question. Ton lampe est casse?
G: N, tu es silencieuse... pourquoi?
V: Quand j'etait petit 2 ou 3. N et G - Pensez-vous que l'Arab a su que les autres Arabs l'ont vu?
G: N + V: Vous pensez que le mot "Arabe" dans le context de cette histoire est un peu raciste ou non?
G: Les autres Arabes l'ont vu???
C: Maintenant, je suis L, mais je suis C.
G: a
G: Bonjour C=L
M: bonjour les filles, je sais que vous aimez moi, mais je dois partir maintenent.
G: C, pourquoi tu a change ton identite?
N: C'est possible. Pourquoi est-ce que Camus n'avais lui donne un nom. Pourquoi est-il seulement L'Arab?
C: Je ne pense que le nome Arabe et raciste. Camus l'utilize pour nous enseignons que le francais si sont raciste avec l'arabe mais Daru ne l'importe pas qui l'arabe est. Seulement importe qu'il est un homme.
N: Bonjour L... C'est Ms. T
V: Dans cet context, oui, parce-que Balducci l'a utilise de distinguisher entre les Europeans superior et les autres inferiors – les Arabs
G: Je ne le trouve pas raciste parce que dans le context de l'histoire, l'Arabe est seulement un Arabe. C'est le temps...
C: G, je change mon identitie parce que L est piu belle, et je veut etre belle
M: G, c'est un reve pour toi, mais je ne sais pas le temps pour tes joues

V: Je pense que les autres Arabs doivent voir l'Arab parce qu'ils savaient que Daru l'a donne sa liberte.
C: M est dans notre conference?
G: Mais, ma petite C, tu es la plus jolie fille du monde... apres moi (HEE HEE)
N: Ils croivent que Daru a lui donne son liberte, mais ils ne savaient pas que c'est un choix, pas necessairement le liberte.
C: Merci, belle
G: Vous pensez qu'il est fou parce qu'il reviens a la prisonne
C: N tu crois que Daru ne pense pas qu'il a un choix?
M: G je repete que tu as besoin un "hobbie".
G: J'ai mal a la ventre. Peut-etre je dois vomir. Je deteste d'etre malade.
C: Oh Oh
N: Non, il n'est pas fou a mon vie mais sa conscience lui a dit que aller a la prision ce que il doit faire.

Translation of InterChange transcript excerpt: French 3 (week 11)

Note: The original French transcripts contains organizational, grammatical, lexical, orthographic, and syntactic errors. Sentences have been reconstituted in the English translation.

G: Where did you finish high school?
N: What is "lamp"?
N: I do not think about the host . . . (he He)
G: Really? Then what do you think about?
V: I finished high school in Garden Grove, CA (it's in southern California), but I was born in Virginia. And "*lamp*" is "a lamp".
G: When did you move to California?
N: I feel stupid . . . pardon the question. Your lamp is broken?
G: N, you are quiet . . . why?
V: When I was little 2 or 3. N and G – Do you think that the Arab knew that the other Arabs saw him?
G: N + V: Do you think that the word "Arab" in the context of this story is a little racist or not?
G: The other Arabs saw him???
C: Now, I am L, but I am C.
G: a
G: Hi C=L
M: Hi girls, I know that you love me, but I must leave now.
G: C, why did you change your identity?
N: It's possible. Why didn't Camus give him a name. Why is he only The Arab?
C: I don't think the name Arab is racist. Camus uses it to teach us that the French are racist with the Arab but Daru doesn't care who the Arab is. It only matters that he is a man.
N: Hi L . . . It's Ms. T
V: In this context, yes, because Balducci used it to distinguish between the superior Europeans and the other inferiors – the Arabs

G: I don't find it racist because in the context of the story, the Arab is only an Arab. It's the time . . .

C: G, I change my identity because L is more beautiful, and I want to be beautiful

M: G, it's a dream for you, but I don't know the time for your cheeks/games [*sic; "games" intended.*]

V: I think that the other Arabs must see the Arab because they know that Daru gave him his freedom.

C: M is in our conference group?

G: But, my little C, you are the prettiest girl in the world . . . after me (HEE HEE)

N: They believe that Daru gave him his freedom, but they didn't know that it's a choice, not necessarily freedom.

C: Thank you, beauty

G: Do you think he is crazy because he's coming back to the prison?

G: N do you believe that Daru doesn't think that he has a choice?

M: G I repeat that you need a "hobby".

G: I have a stomachache. Maybe I have to throw up. I hate being sick.

C: Oh Oh

N: No, he is not crazy in my opinion but his conscience told him to go to prison what he must do.

InterChange transcript excerpt: French 4 (week 11)

A: J bonjour

D: Bonjour, les criticismes commencent

D: Oui, laissez les bonnes temps roulent, et les criticismes commencent!!!!!!

J: oui, bonjour tout le monde

D: J, Merci beaucoup pour votre criticism excellent. Il paru que vous avez ecrit plus que moi dans ma composition. Je pense qu'il me aidera.

J: Bon, Je veux commencer avec A. Je suis d'accord avec ton idee sur le plaisir que Rene trouve dans son soufrance. C'est une idee interessante. Personne ne lui demande pas dans l'histoire pourquoi il ne fais pas d'effort pour ameillereur sa situation. C'est vrai qu'il souffre, il n'y a aucune doute sur cela, mais tu as touche un aspect interessant dans le roman.

A: Je trouve votre idee directrice tres interessante est très provacative. Mais vous introduisez une assumption "le but de Chateaubriand ait ete d'affirmer que la bonheur de l'homme reste sur Dieu" Je pense que cette phrase 'ne va de soi'. Il y a une distinction, dans mon avis entre 'bonheur avec Dieu' et l'idee que la religion est la seule chose peut sauver les humaines.

J: D, Merci a toi. Je pense que je t'ai dit presque tout. La seule chose qui te reste a faire c'est developer tes idees, desquelles tu as assez.

D: A, Vous avez fait, pas supprenant, un bon commencement. Cependant, il y a plusieurs fauts dans votre bruillon, dont il s'agit d'expliquer un peu plus le concept d'hero tragique, et de structure votre composition pour être plus clair dans ce que vous veut dire. Je pense que vous trouvez René un hero ambigue, un idee très interassant à moi parce que c'est la nature de la tragedie; qu'un homme a la puissance de sauver lui-même, mais à cause de ses fauts humains, il est detruit. L'autre idee dont j'ai beaucoup d'interesse est votre opinion que René a plus de sensibilité; c'est a dire qu'il avait un coeur plus capable; que les gens ordinaires. ça c'est la raison pour ses souffrances, et aussi, ironiquement, pour son ecstase. Pour summariser, j'aime beacoup votre plan, et je voudrais lire la composition après vous l'avez fait

J: A, Je ne suis pas d'accord avec I,B. Il ne me semble pas que Rene soit pauvre. Il a le temps pour voyager et faire ce qu'il veut. Il n'a pas besoin de travailler. Je pense que bien quil n'ait pas recu le chateau ou la propriete de la famille cela ne veut pas dire qu'il est pauvre. 'I,C' c'est une idee aussi tres interessante. Rene ne parle jamais de l'aimitié. Il pense toujours à sa misere et à sa soeur, mais comme j'ai déjà dit, il ne cherche pas une solution. Tu devrais developer, peut-etre explorer, lais raison pour lesquelles il fait cela.

A: J, Votre idee directrice evoque beaucoup des idees. Qu'est-ce que les peres symbolise? Est-ce que vous trouvez un lien entre les deux peres, une chretienne et l'autre indien avec votre idee 'bonheur de l'homme reste sur Cieux'. L'autre partie principale de votre idée directrice, "Dieux n'est pas facil a trouver et que ce que fait la difference est les circonstances particulieres de chaque personne" Peut-etre vous peut parler de les differences entre circonstances – et personaltie entre Rene et sa soeur pour expliquer pourquoi Amelie a choisi la religion chretienne pur au fin. Est-ce que vous pensez qu'elle trouve la bonheur vraiment. Peut-etre elle trouve un sorte de paix dans son ame et peut-etre elle trouve un pardon pour sa peché, mais est-ce que vous pensez qu'elle trouve le bonheur. Je pense que Chateaubriand fait un argument que la bonheur est vraiment impossible pour les humains passionés qui existe dans une societe occidentale ou les regles morales existe, mais la seule facon q'on peut vivre avec dignite est avec une systeme relgieuse.

J: D, Je n'ai pas ton brouillon, mai je me souviens de tes idèes. La plus forte, sans doute, est la comparaison que tu fais entre René et le volcan. René est un homme, mais il est parte de la nature, une nature corrompue si tu veux, mais il est seule dans la foule de la meme facon que le volcan est seule dans l'ile. De la meme maniere que le volcan a de (comment est-ce qu'on appelle ca que les volcans ont René a son misere. Aussi, tu fais mention que René cherche quelque chose dans la nature. Vois-tu la relation?? je pense que tu la vois.

D: J, Maintenant, à vous. J'ai quelques remarques que vous pouvez ignorez si vous voulez. Mais voila ce que je pense: J'aime votre idee que Chat. ecrit comment Dieux n'est pas facil a trouver, mais je ne comprend pas votre deuxime aspect du thèse, dans laquelle vous mention 'les circonstances particulieres de chaque personne'. Qu'est ce que vous voudriez dire dans cette phrase? Je recommend que vous expliquiez plus. Je suis d'accord avec l'idee que tous la tristesse a formé la characatere du jeune René, mais est-ce que sa tristesse est la resultat de son ignorance de Dieux, ou est-ce qu'elle est la resultat de la mort et de l'abandonnement de ses parents, et puis, sa soeur. Je ne trouvais pas votre explication de la formation des pensées de Renée sur son enfance très clair. Aussi, j'aime l'idee que vous exprimez du fait que Dieux est un resource pour les afflictions de Rene. Dans la section de votre bruillon ou vous parlez de la recherche de Rene dans le monde, je recommend que vous explique pour quelle raison René a cherché dans l'antiquité pour la vrai, et comment il s'est rendu compte du fait que seulement par

Dieux un homme peut arriver à la piase intèrieur. autre que ça, vous avez
très bonnes idées et structure. Bonne chance, et bonne vacance aussi!!!!!

Translation of InterChange transcript excerpt: French 4 (week 11)

A: J hi
D: Hi, the criticisms begin
D: Yes, let the good times roll, and the criticisms begin!!!!!!
J: yes, hi everyone
D: J, Thanks a lot for your excellent criticism. It seemed that you wrote more than I did in my composition. I think it will help me.
J: Good, I want to begin with A. I agree with your idea about the pleasure that Rene finds in his suffering. It's an interesting idea. No one asks him in the story why he doesn't make any effort to improve his situation. It's true that he suffers, there is no doubt about it, but you have touched an interesting aspect in the novel.
A: I find your thesis statement very interesting and provocative. But you introduce an assumption "Chateaubriand's goal was to affirm that man's happiness depends on God" I think that this sentence "is not self-evident." There is a distinction, in my opinion, between "happiness with God" and the idea that religion is the only thing that can save human beings.
J: D, Thank you. I think that I told you almost everything. The only thing that you have left to do is to develop your ideas, which you have enough of.
D: A, You have made, not surprisingly, a good beginning. However, there are several flaws in your rough draft, of which it is a question of explaining a little more the concept of the tragic hero, and the structure of your composition in order to be more clear in what you mean. I think that you find Rene to be an ambiguous hero, a very interesting idea to me because this is the nature of tragedy; that a man has the power to save himself, but because of his human flaws, he is destroyed. The other idea that interests me a lot is your opinion that Rene has more sensitivity; that is, he had a more capable heart; than ordinary people. that is the reason for his suffering, and also, ironically, for his ecstasy. To summarize, I like your outline very much, and I would like to read the composition after you have done it
J: A, I don't agree with "I,B" [*Note:* Indicates point in the student's outline]. It doesn't seem to me that Rene is poor. He has the time to travel and to do what he wants. He doesn't need to work. I think that although he did not get the castle or the family property that this does not mean that he is poor. "I,C" [*outline*] is also an interesting idea. Rene never speaks about friendship. He always thinks about his misery and his sister, but like I already said, he doesn't look for a solution. You should develop, perhaps explore, the reasons why he does this.
A: J, Your thesis statement evokes a lot of ideas. What do the fathers symbolize? Do you find a link between the two fathers, a Christian and the other an Indian with your idea that "the happiness of man is located in the Heavens." The other main part of your thesis statement, "God is not easy to find and that what makes the difference is the particular circumstances of each person" Maybe you can talk about the differences between cir-

cumstances – and the personality between Rene and his sister in order to explain why Amelie chose pure Christian religion at the end. Do you think that she really finds happiness? Maybe she finds a kind of peace in her soul and maybe she finds forgiveness for her sin, but do you think that she finds happiness. I think that Chateaubriand makes an argument that happiness is really impossible for human passions that exist in a Western society where rules of morality exist, but the only way that one can live with dignity is with a religious system.

J: D, I don't have your rough draft, but I remember your ideas. The strongest, no doubt, is the comparison you make between René and the volcano. René is a man, but he is part of nature, a corrupt nature, if you want, but he is alone in the crowd in the same way that the volcano is alone on the island. In the same way that the volcano has some (how do you call that that the volcanoes have René has his misery. Also, you mention that René is looking for something in nature. Do you see the relationship? I think that you see it.

D: J, Now for you. I have some remarks that you can ignore if you like. But here's what I think: I like your idea that Chateaubriand writes how God is not easy to find, but I don't understand the second aspect of your thesis, in which you mention "the particular circumstances of each person." What do you mean in this sentence? I recommend that you explain more. I agree with the idea that all the sadness shaped the personality of the young René, but is his sadness the result of his ignorance of God, or is it the result of the death and abandonment of his parents, and then, his sister? I didn't find your explanation about the shaping of René's thoughts on his childhood very clear. Also, I like the idea that you express about the fact that God is a resource for Rene's afflictions. In the section of your rough draft where you talk about Rene's search in the world, I recommend that you explain why René searched in antiquity for the truth, and how he realized that only through God can man find inner peace. other than that, you have very good ideas and structure. Good luck, and have a good vacation also!!!!!

Appendix C: Tapescript of face-to-face, spoken interaction in peer-group exchanges (French 4, week 12)

J: Moi, j'ai trouvé que ton introduction est très bon. Je l'aimais bien, beaucoup. La partie du texte... tu sais bien que tu as utilisé les mots de Flaubert à une amie beaucoup.

A: Excuse me.

J: Où est-ce que tu l'as trouvé? Flaubert a écrit à une aime que ??? est ironique.

A: C'est dans le reader.

J: Moi, j'aime ça et la définition que tu as de l'ironie c'est bon aussi.

A: Oui, je pense que l'idée de l'ironie a une définition un peu ambigue et ici les personnes comprend la sorte d'ironie que je voudrais décrire. C'est l'argument plu fort. Où est D?

J: Aussi, je suis d'accord avec l'idée que les [???] subtiles. C'est pour ça tu as une autre bon chose ici. On n'a pas l'impression de voir une tragédie. Cela... aussi. Je pense que les éléments d'une tragédie sont là mais ce n'est pas une tragédie vraiment parce que le personnage principal ne sait pas ce qui se passe.

A: Qu'est-ce que c'est?

J: Le personnage principal ne sait pas ce qui se passe autour d'elle. Qu'est-ce que tu penses quand tu lis une tragédie? Tu veux que le personnage ont une dilemma.

A: Exactement. Il n'a pas une problématique morale de Félicité. Pour un autre réfléchit aux problèmes de son amour – si c'est un amour vrai ou un amour approprié de sa situation ou elle n'a pas de conflits dans son âme ça c'est lequel est la caractéristique principale d'une tragédie dans mon avis. Alors, O.K. Alors, je pense que votre composition a beaucoup d'idées très bien et vous avez pris une attaque plus différente que les autres. Ca c'est une bon chose. Le paradoxe que Flaubert entourait la situation triste et pitoyable et l'ironie existe dans lequel en même temps sont devenus des ironies elles-mêmes. Je ne comprends exactement cette phrase.

J: Oui. Ce n'est pas clair. Ce que je voulais dire c'est que la situation est triste et pitoyable. Cette situation n'est pas ironique dans le sens que l'auteur [???] l'ironie sur Félicité mais sur plus ou moins l'ironie c'est... c'est difficile.

A: Travaillez de clarifier ce que c'est. Je pense que de votre développement du de l'ironie qui existe qu'existe dans le nom de Félicité est très bon détail d'expliquer et de te concentrer sur les détails c'est plus bon de parler au sens général, global de l'histoire parce que dans quand vous parlez des mo- tifs des idées générales vous il y a une tendance de résumer plus et vous évitez cette problème. C'est très bon. Alors une autre chose qui est très in- téressante dans votre essai composition est votre développement de la situ- ation de Mme Aubain et j'ai une idée pour vous de montrer une certaine ironie entre le fait que peut-être ça c'est votre idée directrice que l'ironie parce que O.K. Félicité est très triste à cause de ces choses – les morts, les choses comme ça. Et parce qu'elle a un amour pour les personnes et les choses elle grant cet amour est un peu plus ridicule dans quelque situation. La tristsse de Mme Aubain l'angoisse ne reste pas dans mon avis donc peut-être j'ai quelques idées de mon [???] que je place dans le texte, mais Mme Aubain la tristesse, l'angoisse. Oui, c'est parce que sa fille et son fils sont morts et bien cette angoisse est un problème d'elle parce que et elle n'était pas heureuse parce que sa situation sociale est malgré while tandis que Félicité est heureuse, la mort est la cause, pas la situation sociale. Vous comprenez? Ca c'est excellent. Et je vous conseille de concentrer sur cette ironie de cette problème. Et dans ce sens je pense que Flaubert a affirmé la supériorité de Félicité sur Mme Aubain. La tristesse de Félicité est très réelle quand la tristesse de Mme Aubain, vous le comprenez, ne vous touche pas. Comprenez? Très bien.

Translation of face-to-face tapescript (French 4, week 12)

J: I found your introduction very good. I liked it a lot, very much. The part of the text . . . you know that you used Flaubert's words to a friend very well.

A: Excuse me.

J: Where did you find it? Flaubert wrote to a friend that ??? is ironic.

A: It's in the reader.

J: I like that and the definition that you have of irony is good, too.

A: Yes, I think that the idea of irony has a slightly ambiguous definition and here the people understand the kind of irony that I want to describe. It's a stronger argument. Where is D?

J: Also, I agree with the idea that the [???] are subtle. It's because of that that you have another good thing here. We do not feel we are seeing a tragedy. That . . . also. I think that the elements of a tragedy are there but it's not really a tragedy because the main character doesn't know what is happening.

A: What is this?

J: The main character doesn't know what is happening around her. What do you think when you read a tragedy? You want the character to have a dilemma.

A: Exactly. There is no moral problematic for Felicity. For another, she reflects on the problems of love – if it's true love or a love appropriate to her situation or she doesn't have conflicts in her soul and that is the main characteristic of a tragedy in my opinion. Then, O.K. Then, I think that your composition has lots of very good ideas and you have taken a point of attack very different from the others. That's a good thing. The paradox with which Flaubert surrounds the situation is sad and pitiful and the irony exists in that which at the same time becomes ironic itself. I don't exactly understand this sentence.

J: Yes. It's not clear. What I wanted to say is that the situation is sad and pitiful. This situation is not ironic in the sense that the author [???] the irony on Felicity but on more or less the irony it's . . . it's difficult.

A: Work on clarifying what it is. I think that your development of the irony which exists in the name Felicity is a very good detail to explain and to concentrate on details it's better than talking generally, globally about the story because in when you talk about motifs of general ideas you there is a tendency to summarize more and you avoid this problem. This is good. Then another thing that is very interesting in your essay composition is your development of Mme Aubain's situation and I have an idea for you to show a certain irony between the fact that perhaps that is your thesis statement that irony because O.K. Felicity is very sad because of these things – the deaths, things like that. And because she has a love for people and things she grants this love is a little more ridiculous in some situations. Mme Aubain's sadness anxiety doesn't remain in my opinion thus perhaps I have some ideas about my [???] that I place in the text, but Mme Aubain sadness, anxiety. Yes, that's because her daughter and son are dead and well this anxiety is her problem because she wasn't happy because of what her social situation is while Felicity is happy, death is the reason, not the social situation. Do you understand? This is excellent. And I advise you to concentrate on this irony of this problem. And in this sense I think that Flaubert affirmed the superiority of Felicity over Mme Aubain. Felicity's sadness is very real when Mme Aubain's sadness, you understand it, doesn't affect you. Do you understand? Very good.

References

Armstrong, K. M., & Yetter-Vassot, C. (1994). Transforming teaching through technology. *Foreign Language Annals, 27,* 475–486.

Barnett, M. (1989). Writing as process. *French Review, 63,* 31–44.

Flower, L. S. (1988). The construction of purpose in writing and reading. *Occasional Paper 4.* Berkeley: Center for the Study of Writing.

Flower, L. S., & Hayes, J. R. (1980). The dynamics of composing: Making plans and juggling constraints. In L. W. Gregg & E. R. Steinberg (Eds.), *Cognitive processes in writing* (pp. 31–50). Hillsdale, NJ: Lawrence Erlbaum Associates.

Garrard, L., Rusterholz, B. L., & Long, S. S. (1993). *En train d'écrire.* New York: McGraw-Hill.

Gaudiani, C. (1981). *Teaching writing in the foreign language classroom.* Washington, DC: Center for Applied Linguistics.

Hayes, J. R., & Flower, L. S. (1980). Identifying the organization of writing processes. In L. W. Gregg & E. R. Steinberg (Eds.), *Cognitive processes in writing* (pp. 31–50). Hillsdale, NJ: Lawrence Erlbaum Associates.

Herron, C., & Moos, M. (1993). Electronic media in the foreign language and literature classroom: A fusion between science and the humanities. *Foreign Language Annals, 26*(4), 479–490.

Holdstein, D. H. (1987). *On composition and computers.* New York: Modern Language Association.

Holdstein, D. H., & Selfe, C. L. (Eds.). (1990). *Computers and writing: Theory, research, practice.* New York: Modern Language Association.

Hunt, K. W. (1970). Syntactic maturity in school children and adults. *Monographs of the Society for Research in Child Development, 35*(1), no. 134. Chicago: University of Chicago Press.

Kern, R. G. (1995). Restructuring classroom interaction with networked computers: Effects on quantity and quality of language production. *Modern Language Journal, 79*(4), 457–476.

Kern, R. G., & Schultz, J. M. (1992). The effects of composition instruction on intermediate level French students' writing performance: Some preliminary findings. *Modern Language Journal, 76*(1), 1–13.

Lanham, R. A. (1993). *The electronic word: Democracy, technology, and the arts.* Chicago: University of Chicago Press.

Ong, W. (1977). *Interfaces of the word.* Ithaca, NY: Cornell University Press.

Schultz, J. M. (1991a). Mapping and cognitive development in the teaching of foreign language writing. *French Review, 64*(6), 978–988.

Schultz, J. M. (1991b). Writing mode in the articulation of language and literature classes: Theory and practice. *Modern Language Journal, 75*(4), 411–417.

Schultz, J. M. (1994). Stylistic reformulation: Theoretical premises and practical applications. *Modern Language Journal, 78*(2), 169–178.

Siskin, J. H., Krueger, C. L., & Fauvel, M. (1996). *Tâches d'encre: Cours de composition.* Lexington, MA: D. C. Heath.

Williams, N., & Holt, P. (1989). *Computers and writing.* Oxford: Blackwell.

7 Networked multimedia environments for second language acquisition

Dorothy M. Chun
Jan L. Plass

Introduction

Networked environments have been used for many years as both a delivery medium and a collaboration tool in second language acquisition. Typical examples preceding the studies reported on in this volume include the use of e-mail for asynchronous collaboration (e.g., Esling, 1991; Barson, Frommer, and Schwartz, 1993; Cononelos & Oliva, 1993; Oliva & Pollastrini, 1995; Warschauer, 1995; Brammerts, 1996; Kern, 1996), support for "writing as process," including peer-review software (e.g., Michaels, 1993), and on-line discussions for synchronous collaboration between students and for negotiating meaning and developing discourse competence and sociocultural competence (e.g., Beauvois, 1992; Kelm, 1992, 1996; Kern, 1995; Pinto, 1996; Sanchez, 1996; Warschauer, 1996a, 1997; Chávez, 1997). All of the aforementioned work, however, is based on a primarily verbal presentation of information and text-based communication.

In recent years, use of the World Wide Web for delivery of language learning materials has been expanding rapidly (e.g., Godwin-Jones, 1996; Peterson, 1997; Blyth, 1998). There is a plethora of Web sites for language teaching and learning that incorporate the multimedia capabilities of the Web and *present* information in the form of visuals and audio in addition to text. However, the vast majority of learner *production* activities involve only text-based responses from the learner (e.g., answering multiple-choice questions about content or grammar, typing in answers to content questions or grammatical exercises, filling in tables with information discovered in the various Web sites, and writing short answers or essays [Moehle-Vieregge, Bird, & Manteghi, 1996]). Follow-up activities suggested on Web sites do often require students to compare notes with each other, discuss what they found, or present their findings orally to the class. Although these activities may be inspired by hypermedia environments, however, they are usually carried out in more traditional, non-networked means.[1]

1 An exceptional project that involved international collaboration among students creating a bilingual audiovisual Web documentary is described in Barson and Debski (1996).

This chapter is concerned with the use of networked hypermedia environments that not only present learners with information in various modes (visual, audio, and verbal/textual), but also require learners to engage in productive tasks and activities in a variety of modes. These environments can include synchronous or asynchronous methods of student collaboration, and they employ video, images, sound, and text for both the presentation and the negotiation of information, which results in a different set of questions regarding design and use of these environments. This chapter will first describe a Web-based project, netLearn, which is currently being developed at the University of California, Santa Barbara (UCSB) for second-year German students. The underlying purposes of the project are to provide a set of hypermedia tools on the Web that help learners attain second language competencies and skills, and, using netLearn itself as a research tool, to study how students' interaction and learning in a hypermedia environment might differ qualitatively from stand-alone multimedia environments or text-based networking environments. Of importance is that the project is also based on an integrated approach to the design of networked multimedia programs (i.e., on the integration of interface design issues with principles of language acquisition). These issues will be discussed in the second part of the chapter.

Networked multimedia environments for language learning

The unique attributes of networked multimedia environments, such as instant access to a wealth of primary information on the World Wide Web, the capabilities of synchronous and asynchronous communication and collaborative work, and the use of multiple modes and nonlinear forms of presenting information, make this medium a strong candidate for use in language learning and acquisition. The use of networked environments for learning in general, and for second language acquisition in particular, raises many questions regarding the design of these environments that differ from the traditional design of text-based and stand-alone systems. This section describes the goals of language instruction and the existing instructional materials designed to meet these goals. There are currently numerous multimedia programs for language learning, but most of them tend to be stand-alone programs that are not networked (e.g., Barson, 1989; Lyman-Hager, Davis, Burnett, & Chennault, 1993; Chun & Plass, 1995, to list but a few). In addition, there are many uses of networking functions for enhancing language acquisition, but they are predominantly text-based functions. What remains relatively unexplored is the development of *networked multimedia* materials (see Figure 1). This is an important avenue for instructional research and development because many

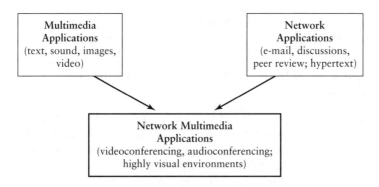

Figure 1   Multimedia, networked, and networked multimedia instructional materials.

language instructors believe that the use of the Web represents a paradigm shift in how languages are taught and learned, but they have not considered the necessity of integrating interface design in a networked environment with underlying principles of language acquisition in the development of Web-based materials.

Language learning involves a number of different skills, for instance, the traditionally recognized skills of listening comprehension, speaking, reading, and writing. In addition, more recent definitions of proficiency in a second language involve competence above and beyond grammatical or syntactic competence to include discourse competence (e.g., issues of coherence, cohesion, and rhetorical organization), and several types of pragmatic competence (e.g., sociolinguistic competence, illocutionary competence, and sociocultural competence [Canale & Swain, 1980; Bachman, 1990; Kramsch, 1993, 1995]). Current approaches and methodologies for teaching second languages reflect the new emphases on developing competencies beyond the linguistic/grammatical domain. More important, the availability and use of current technologies that support computer-assisted language learning (CALL) and computer-mediated communication (CMC) raise the critical question of whether or not there is indeed a paradigm shift in how languages are taught and learned (Kaiser, 1997). The Internet and the World Wide Web are ideal communication tools and networking tools, as they provide the medium both for conveying thoughts and for negotiating with others. This makes them particularly useful for second language acquisition because the ultimate goal of learning a new language is to be able to successfully express one's own ideas and to comprehend the thoughts of others, in other words, to understand and to be understood. The problem is to design learning environments that take full advantage of the current networked multimedia environments while remaining firmly grounded in principles of second language acquisition.

Example of a networked hypermedia environment: Project netLearn

Project netLearn, currently under development at UCSB and targeting second-year language learners, implements multimedia materials on the World Wide Web that contain components for enhancing proficiency in the traditional areas of listening comprehension, speaking, reading comprehension, and writing, as well as in communicative competence, discourse competence, and pragmatic competence. Built into these components are activities that utilize (1) Web access to "primary data" and authentic cultural information, (2) specific networking capabilities that allow for synchronous and asynchronous communication and collaborative work, and (3) the capability of presenting information nonlinearly in multiple modes (text, graphics, sound). These components are intended to implement principles of interface design that support the cognitive processes of the learner. The goal is to create an environment that engages learners in meaningful activities that are rooted in reality. Instead of giving learners individual self-contained assignments, they are presented with a general problem whose solution is nontrivial (i.e., it requires several different activities and steps). Learners have the freedom to choose both the order in which they tackle a task and the tools that they use in order to accomplish their goal. For example, learners are not explicitly told to "listen to this first," "read that next," or "write this now," but they are given the opportunities to access information in different modes and to respond in different modes in order to complete their task. In other words, a variety of tools are implemented so that learners can decide for themselves how they would like to solve a problem or accomplish a task. In addition, as they are carrying out the various tasks, they are creating a database of information that is stored in their own Web space and is a collection of what each individual has created.

NETWORKED MULTIMEDIA TOOLS

Specifically, the kinds of tools that we have incorporated into netLearn include listening tools, speaking tools, reading (decoding) tools, writing tools, tools to facilitate communication and negotiation, and tools providing access to cultural information. The so-called netTools provided in netLearn thus include: netWrite, which is an open-ended "notebook" function that gives learners the ability to write documents, anything from compiling their own notes to writing a report, a letter or an essay; netRead, which provides two tools for reading, both a glossary created specifically for a given text and access to an on-line German-English dic-

TABLE 1. SLA SKILLS AND COMPETENCIES AND THE GENERIC TOOLS THAT
SUPPORT THEM

Skills/competencies	Generic tools
Listening	netListen to hear audio narration, voice-mail messages
Speaking	netRecord to record voice-mail messages
Reading	netRead to read textual information, e.g., letters, essays, literary documents; to access glossaries or dictionaries netMail to read e-mail
Writing	netWrite to write letters or notes, application forms netDiscuss to participate in text-based, asynchronous discussions netMail to write and send e-mail
Communicative	All of the above, plus . . . netChat to conduct synchronous text-based discussions netAudio/VideoConference to conduct synchronous conversations or discussions with audio and/or video components
Sociolinguistic and illocutionary	netDiscuss netChat netAudio/VideoConference
Organizational	netPack to collect and store one's own information netNavigator to navigate successfully between information points within the netLearn program as well as to return to the program from any other website

tionary; netListen, which also has dual components, providing audio recordings of various texts or information, as well as access through Real Audio to on-line audio sources, such as on-line radio stations (e.g., Deutsche Welle and other news sources); netChat, which is a synchronous text-based conferencing tool; netAudio/VideoConference, which allows for either audioconferencing or videoconferencing depending on the availability of the necessary hardware; netDiscuss, which functions as a listserv or bulletin board to on-line discussion; netRecord, which allows learners to record various kinds of information required in a spoken form (e.g., leaving a voice message on an answering machine). Finally, each student has his/her own netPack, which is each learner's own individual digital "space" for storing pieces of information that have been collected and files that have been created.

Table 1 links specific second language acquisition (SLA) competencies with the Web-based tools in netLearn designed to facilitate instructional strategies to engage learners in higher-level cognitive processes involved in these competencies. These tools are designed to be used in a constructivist learning environment (i.e., in an environment in which learners create or construct new knowledge, described in more detail later in the section titled "Design of language instruction based on a constructivist approach"). The actual design and implementation of the instruction by the instructor will determine the level of learner activity in using these tools.

TASKS/ACTIVITIES

In our prototype of the netLearn environment, students are presented with the prospect of studying abroad for a year. They must prepare themselves by going through an application process, requesting letters of recommendation from instructors, writing a statement of purpose, and gathering the necessary documents. They must arrange for housing abroad (e.g., find a roommate and a place to live). They must make travel arrangements, both for the transatlantic trip and for travel within Europe. In the following paragraphs, some of the individual activities and their specific goals will be described. What must be borne in mind, however, is that, in constructivist learning environments, learners have the freedom to approach these tasks in the order of their choice, using the tools that they find most helpful.

At the beginning, learners are given their "mission": The stage is set with learners receiving a letter congratulating them on their achievements in language learning and inviting them to apply to study abroad at a European university. They have the option of hearing this letter read to them by a native speaker of German and of looking up unfamiliar words that have been annotated by the creators of the program. In addition, there is a link to an on-line English–German dictionary so that they can look up words that have not been specifically glossed. After reading and/or hearing the letter, they can choose any one of three subgroups of activities in any order of preference: Preparing for Study Abroad, Arranging Housing, or Making Travel Arrangements. Each of the subgroups contains a variety of activities: listening activities, speaking activities, reading activities, writing activities, collaborating activities, and activities requiring negotiation.

In order to arrange for housing, the learner consults the second subgroup, Arranging Housing, and is presented with a menu of different tasks. A "Housing Wanted" card can be filled out: The learner types in information (e.g., regarding what type of housing is desired, whether roommates are desired, how much he or she can afford to pay in rent). The learner can read other students' cards that have been posted in order to find a roommate. The learner can record his or her own descriptions of an ideal roommate and post it for others to listen to. In addition, the learner can listen to recordings in which other learners describe the type of roommate they are seeking. After reading about and listening to others' postings, students can contact prospective roommates, either by e-mail or by audioconferencing or videoconferencing, depending on availability of necessary hardware and software. For example, if the learners have access to a camera and to videoconferencing software, they can converse and negotiate with a potential roommate. In addition, depending on the city in which the learner is seeking housing, it might be possible to simulate searching for an actual apartment. For example, a rental agency in Berlin has a Web site with "authentic information": It posts listings for apartments available in Berlin and provides a brief description and photographs of each apartment (Moehle-Vieregge et al., 1996, p. 107). Students desiring to study in Berlin could choose their favorite apartment and negotiate with potential roommates regarding price, who will get which room, and so on.

In the process of carrying out these activities, learners can create various documents, graphics files, audio files, even videos, all of which are stored as they are created in the learner's netPack. In the case of study abroad, the learner collects all of the elements that are potentially relevant and necessary for study abroad, and it is this collection of work that demonstrates to the instructor what the student has learned through the course of the project.

Ideally, then, the use of a networked multimedia environment can provide opportunities in separate, yet related, activities for practicing the different skills of listening, speaking, reading, and writing, as well as for enhancing communicative and pragmatic competence. By having opportunities to exchange information with others in different modes, and to investigate and process authentic information, learners are challenged beyond grammatical or syntactic competence to demonstrate discourse competence and pragmatic competence. For example, in negotiating with potential roommates, they must show pragmatic competence, first in presenting themselves and describing their needs, and second in discussing the desires of their potential roommate and determining whether they will be compatible. They may need to demonstrate sociolinguistic competence in rejecting a potential roommate, or illocutionary competence in trying to persuade a reluctant prospect to consider becoming a roommate. In addition, the possibility of communicating with others in different modes takes advantage of the multimedia capabilities of the Web. Learners can engage in synchronous discussions (e.g., "chat" functions) that either could be text-based, real-time discussions or could involve audioconferencing or videoconferencing. They can participate in "collaborative" functions (e.g., by using white boards to simultaneously work on the same document or file). All of the foregoing capabilities, in their concurrent availability, create a new type of environment that gives learners the freedom to use the method of communication or information exchange or

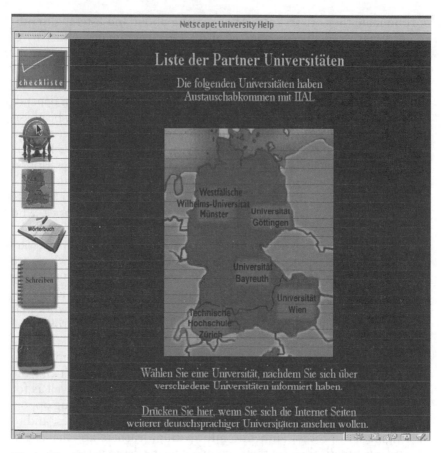

Figure 2   Screen shot from netLearn with navigation bar on the left.

retrieval they prefer. Learners are, in essence, constructing their own meaning.

With regard to navigation tools, in addition to the standard tools found in Web browsers (e.g., the "back" or "forward" buttons), netLearn contains tools to keep students in the learning environment or to guide them back if they leave it. There is a separate navigation bar on the left side of the screen that allows users, first, to return to the point in the netLearn that they left, particularly if a link to another Web site or additional links to multiple Web sites had been followed, and second, to access certain standard components of the netLearn program at any time (see Figure 2). There is access to an on-line dictionary (*Wörterbuch*); to a notebook (*Schreiben* [writing]), where learners can write notes to themselves or compose a written document; to audio information (on certain pages, when appropriate); and to their personal netPack for stor-

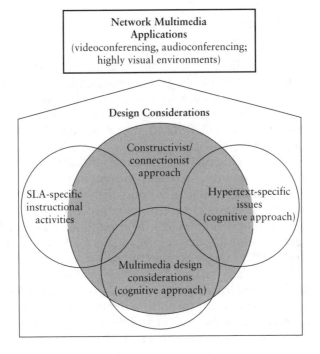

Figure 3 Design considerations for networked multimedia language learning environments.

ing files and organizing the different pieces of information that they have gathered.

Yet to be implemented in the program netLearn are "administrative tools" for instructors and researchers (e.g., tools for determining accessibility of specific information and for creating log files for research purposes that track which pages learners have visited and what kind of information has been accessed – textual, graphic/video, audio).

Integrated design approach: Designing networked multimedia environments

In this section, we discuss the design principles on which netLearn is based and on which future development of Web-based materials, as well as future research studies, can be based. As illustrated in Figure 3, we suggest that the design of networked multimedia applications for language learning be based on principles of second language acquisition and constructivist learning, as well as on a cognitive approach to the use of hypertext and multimedia.

Design of language instruction based on a constructivist approach

The development of theories of second language acquisition has paralleled that of learning theories in general, progressing from behaviorism to cognitivism, and most recently, in the case of theories of language learning, to connectionism. In connectionist models, *"knowledge is in the connections themselves,* rather than in the units themselves" (Rumelhart & McClelland, 1986, p. 132; emphasis added). Some connectionist models also take an interactionist perspective in which all the connections can be modified as one interacts with the environment. This interactionist view of learning is similar to constructivist approaches to learning, which describe learning as a constructive process in which the learner builds an internal representation and interpretation of knowledge by internalizing and transforming new information (e.g., Bednar, Cunningham, Duffy, & Perry, 1992; Greene & Ackerman, 1995).

Based on these underlying theories, pedagogical approaches in second language teaching and learning have also shifted emphasis from acquiring skills or learning content (product-oriented processes) to the interaction of the learner with the content and with the environment (process-oriented approaches). These process-oriented approaches are very much in accordance with both the constructivist approaches to learning and the emphasis on developing communicative language proficiency, as distinguished from grammatical competence. The next step is to integrate principles of language instruction based on a constructivist approach with principles of designing networked multimedia learning environments.

Constructivist approaches to learning advocate allowing learners not only to interact directly with information to be learned, but also to add their own information and construct their own relationships. In the more traditional model of learning, the "learning-as-knowledge-absorption model," the learner is viewed as a passive recipient of knowledge. The purpose of instructional materials is to present information, and the goal of the learner is to absorb or acquire information. In contrast, in the "learning-as-knowledge-construction model," the learner is viewed as an active processor of information and constructor of new knowledge. The purpose of instructional media in this case is to foster active cognitive processing, and the goal of the learner is to make sense of the material and to create new material. Multimedia programs aimed at fostering knowledge absorption simply present information. On the other hand, multimedia programs based on knowledge construction add options to suit the individual learning strategies of active learners, such as options to see animations or videos, to receive text commentary on the material, or to hear audio supplements (Mayer, 1997). Furthermore, learners can be asked or encouraged to respond in modes other than the text mode, that is, by employing visual and audio forms of information in addition to text. In this way, multimedia programs based on a constructivist model can potentially enhance language learning by facilitating comprehension in listening and reading and, by providing opportunities for learners to construct and negotiate meaning, in speaking, writing, and other symbolic modes. Networked multimedia environments provide opportunities for asynchronous and synchronous dialogue in which meaning can be negotiated in modes other than written or printed text. The interactions between and among learners, as well as the interaction of the learner with authentic material in the Web environment, enhance the "learning-as-knowledge-construction" process.

Design issues specific to learning with networked multimedia

The design of multimedia and hypermedia materials must be based on the underlying question of how to integrate SLA principles with the capabilities of the learning environment (e.g., Hemard, 1997; Watts, 1997). Four general capabilities or features of the World Wide Web that have the potential to enhance language learning are: the universal availability of authentic materials, the communication capabilities through networking, the multimedia capabilities, and the nonlinear (hypermedia) structure of the information. All four areas have been separate topics of research, though not necessarily with regard to language learning or considered in combination with one another.

One of the important principles of communicative language teaching is that authentic language should be used in instruction whenever possible (Omaggio-Hadley, 1993). Authentic materials are easily accessed and instantly retrievable on the Web, but the sheer volume of available information, particularly when in a foreign language, is daunting. Instruction must be designed to provide guidance to the learner. Preselecting certain sites or providing specific search criteria can help learners sift through the mass of information. As a concrete example, in the netLearn program, students need to select a university abroad at which to study. The program provides the URLs for five recommended universities in geographically diverse areas that the student can begin exploring (see Figure 2), and then lists an additional set of URLs for the dozens of other universities that have Web sites. (The last instruction on the screen, *Drücken Sie hier, wenn Sie sich die Internet Seiten weiterer deutschsprachiger Universitäten ansehen wollen*, means "Click here if you want to look at the Internet sites of other German-speaking universities.") Learners are thus directed to authentic Web sites but are not overwhelmed initially by having to choose from a lengthy list.

The second capability of the Web – to foster and enhance communication – has been documented in a wide range of studies and papers on networked environments for language learning (e.g., Barson et al., 1993; Chun, 1994; Kern, 1995; Warschauer, 1995, 1996b; Kelm, 1996; Chávez, 1997; Ortega, 1997, as well as the chapters in this volume, to name but a few). As stated earlier, however, the great majority of these networked environments are text-based. Will networked multimedia environments (e.g., environments that allow for audioconferencing and videoconferencing) also be effective in developing learners' linguistic, pragmatic, and sociocultural competence? This is a critically important area of future research. In the netLearn program, for example, tools for learners to record themselves, to listen to other students' recordings, and to conduct audioconferencing and videoconferences are built into the program, taking advantage of the technological capabilities. Furstenberg (1997) has noted that such interactive technologies enable users to incorporate speech acts, intonation, and nonverbal signals into their forms of communication in an unprecedented way.

Studies are planned at UCSB in the near future to investigate the dynamics of how learners use the recording and conferencing tools. By comparing what learners write in their e-mail messages or contributions to a listserv with what they say in recordings or in audioconferences, we hope to gain insight into their developing competencies and how the written and spoken language they produce on the same topic might differ (e.g., whether different types of speech acts or other pragmatic signals are used in the written versus the spoken mode).

The third area, the potential of multimedia environments, which overlaps to some degree with the second area of enhancing communication, has been investigated in a relatively large body of research on stand-alone environments for language learning (e.g., Lyman-Hager et al., 1993; Chun & Plass, 1996a, 1996b, 1997; Steffensen, Goetz, & Cheng, 1996). Chun and Plass (1997) argue that multimedia information may aid in the comprehension of information by supporting the various cognitive processes involved in comprehension. In addition, the emerging research results strongly suggest an interaction between individual differences in learners, the learning task, and the multimedia information provided. For example, students who are classified as visualizers (based on their behavior of selecting visual information for unknown vocabulary words) learn lexical items better when these words are presented in a visual mode (e.g., pictures, videos), whereas students who are classified as verbalizers (based on their behavior of selecting verbal information for unknown vocabulary words) learn lexical items better when these words are presented in a verbal mode (e.g., written translations) (Plass, Chun, Mayer, & Leutner, 1998). The effects of multimedia in a networked environment, however, have yet to be investigated. One hypothesis to be tested is that having learners create multimedia responses in a Web-based environment in order to carry out a task will result in better retention and improved

TABLE 2. STUDENTS' EVALUATION OF NETLEARN NAVIGATIONAL TOOLS

Questionnaire item	Mean	SD
• I often lost track of where I was in the program or what I was doing.	3.23	1.01
• The structure of the program was obvious to me.	2.62	1.19
• The navigation within the program was clear.	2.15	0.90
• The program provided adequate information for navigating within the program.	2.69	1.03

competence in the areas currently being targeted. For example, in the netLearn program, if learners can both read and hear a "housing wanted" posting, or if learners must both write and record their own "roommate search," they may develop multiple routes for storing and retrieving vocabulary items or grammatical constructions. This is a question for future research.

The fourth area, the potential of hypertext structures to foster learning, has been discussed in a number of studies and papers, though not specifically with regard to language learning (e.g., Jonassen & Grabinger, 1990; Spiro & Jehng, 1990; Spiro, Feltovich, Jacobsen, & Coulson, 1992) and will be summarized only briefly here. Spiro and Jehng (1990), for instance, suggest that the design of hypertexts should be based on a "cognitive flexibility theory" in order to allow the reader to access information in various sequences and to return to the same place on different occasions, coming from different directions. A central claim of the theory is that revisiting the same material, in rearranged contexts and from different conceptual perspectives, aids in advanced knowledge acquisition. However, Rouet and Levonen (1996) suggest that "hypertext efficiency involves a trade-off between the power of the linking and search tools it provides and the cognitive demands or costs these tools impose on the reader" (p. 20).

For language learning, consideration of the potential disadvantages of hypertext and hypermedia environments is rapidly becoming a primary area of current research. In a pilot study of the netLearn program, we asked users to evaluate the navigational tools in the program. Learners were asked to respond to the statements in Table 2 on a scale of 1–5, with 1 = strongly agree and 5 = strongly disagree. The responses of the thirteen learners ranged from 1 to 5, and the means and standard deviations indicate very mixed reactions (i.e., some users found navigation very clear and adequate, whereas others had the opposite reaction). This ambiguity was also reflected in the separate written comments of the users. Investigating the potential cognitive overload of navigating in a hypermedia environment is another area to be studied in the future with netLearn.

Another potential source of cognitive overload is the structure of hypermedia itself. Structural information within a knowledge domain is traditionally contained in the sequential or spatial arrangement of the information in linear text, such as in a book, and is identified and perceived by the reader in this form. In hypermedia systems, on the other hand, structural information is coded in the form of links between nodes and thus has to be decoded in a different way. For the learner unfamiliar with these environments, this may add to the cognitive overhead in solving a learning task. Furthermore, for a second language learner, there is the additional burden of decoding not only the different structure of the information but the basic vocabulary and syntax of the text itself. Specifically, if the learner does not understand the word or phrase in the foreign language that constitutes the "hot link," then clicking on the link and being taken to another node may further confuse the learner rather than help. Developers of second language hypertext programs must thus be particularly sensitive to keeping this burden to a minimum. On the other hand, one of the potential strengths of hypermedia systems is that, by their very nature, they can help learners link information that the learners might otherwise not have connected. In particular, if information is provided in multiple modes, such as visual as well as audio, comprehension might be facilitated for certain types of learners who would benefit from having multiple forms of input to help decode a piece of information in the foreign language.

In sum, the approach taken in this chapter has been to consider each of the four features of hypermedia environments (the universal availability of authentic materials, the communication capabilities through networking, the multimedia capabilities, and the nonlinear [hypermedia] structure of the information) and to integrate each with the goal of supporting cognitive processes in learning in a constructivist learning environment. Comparable to the notion that multimedia information may aid comprehension of information by supporting the various cognitive processes involved in comprehension (Chun & Plass, 1997), we argue that the design of a hypermedia language learning environment has to be based on the goal of supporting the cognitive processes involved in processing the instructional materials in a networked environment while ensuring a reduction of the impact of inhibiting factors such as extraneous cognitive load resulting from navigational requirements of hypertext.

Specifically, as a way of integrating (1) the learning approach (constructivism) and the accompanying cognitive processes with (2) the learning environment (networked multimedia), the tools implemented in netLearn include: tools for communication between learners (e.g., chat room, e-mail, conferencing, bulletin board), tools for learners to construct their own information database (e.g., bag/pack metaphor for collecting and storing information), tools for navigation through the Web (e.g., tools to keep students in the learning environment or guide them back if they leave it; help tools), and administrative tools for instructors and researchers (e.g., determining accessibility of specific information, creating log files for research purposes of both user actions and their navigational routes). The multimedia capabilities of visualization and of adding sound allow these tools to be more realistic and easier to use than traditional text-based environments.

Furstenberg (1997) stresses using electronic media to foster more authentic exchanges and to enrich students' interactions. The tasks that students perform should "exploit the associative nature of hypertext or hypermedia so that students can collaboratively discover and construct new connections, which they combine in a coherent whole" (ibid.). She sees the role of the instructor or Web designer as that of designing "tasks that enable students to tell us what they have seen, learned, or understood and that enable students to work collaboratively to create valid arguments, contexts, and stories that they can support, illustrate, and justify" (p. 24). Similarly, Warschauer (1997) recommends that computer-mediated communication activities be experiential and goal-oriented, and that tasks be consistent with principles of situated learning (i.e., that learners engage in meaningful tasks and solve meaningful problems that are of interest to the learners and can also be applied in multiple contexts). The concept of situated learning is common to both constructivist approaches and sociocultural theory. By using multimedia components in networked activities (e.g., audioconferencing and videoconferencing in netLearn), learners have the opportunity for authentic exchanges in which to practice conversational strategies that lead to improved sociolinguistic and pragmatic competence. In addition, as conferencing expands to include international partners, cross-cultural communities are created that enrich the language learning experience.

Summary and conclusions

The increasing use of networked multimedia environments (in particular the World Wide Web) for language learning leads to questions such as how to reconcile instructional design with principles of second language acquisition, how best to support the cognitive processes involved in second language learning, and how to capitalize on the unique capabilities of the Web. So far, the Web has been used primarily as a source of authentic linguistic and cultural data for language learning and as a platform for written networked communication – features that have been exploited for a number of years in Web-based programs. Networked environments that allow learners to communicate using the full range of multimodal forms are relatively new, however. We have described netLearn, a prototype application currently under development, as one example of how SLA-based design principles might be implemented in the creation of instructional materials.

In a *networked multimedia* environment, the most important criteria for implementing language instruction are (1) that the cognitive processes involved in developing linguistic and pragmatic competence must be supported, and (2) that the problems of hypermedia environments that could diminish the potentially positive effects must be avoided. Much remains to be learned about the cognitive processes of learners when they use these environments. Further studies on the use of these instructional materials (e.g., the netLearn program) and on how language learners process information in such environments will need to address some questions with regard to these two criteria.

First, from the perspective of studying the cognitive processes involved in learning with hypermedia materials, the following questions are important for language learning: How do the cognitive processes of users in networked multimedia environments differ from those used for purely text-based networked communication (e.g., videoconference exchanges versus e-mail exchanges)? How do learner interactions differ in written versus spoken on-line discussions? Are different speech acts and different types of pragmatic signals used in different discussion modes, resulting in different types or degrees of pragmatic competence? Do these reflect potentially different cognitive processes? How does the presentation of information in textual, graphic, video, and audio modes support cognitive processes in language learning? Do the different modes reinforce each other by providing learners with multiple retrieval routes for learning words (linguistic competence) or concepts (sociocultural competence) in the second language? Do individual differences among learners result in their using different cognitive processes and therefore benefiting differently from multimodal stimuli? For example, are visual metaphors better understood by certain learners when combined with textual cues but better understood by other learners when combined with audio cues?

Second, in order to avoid the potential drawbacks of networked multimedia environments, a critical perspective is needed when designing these environments. It is imperative not to underestimate the cognitive resources that learners must use to navigate in hypermedia environments and additionally not to overload learners with an excessive amount of input that cannot be processed efficiently. Some questions to be studied include: In what ways might multimedia (e.g., videoconferencing) or the structure of hypermedia (causing, for example, navigational problems) potentially distract from or interfere with enhancing different types of competence? Does providing information in multiple modes create a cognitive overload for certain users? For example, does communicating via videoconferencing make greater cognitive demands on certain types of learners than text-based conferencing (but, on the other hand, provide additional scaffolding for other types of learners)?

Therefore, before assuming that hypermedia environments are inherently beneficial to language learning because they allow immediate access to authentic material and facilitate communication, we need to understand some basic principles of how individual learners process and retain information in different modes and how they integrate this information into the different aspects of their L2 competence. We must be specific in isolating the features of networked multimedia that can enhance particular competencies of different kinds of learners and in determining at what point cognitive overload resulting from the medium can hinder the language acquisition processes for certain learners.

References

Bachman, L. (1990). *Fundamental considerations in language testing*. Oxford: Oxford University Press.

Barson, J. (1989). Stay Tooned [computer program]. Stanford, CA: Stanford University.

Barson, J., & Debski, R. (1996). Calling back CALL: Technology in the service of foreign language learning based on creativity, contingency, and goal-oriented activity. In M. Warschauer (Ed.), *Telecollaboration in foreign language learning* (pp. 49–68). Honolulu: Second Language Teaching and Curriculum Center, University of Hawaii.

Barson, J., Frommer, J., & Schwartz, M. (1993). Foreign language learning using e-mail in a task-oriented perspective: Inter-university experiments in communication and collaboration. *Journal of Science Education and Technology, 2*(4), 565–584.

Beauvois, M. H. (1992). Computer-assisted classroom discussion in the foreign language classroom: Conversation in slow motion. *Foreign Language Annals, 25*(5), 455–464.

Bednar, A. K., Cunningham, D., Duffy, T. M., & Perry, J. D. (1992). Theory into practice: How do we link? In A. K. Bednar, D. Cunningham, T. M. Duffy, & J. D. Perry (Eds.), *Constructivism and the technology of instruction* (pp. 17–34). Hillsdale, NJ: Lawrence Erlbaum Associates.

Blyth, C. S. (1998). *Untangling the Web: St. Martin's guide to language and culture on the Internet*. New York: St. Martin's Press.

Brammerts, H. (1996). Language learning in tandem using the Internet. In M. Warschauer (Ed.), *Telecollaboration in foreign language learning* (pp. 121–130). Honolulu: Second Language Teaching and Curriculum Center, University of Hawaii.

Canale, M., & Swain, M. (1980). Theoretical bases of communicative approaches to second language teaching and testing. *Applied Linguistics, 1,* 1–47.

Chávez, C. L. (1997). Students take flight with Daedalus: Learning Spanish in a networked classroom. *Foreign Language Annals, 30*(1), 27–37.

Chun, D. M. (1994). Using computer networking to facilitate the acquisition of interactive competence. *System, 22*(1), 17–31.

Chun, D. M., & Plass, J. L. (1995). Project *CyberBuch:* A hypermedia approach to computer-assisted language learning. *Journal of Educational Multimedia and Hypermedia, 4*(1), 95–116.

Chun, D. M., & Plass, J. L. (1996a). Effects of multimedia annotations on vocabulary acquisition. *Modern Language Journal, 80,* 183–198.

Chun, D. M., & Plass, J. L. (1996b). Facilitating reading comprehension with multimedia. *System, 24*(4), 503–519.

Chun, D. M., & Plass, J. L. (1997). Research on text comprehension with multimedia. *Language Learning and Technology, 1*(1), 60–81.

Cononelos, T., & Oliva, M. (1993). Using computer networks to enhance foreign language/culture education. *Foreign Language Annals, 26*(4), 527–534.

Esling, J. H. (1991). Researching the effects of networking. In P. Dunkel (Ed.), *Computer-assisted language learning and testing: Research issues and practice* (pp. 111–131). New York: Newbury House.

Furstenberg, G. (1997). Teaching with technology: What is at stake? *ADFL Bulletin, 28*(3), 21–25.

Godwin-Jones, R. (1996). Creating language learning materials for the World Wide Web. In M. Warschauer (Ed.), *Telecollaboration in foreign language learning* (pp. 69–82). Honolulu: Second Language Teaching and Curriculum Center, University of Hawaii.

Greene, S., & Ackerman, J. M. (1995). Expanding the constructivist metaphor: A rhetorical perspective on literacy research and practice. *Review of Educational Research, 65*(4), 383–420.

Hemard, D. P. (1997). Design principles and guidelines for authoring hypermedia language learning applications. *System, 25*(1), 9–27.

Jonassen, D. H., & Grabinger, R. S. (1990). Problems and issues in designing hypertext/hypermedia for learning. In D. H. Jonassen & H. Mandl (Eds.), *Designing hypermedia for learning* (Vol. NATO ASI Series Vol. F 67, pp. 3–25). Heidelberg: Springer-Verlag.

Kaiser, M. (1997, April). Digital technologies and foreign language pedagogy: New tools and new paradigms? Paper presented at the Berkeley Language Center Symposium, Berkeley.

Kelm, O. (1996). The application of computer networking in foreign language education: Focusing on principles of second language acquisition. In M. Warschauer (Ed.), *Telecollaboration in foreign language learning* (pp. 19–28). Honolulu: Second Language Teaching and Curriculum Center, University of Hawaii.

Kelm, O. R. (1992). The use of synchronous computer networks in second language instruction: A preliminary report. *Foreign Language Annals, 25*(5), 441–454.

Kern, R. G. (1995). Restructuring classroom interaction with networked computers: Effects on quantity and characteristics of language production. *Modern Language Journal, 79*(4), 457–476.

Kern, R. G. (1996). Computer-mediated communication: Using e-mail exchanges to explore personal histories in two cultures. In M. Warschauer (Ed.), *Telecollaboration in foreign language learning* (pp. 105–119). Honolulu: Second Language Teaching and Curriculum Center, University of Hawaii.

Kramsch, C. (1993). *Context and culture in language teaching.* Oxford: Oxford University Press.

Kramsch, C. (Ed.). (1995). *Redefining the boundaries of language study.* Boston: Heinle and Heinle.

Lyman-Hager, M. A., Davis, J. N., Burnett, J., & Chennault, R. (1993). Une vie de boy: Interactive reading in French. In F. L. Borchardt & E. M. T. Johnson (Eds.), *Proceedings of the CALICO 1993 Annual Symposium on "Assessment"* (pp. 93–97). Durham, NC: Duke University.

Mayer, R. E. (1997). Multimedia learning: Are we asking the right questions? *Educational Psychologist, 32*(1), 1–19.

Michaels, G. (1993). MacCollaborator [computer program]. Santa Barbara: University of California, Santa Barbara.

Moehle-Vieregge, L., Bird, S. R., & Manteghi, C. (1996). *Surf's up: Website workbook for basic German.* Guilford, CT: Audio-Forum.

Oliva, M., & Pollastrini, Y. (1995). Internet resources and second language acquisition: An evaluation of virtual immersion. *Foreign Language Annals, 28*(4), 551–563.

Omaggio-Hadley, A. (1993). *Teaching language in context.* (2nd ed.). Boston: Heinle & Heinle.

Ortega, L. (1997). Processes and outcomes in networked classroom interaction: Defining the research agenda for L2 computer-assisted classroom discussion. *Language Learning and Technology, 1*(1), 82–93.

Peterson, M. (1997). Language teaching and networking. *System, 25*(1), 29–37.

Pinto, D. (1996). What does "schMOOze" mean?: Non-native speaker interactions on the Internet. In M. Warschauer (Ed.), *Telecollaboration in foreign language learning* (pp. 165–184). Honolulu: Second Language Teaching and Curriculum Center, University of Hawaii.

Plass, J. L., Chun, D. M., Mayer, R. E., & Leutner, D. (1998). Supporting visual and verbal learning preferences in a second language multimedia learning environment. *Journal of Educational Psychology, 90*(1), 25–36.

Rouet, J., & Levonen, J. J. (1996). Studying and learning with hypertext: Empirical studies and their implications. In J. Rouet, J. J. Levonen, A. Dillon, & R. J. Spiro. (Eds.), *Hypertext and cognition* (pp. 9–23). Mahwah, NJ: Lawrence Erlbaum Associates.

Rumelhart, D. E., & McClelland, J. L. (1986). PDP models and general issues in cognitive science. In D. E. Rumelhart & J. L. McClelland (Eds.), *Parallel distributed processing: Explorations in the microstructure of cognition* (pp. 110–149). Cambridge: MIT Press.

Sanchez, B. (1996). MOOving to a new frontier in language learning. In M. Warschauer (Ed.), *Telecollaboration in foreign language learning* (pp. 145–163). Honolulu: Second Language Teaching and Curriculum Center, University of Hawaii.

Spiro, R. J., Feltovich, P. J., Jacobsen, M. J., & Coulson, R. L. (1992). Cognitive flexibility, constructivism, and hypertext: Random access instruction for advanced knowledge acquisition in ill-structured domains. In T. M. Duffy & D. H. Jonassen (Eds.), *Constructivism and the technology of instruction: A conversation* (pp. 57–75). Hillsdale, NJ: Lawrence Erlbaum Associates.

Spiro, R. J., & Jehng, J.-C. (1990). Cognitive flexibility and hypertext: Theory and technology for the nonlinear and multidimensional traversal of complex subject matter. In D. Nix & R. Spiro (Eds.), *Cognition, education and multimedia: Exploring ideas in high technology* (pp. 163–205). Hillsdale, NJ: Lawrence Erlbaum Associates.

Steffensen, M. R., Goetz, E. T., & Cheng, X. (1996, April). Imaginative aspects of comprehension in first and second language. Paper presented at the annual meeting of the American Educational Research Association, New York.

Warschauer, M. (1995). *E-mail for English teaching.* Alexandria, VA: TESOL.

Warschauer, M. (1996a). Comparing face-to-face and electronic discussion in the second language classroom. *CALICO Journal, 13*(2–3), 7–26.

Warschauer, M. (Ed.). (1996b). *Telecollaboration in foreign language learning.* Honolulu: Second Language Teaching and Curriculum Center, University of Hawaii.

Warschauer, M. (1997). Computer-mediated collaborative learning: Theory and practice. *Modern Language Journal, 81,* 470–481.

Watts, N. (1997). A learner-based design model for interactive multimedia language learning packages. *System, 25*(1), 1–8.

8 An electronic literacy approach to network-based language teaching

Heidi Shetzer
Mark Warschauer

Introduction

Since the early 1990s, English-language teaching professionals have tried a variety of ways to make use of the Internet to promote language learning and practice. These range from the creation of self-access on-line quiz collections to the use of authentic on-line materials as input for content-based projects and activities (Hegelheimer, Mills, Salzmann, & Shetzer, 1996).[1]

However, the Internet is much more than just a teaching tool. It is becoming one of the primary media of literacy and communication practices. The estimated number of worldwide users of the Internet topped 130 million in August 1998 (Nua Ltd., 1998) and continues to grow at a rate of 40%–50% a year, with growth rates in China, Indonesia, and other developing countries as great as or greater than in the United States (Glave, 1998). E-mail is now surpassing face-to-face and telephone conversation as the most frequently used communication tool in certain business sectors (American Management Association International, 1998), while Internet-based publishing and collaboration are transforming scientific research (Harnad, 1991). Meanwhile, students of all ages must learn to find, share, and interpret on-line information as part of a necessary shift from *just in case* to *just in time* learning (Lemke, 1998). Even in the personal sphere, the Internet has become a major arena for entertainment and socializing in the United States and other developed countries. Thus, it is no exaggeration to say that the development of literacy and communication skills in new on-line media is critical to success in almost all walks of life. Finally, with an estimated 85% of the electronically stored information in the world in the English language (Crystal, 1997), the overlap between English language learning and the development of electronic literacy is especially pronounced.

---

1 For examples of self-access on-line quiz collections, see Dave's ESL Café (http://www. eslcafe.com) or InternetTESL Self-Study Quizzes (http://www.aitech.ac.jp/~iteslj/ quizzes/). For content-based projects and activities, see, in addition to Hegelheimer et al., OPPortunities in ESL Theme-Based Pages (http://darkwing.uoregon.edu/~leslieob/ themes.html).

Therefore, whereas previously educators considered how to use information technology in order to teach language, it is now essential also to consider how to teach language so that learners can make effective use of information technology. Working toward both these objectives, rather than just the first one, is what distinguishes an electronic literacy approach to network-based language teaching.

In developing and implementing an electronic literacy approach, a number of questions must be addressed. How should ESL and EFL teachers make best use of new on-line opportunities to maximize language study and practice while also helping students develop computer-based communication and literacy skills? What strategies for communicating and networking should students be taught? What goals should language teachers aim for and what kinds of on-line projects could students carry out to accomplish those goals? Which are the most crucial electronic resources and tools that teachers should learn so that they can teach them to their students? How can teachers encourage students to become autonomous learners who can continue to learn how to communicate, conduct research, and present their ideas effectively using information technology beyond the confines of the class or the semester?

To address these questions, we begin by presenting a conceptual framework for the development of electronic literacy. We then discuss classroom applications derived from this framework. Finally, we examine the research implications of an electronic literacy approach.

An electronic literacy framework

An electronic literacy framework is based on several premises. First, it assumes that becoming literate is not just a matter of learning how to decode and put to paper letters and words, but rather a matter of mastering processes that are deemed valuable in particular societies, cultures, and contexts. Thus, just as the development of the printing press helped to redefine literacy in Europe and, eventually, the whole world (Eisenstein, 1979), the spread of on-line communication is reshaping literacy today, and this time at a much faster pace (Warschauer, 1999). Within the industrialized world, virtually all academic and professional writing now involves computer use, and, according to some predictions, most reading will likely take place on computer screens within a few decades (Bolter, 1991). Literacy is a shifting target, and we have to prepare students for their future rather than our past.

An electronic literacy approach also assumes that there is not just one literacy, but many kinds of literacy, depending on context, purpose, and medium. Although reading and writing on-line are closely related to reading and writing in print, the two literacy contexts are also sufficiently different to demand theoretical and practical attention.

Finally, an electronic literacy framework differs sharply from the notion of *computer literacy*, a concept now largely discredited for its minimalist focus on matters such as how to turn a computer on and operate simple programs (Papert, 1980). Rather, an electronic literacy framework considers how people use computers to interpret and express meaning. Electronic literacy thus involves what has been called information literacy – the ability to find, organize, and make use of information – but electronic literacy is broader in that it also encompasses how to read and write in a new medium.

We divide electronic literacy skills into three broad, overlapping areas: communication, construction, and research (cf. Eisenberg & Johnson, 1996; Eisenberg & Berkowitz, 1998; Lemke, 1998). In the rest of this section, we will examine these three areas conceptually, and then discuss practical applications in the following section.

Communication

By allowing us to communicate with groups of people all over the world, simultaneously, at little cost, and in an archived format that allows us to record, reflect on, and refine our previous words as well as those of our interlocutors, computer-mediated communication serves as an intellectual amplifier, bringing about a revolution in human interaction and cognition (Harasim, 1990; Harnad, 1991). It is no surprise that such a powerful communications tool is transforming how we interact in business, education, and personal life.

Yet, like many powerful tools, computer-mediated communication is difficult to master and, if used poorly, can do as much harm as good. Several features of computer-mediated communication deserve attention.

Computer-mediated communication (CMC) has been found to exhibit certain characteristics typical of written communication, certain characteristics typical of spoken communication, and other characteristics unique to the computer medium (Collor & Bellmore, 1996; Werry, 1996; Yates, 1996). For example, CMC includes its own forms of salutation and greetings and, in some forms, its own special uses of abbreviations and symbols (Werry, 1996). On-line forums develop their own complex rules for turn taking and topic shifting, which differ greatly from those of other oral or written media. Just as in all communication, those who master the particular stylistic and sociolinguistic features required by the context and medium will best reach their audience.

Computer-mediated communication strips away factors that tend to control or delimit face-to-face conversation. CMC reduces social context clues related to race, gender, handicap, accent, and status, as well as non-verbal cues, such as frowning and hesitating (Sproull & Kiesler, 1991). CMC also allows individuals to contribute at their own time and pace, neutralizing the advantage of those who tend to speak out loudest and interrupt the most (ibid.). The result is free-flowing communication that, if handled well, can result in the fruitful exchange of ideas but, if handled poorly, can quickly erupt into hostile outbursts. In the "Class-room applications" section of this chapter, we offer suggestions for struc-turing effective electronic literacy activities.

The result is that learning how to communicate effectively via computer involves more than just translating from one communications medium to another; it involves new ways of interacting and collaborating. To use an urban metaphor, the Internet is analogous to the typical postmodern city, such as Los Angeles; it is "pluralistic, chaotic, designed in detail yet lacking universal foundations or principles, continually changing, linked by centreless flows of information" (Relph, 1991, pp. 104–105). And the newcomer to the Internet, as to Los Angeles, must learn to negotiate the decentered terrain.

Construction

Construction more or less corresponds to what would be considered "writ-ing" in traditional pedagogy. However, the term "construction" is used to designate three important shifts: (1) from essay to hypertext, (2) from words to multimedia, and (3) from author to co-constructor.

Although essays are never read in a linear fashion, they at least appear in a linear form. The hypertext that appears on the World Wide Web, with its decentralized linkages to other materials at the same Web site or to other Web sites around the world, represents a radically different way of presenting information. Hypertext is far from replacing traditional linear genres of writing, but at the very least is supplementing them as an important new way of way of presenting written information and ideas (Bolter, 1991; Lanham, 1993). Creating a good hypertext involves many challenges, from the rhetorical to the organizational to the technical.

Hypertext authoring is not only a matter of reconceptualizing how to arrange words; it also involves creative use of other media, such as graphics, audio, and video. Document appearance has been an impor-tant feature since long before the Internet. However, with each decade of the electronic era, the value of the visual is growing, as witnessed by changes in everything from newspaper styles to television news to school textbooks (Kress, 1998). The Internet represents a further extension of this, with quality Web documents judged as much for their appearance and presentation as for their texts. It is not a matter of starting with a text and then prettifying it, but rather of knowing how to combine var-ious media to communicate most effectively to an audience (Kress, 1998; Lemke, 1998).

Finally, on-line construction of documents is generally a collaborative process, in several ways. First, most Web sites are the joint effort of a team of people rather than just one person. Second, Web sites inevitably link to the work of other sites and authors; whereas this is also done via footnoting in traditional texts, it becomes a much more dynamic form of interaction in Web site design, as the original author(s) must consider that the reader will link to the other site in the middle of reading and thus engage in the two (or more) pieces in a back and forth fashion. In this sense, then, the readers also become co-constructors, as they play a more active role in piecing together texts to make meaning (Landow, 1992). Finally, the hypertext author must consider the possible interaction and response not only of the intended audience, but also of a much broader audience that might happen across the Web site.

Research

The amount of information available worldwide to the average individual has exploded in recent years, and an increasing amount of it is available on-line. Knowing how to navigate Internet sources, search for information, and critically evaluate and interpret what is found represents perhaps the most crucial set of electronic literacy skills.

To understand how research, and other related skills such as reading, have changed in the on-line environment, let us examine the example of a student who is assigned to do a research project on a contemporary topic. In a traditional print environment, the student will go to the library, gather some source material, bring it home, read through it, and write up an essay to turn in to the teacher. The student would assume that the sources were valid because they were (*a*) published in a book, and (*b*) included in the library's holdings. If any questions came up about the sources, the student could clear these up with the teacher later.

Students looking for information on the Internet would have to use very different reading and research strategies. On the Internet, reading skills are intimately bound up with searching and evaluation skills, just to find the material that one wants. This involves first knowing how to use search engines effectively and then being able to skim and scan to see if what was found is remotely of interest, while simultaneously making judgments as to its source, validity, reliability, and accuracy – and then making on-the-spot judgments about whether to continue perusing that Web page, go to other links from the same page, go back to the search engine, or give up the Internet altogether for this particular investigation and try another source. Thus, reading in the on-line realm by necessity becomes critical literacy – because those who cannot make critical evaluations cannot even find what they need to read on the Internet.

Finally, as suggested earlier, on-line reading and research also involve the ability to critically evaluate not only texts, but also multimedia documents. One important advantage of having students construct multimedia work is that they will then be in a better position to critically interpret multimedia documents produced by others.

One other principle of electronic literacy intersects with all of the others, and that is learner autonomy. Lemke (1998) distinguishes between a *curricular learning paradigm,* which dominates much of education today, and an *interactive learning paradigm* of libraries and research centers. In the former, someone else decides what you need to know and when you need to know it; in the latter, determining your own learning goals and interests is the key feature of the educational process. Flexible, autonomous, lifelong learning is essential to success in the age of information (Reich, 1991; Rifkin, 1995). Autonomous learners know how to formulate research questions and devise plans to answer them. They answer their own questions through accessing learning tools and resources online and off-line. Moreover, autonomous learners are able to take charge of their own learning by working on individual and collaborative projects that result in communication opportunities in the form of presentations, Web sites, and traditional publications accessible to local and global audiences. Language professionals who have access to an Internet computer classroom are in a position to teach students valuable lifelong learning skills and strategies for becoming autonomous learners.

Table 1 summarizes some of the key differences between an electronic literacy approach and earlier approaches to language and literacy instruction.

Classroom applications

The framework described in this section is designed to be used as a tool for planning tasks and projects for the language classroom that use computers and the Internet as tools for personal and professional empowerment. The framework expands on the three areas already discussed: communication, construction, and research. Within each section of the framework, skills and activities are suggested to promote autonomous learning and meaningful language use.

Access to technological tools and resources varies from context to context, and technologies change rapidly. Therefore, the following list allows instructors the flexibility to select and choose from the technologies available in their particular teaching context.

Electronic literacy and language use

Communication
- How to contact *individuals* to ask a question, give an opinion, give advice, or share knowledge. How to respond to questions, replies, feedback, advice, or other communication.

TABLE I. EARLIER APPROACHES VERSUS ELECTRONIC LITERACY APPROACH

	Earlier approaches	Electronic literacy approach
Communication	Based on speaking and listening	Also includes computer-mediated communication
Construction	Based on linear texts	Also includes hypertexts
	Excludes nonprint media	Combines texts and other media
	Tends to focus on individual writing	Strong focus on collaboration
Reading & research	Restricted to print sources	Includes on-line sources
	Focuses on linear texts	Also includes hypertexts
	Excludes nonprint media	Combines texts and other media
	Tends to separate reading skills from critical evalua-tion skills	Views critical evaluation as central to reading
	Focuses on library search skills	Includes searching and navigating on-line sources
Learning paradigm	Often based on curricular learning paradigm	Based on interactive learning paradigm, with emphasis on autonomous learning

- How to contact *groups* of people using a variety of on-line technologies in order to read for comprehension, ask a question, share an opinion, give advice, share knowledge, conduct surveys, and post summaries and original research. How to be contacted and interact with groups of people.
- How to participate in *collaborative projects* with people in different places to accomplish a shared goal (i.e., how to set up and participate in communication networks).
- How to select the available *asynchronous technologies* such as e-mail, e-mail lists, Web bulletin boards, and news groups.
- How to select the *synchronous technologies* such as MOOs, chat rooms, IRC, person-to-person and group videoconferencing via CU-See Me, Internet Phones, or other tools.
- Understanding *implications:* netiquette issues, privacy issues, safety issues, corporate advertising issues.

Construction
- How to *create* Web pages and Web sites, individually and collabora-tively, through effective combination of texts and other media in hyper-text format.

- How to *store, maintain, and manage* Web sites so they can be viewed locally and globally.
- How to *market* Web sites and encourage communication about topics presented in Web sites.
- How to select the available *Web technologies:* Hypertext Markup Language (HTML), Web page creation software programs, Web page storage options.
- Understanding *implications:* Copyright issues, intellectual property issues, corporate advertising issues, safety issues, and censorship issues.

Research
- How to come up with *questions* to investigate, how to develop keywords, how to categorize and subcategorize, how to map ideas and concepts (nonlinear idea development).
- How to *find information* on-line using Web indices, search engines, and other specialized search tools.
- How to *evaluate and analyze* the value of information and tools.
- How to determine *authority and expertise.*
- How to identify *rhetorical techniques* of persuasion.
- How to *distinguish* primary and secondary sources.
- How to *cite* on-line sources and give credit to others.
- How to select the available *search technologies:* search indices and engines, software packages for brainstorming, and so on.
- Understanding *implications:* corporate advertising issues, authority issues, privacy issues, quality issues, theft/crime issues.

Each section of the framework suggests potential implications with the activities that are listed. Many of these implications challenge the boundaries of traditional teaching. Teaching students to ask questions and find answers in a global, on-line context raises provocative sociopolitical issues that teachers need to comprehend in order to effectively teach strategies for autonomous learning and language use. Instructors are encouraged to draw from the suggestions presented here to develop new, integrative activities that combine all three parts of the framework.

Communication

Many of the ideas presented in the communication section of the framework encourage the teaching of speech acts and conversational strategies and functions reminiscent of notional-functional syllabi. In this case, though, they are taught not as part of an abstract syllabus but in response to the real needs of students as they engage in authentic interaction. Through e-mail and other electronic communication tools, students have the opportunity to contact speakers of the language studied in the classroom, and they also have the opportunity to encounter and study asynchronous and synchronous examples of the language in practice. The Internet opens multiple communication channels for interpersonal communication, group discussion, and information sharing.

For explicit language practice, in the networked computer laboratory, students might *study questions that other people ask and the responses given to the questions* in public places on the Internet. This can be done by studying the language of e-mail discussion groups, news groups, and Web bulletin boards, for example. The teacher could bring in examples of questions and answers she has collected from these media for an initial class discussion (with permission from the authors). She could start with questions and answers posted on e-mail lists, for instance. Next, students could be taught how to find and subscribe to e-mail lists for their own monitoring and communication. Each student could choose an e-mail list to join and monitor during the semester or quarter for language study activities.

Students can also *compose answers in response to the questions other people ask* in public forums as an experiential learning activity. Students can select a question and respond either publicly to the forum or privately by sending an e-mail message directly to the person who posted the message. Students can print out the question and their response and any replies that happened after they made contact. These could be used as part of communication-based journal entries.

Besides asking and answering questions, students can also *study opinions given in public forums and reactions to the opinions* made by other people participating in the discussions. To initiate the class activity, the teacher can distribute examples of people giving opinions and reactions to different ideas. The class could study these examples and develop their own hypotheses about the best way to phrase opinions to share in public spaces.

Another type of communication opportunity on-line is the ability to *share recommendations* for useful resources and tools found on and off the Internet. Students can do research on the Web, for example, and share their results on an e-mail list relevant to the topic of their research. Students can also *ask for recommendations* of Web sites and journal articles related to their topic. They can then summarize and post the results they have collected for the entire on-line forum. These activities happen repeatedly on academic e-mail lists. Students can thus be taught important networking skills with immediate relevance to their academic work.

Many instructors like their students to *survey groups of people* and report their results in class (see, for example, Ady, 1995; Kendall, 1995). Students can work in groups to develop research questions, write up surveys, contact survey participants via the Internet, and interpret survey results. They can also post and discuss their results on-line.

Integrating communication-focused activities such as these takes a good deal of preparation, organization, and time. In many cases, instructors must first learn how to use the associated Internet communication forums (e.g., e-mail discussion lists, Web discussion boards) themselves in order to understand how they can be used for structuring language practice opportunities. It might also take considerable time to collect examples of on-line communicative acts. Thus, professional development and institutional implications are involved: Teachers need to learn how to use tools, and they also need support and encouragement from their teaching institutions to design classes that contain the components desired.

If students join and participate in on-line discussion forums, they, as well as their teachers, might encounter a range of problems dealing with netiquette, privacy, and safety. These are all topics that should be included into the classroom lessons. Students can discuss together the role of proper netiquette (polite on-line behavior) as well as basic notions of on-line privacy. They need to be made aware that electronic messages sent to public forums on-line are often archived and permanently made available to the public. Teachers can integrate on-line "street smart" strategies into their lessons to promote effective, safe on-line communication practices. The goal should be that students learn to effectively network and promote their ideas on-line, without taking unnecessary risks.

Construction

Creating Web pages and Web sites is an increasingly common activity in business and academic environments. Using tools available in the learning context, such as text editors for writing HTML or Web page creation software, students can create their own Web sites to express themselves through text, graphics, audio, and video. What is unique about having students create Web pages for communication and expression is that their work may be stored on a world-accessible Web server. This provides opportunities for public on-line publishing that can result in students receiving rapid attention and feedback for their writing.

Some teachers might assist students to publish their writing in the teacher's own Web server space or publish student work in on-line magazines devoted to publishing student writing. In this case, the editing and/ or maintenance of these documents is in the hands of people other than the students. An alternative is to teach students how they can publish, maintain, and control their own writing on-line. Students can be taught how to manage their own Web sites by controlling their own Web server space, which is now made available free through many venues. Essentially, this lets students become the writers, editors, and publishers of their own information and provides personal power that might bring results well beyond the language classroom. For example, some students might create on-line résumés and portfolios of their professional work to help them apply for jobs in their countries or elsewhere. Students in the Business English Program at the University of California, Santa Barbara (UCSB), create portfolio Web sites consisting of professional biographies, résumés, and useful resource pages for projecting their professional on-line presence.

Students can also be encouraged to market their creations to the Internet community to get feedback on their work and to encourage a dialogue with others who share similar interests. Students can announce their work on e-mail lists, register their work with search engines and indices, and do research on the Web for information on how to further promote their work. Web page creation can be a supplementary component to a language class that meets occasionally in a computer lab, or it can be a course in itself, such as the "English through Web Page Creation" course offered in the English Language Program at UCSB, which involves students in a series of increasingly complex Web design projects resulting in on-line publishing of student-created sites.

The teaching challenges that arise when students create Web pages include issues of plagiarism and copyright violation. The ease with which images or text can be copied from one Web page to another raises intellectual property issues that need to be discussed in the classroom. Students need to be taught how to ask for permission to copy graphics that are not from copyright-free image archives. They also need to learn to properly cite works created by others.

Research

The Internet is a powerful tool for finding information from educational organizations, governmental organizations, businesses, and individuals. With on-line search tools such as search engines and indices, students can learn how to answer questions they devise themselves or that their teachers devise for them. Research tasks that can be done using on-line tools can be learning activities themselves or can be a part of larger projects that integrate listening, speaking, reading, and writing tasks.

In order to promote autonomous learning, teachers might progress from teacher-directed projects, which provide necessary scaffolding for beginning Internet users, to student-directed projects. Beginning steps might include having students scan preselected Web sites for answers to specific questions or to complete an on-line "scavenger hunt" (i.e., a contest involving a timed search for on-line information). Later, students can use Web search engines and indices to answer other specific questions. Later still, they might jointly conduct research on a topic agreed upon by the entire class for compilation into a document to be shared by all, such as a handout or a Web page. After doing initial training activities such as these, students should have mastered the basics of searching for information and will likely be ready to do a research activity based on their own interests. Combinations of group discussion, teacher–student meetings, dialogue journals, and needs analysis questionnaires can be used to help students define their interests and establish research questions. Students can then write a statement of interest that explains and proposes their research, or develop learning contracts (Davidson, 1997) to structure their projects and determine final outcomes. The research itself can involve collaboration and communication with their peers or with distant interlocutors, and can result in on-line publication, thus achieving an integration of communication, construction, and research.

Research implications of an electronic literacy approach

Finally, we examine the concept of "research" in a slightly different guise than that described earlier. We now look at professional research into the learning process itself. Here we are concerned not so much with general research into network-based language learning (as discussed throughout this book), but with the specific kind of research meant to yield insight into the development of electronic literacies.

In this regard, we would contend that, just as the *development* of electronic literacies affects notions of student research, so the *investigation* of electronic literacies affects notions of professional research. In our opinion, excellent models of research on electronic literacies (1) involve teachers themselves as autonomous investigators involved in lifelong learning (rather than having research relegated exclusively to outside experts); (2) involve students as well as co-investigators into their own learning processes (because students are essential co-constructors of knowledge in a learner-centered classroom); and (3) take advantage of the new types of collaborative interaction and co-construction of knowledge facilitated by electronic communication.

An outstanding model of this type of research is provided by Heath (1992), who corresponded by distance with the teacher and students in a 9th-grade English class as they collaboratively investigated the students' uses of oral and written language in the classroom and community. Although Heath's project did not involve electronic communication (as either an object of study or a medium of interaction), it is not hard to imagine the advantages of similar action-research projects involving students, teachers, and, where appropriate, outside researchers jointly communicating via e-mail or the World Wide Web about their own electronic literacy practices. One of us has, in fact, successfully employed such triangular electronic communication in investigating electronic literacy practices (see Warschauer, Chapter 3, this volume).

We do not contend that action research is the only viable model for investigating electronic literacies, just that it is a research approach especially congruent with this topic of investigation. Teachers and students can work collaboratively to look at the types of language they use in different media, their attitudes toward communicating in a variety of media, and the problems and successes that arise as they try to implement their own goals related to technology-enhanced learning and teaching. Computer-assisted discussion sessions, on-line dialogue journals, and other forms of electronic communication provide an excellent means for engaging interactively while saving interactions for future reflection. Writing up their analyses in the form of on-line presentations can provide opportunities to further practice what they have learned, and also to get feedback and input rapidly from the broader language teaching and learning community. Such a process provides opportunities for both teachers and students to reflect critically on the issues they discovered during their research and to revise future teaching, learning, or research plans (Ross, Bondy, & Kyle, 1993; Eby & Kujawa, 1994; Richards & Lockhart, 1994; Shetzer, 1997).

To return to our earlier urban metaphor, it has been noted that the postmodern city "renders doubtful most of the conventional ways of thinking about landscapes and geographical patterns. It is also a serious challenge for cartographers" (Relph, 1991, p. 105). We would contend that the rapid growth of the Internet equally complicates the work of those of us who are trying to map out theories of language and literacy development. By engaging students, teachers, and scholars in collaborative investigative activity, we can at least begin to describe the terrain of electronic literacy and inquire into its myriad sources of diversity.

References

Ady, J. (1995). Survey across the world. In M. Warschauer (Ed.), *Virtual connections: On-line activities and projects for networking language learners* (pp. 101–103). Honolulu: Second Language Teaching and Curriculum Center, University of Hawaii.

American Management Association International (1998). E-mail tops telephone, say HR execs at 69th annual human resources conference [Article]. Retrieved May 29, 1998, from the World Wide Web: *http://www.amanet.org/survey/hrc98.htm*

Bolter, J. D. (1991). *Writing space: The computer, hypertext, and the history of writing.* Hillsdale, NJ: Lawrence Erlbaum Associates.

Collor, M., & Bellmore, N. (1996). Electronic language: A new variety of English. In S. C. Herring (Ed.), *Computer-mediated communication: Linguistic, social and cross-cultural perspectives* (pp. 13–28). Amsterdam: John Benjamins.

Crystal, D. (1997). *English as a global language.* Cambridge: Cambridge University Press.

Davidson, F. (1997). Contract learning [On-line article]. Retrieved August 25, 1998, from the World Wide Web: *http://ux6.cso.uiuc.edu/~fgd/contract.learning.text*

Eby, J. W., & Kujawa, E. (1994). *Reflective planning, teaching, and evaluation: K–12.* New York: Macmillan.

Eisenberg, M., & Berkowitz, B. (1998). *Curriculum initiative: An agenda and strategy for library media programs.* Norwood, NJ: Ablex.

Eisenberg, M., & Johnson, D. (1996). Computer skills for information problem solving: Learning and teaching technology in context [ERIC Document]. Retrieved August 20, 1998, from the World Wide Web: *http://ericir.syr.edu/ithome/digests/computerskills.html*

Eisenstein, E. L. (1979). *The printing press as an agent of change: Communications and cultural transformations in early-modern Europe* (Vols. 1–2). Cambridge: Cambridge University Press.

Glave, J. (1998, February 16). Dramatic Internet growth continues. *Wired News.* Retrieved August 25, 1998, from the World Wide Web: *http://www.wired.com/news/news/technology/story/10323.html*

Harasim, L. (1990). On-line education: An environment for collaboration and intellectual amplification. In L. Harasim (Ed.), *On-line education: Perspectives on a new environment* (pp. 39–64). New York: Praeger.

Harnad, S. (1991). Post-Gutenberg galaxy: The fourth revolution in the means of production and knowledge. *Public-Access Computer Systems Review, 2*(1), 39–53.

Heath, S. B. (1992). Literacy skills or literate skills? Considerations for ESL/EFL learners. In D. Nunan (Ed.), *Collaborative language learning and teaching* (pp. 40–55). Cambridge: Cambridge University Press.

Hegelheimer, V., Mills, D., Salzmann, A., & Shetzer, H. (1996, March). *World Wide Web activities that work (and why!).* International Conference of Teachers of English to Speakers of Other Languages, Chicago, Illinois (available on-line at *http://deil.lang.uiuc.edu/resources/Tesol/WWW_Activities.html*).

Kendall, C. (1995). Cyber-surveys. In M. Warschauer (Ed.), *Virtual connections: Online activities and projects for networking language learners* (pp. 97–100). Honolulu: Second Language Teaching and Curriculum Center, University of Hawaii.

Kress, G. (1998). Visual and verbal modes of representation in electronically mediated communication: The potentials of new forms of text. In I. Snyder (Ed.), *Page to screen: Taking literacy into the electronic era* (pp. 53–79). London: Routledge.

Landow, G. P. (1992). *Hypertext: The convergence of contemporary critical theory and technology.* Baltimore: Johns Hopkins University Press.

Lanham, R. A. (1993). *The electronic word: Democracy, technology, and the arts.* Chicago: University of Chicago Press.

Lemke, J. L. (1998). Metamedia literacy: Transforming meanings and media. In D. Reinking, M. McKenna, L. Labbo, & R. D. Kieffer (Eds.), *Handbook of literacy and technology: Transformations in a post-typographic world* (pp. 283–301). Mahwah, NJ: Lawrence Erlbaum Associates.

Nua Ltd. (1998). How many on-line? [On-line article]. Retrieved August 25,

1998, from the World Wide Web: *http://www.nua.ie/surveys/how_many_ on-line/index.html*

Papert, S. (1980). *Mindstorms: Children, computers, and powerful ideas.* New York: Basic Books.

Reich, R. (1991). *The work of nations: Preparing ourselves for 21st century capitalism.* New York: Knopf.

Relph, E. (1991). Post-modern geography. *Canadian Geographer, 35*(1), 98–105.

Richards, J. C., & Lockhart, C. (1994). *Reflective teaching in second language classrooms.* New York: Cambridge University Press.

Rifkin, J. (1995). *The end of work.* New York: Tarcher/Putnam.

Ross, D., Bondy, E., & Kyle, D. W. (1993). *Reflective teaching for student empowerment.* New York: Macmillan.

Shetzer, H. (1997). Critical reflection on the use of e-mail in teaching English as a second language. Unpublished master's thesis. University of Illinois, Urbana-Champaign.

Sproull, L., & Kiesler, S. (1991). *Connections: New ways of working in the networked organization.* Cambridge, MA: MIT Press.

Warschauer, M. (1999). *Electronic literacies: Language, culture, and power in on-line education.* Mahwah, NJ: Lawrence Erlbaum Associates.

Werry, C. C. (1996). Linguistic and interactional features of Internet Relay Chat. In S. C. Herring (Ed.), *Computer-mediated communication: Linguistic, social and cross-cultural perspectives* (pp. 47–63). Amsterdam: John Benjamins.

Yates, S. J. (1996). Oral and written linguistic aspects of computer conferencing: A corpus-based study. In S. C. Herring (Ed.), *Computer-mediated communication: Linguistic, social and cross-cultural perspectives* (pp. 29–46). Amsterdam: John Benjamins.

9 Task-based language learning via audiovisual networks

The LEVERAGE project

Christoph Zähner
Agnès Fauverge
Jan Wong

Introduction

The LEVERAGE project was part of the European Advanced Communications Technologies and Services (ACTS) program. The project's primary aim was to establish how well broadband telecommunications networks are suited to educational (and especially language learning) needs in today's multilingual and multicultural Europe. A number of partners from six European countries were involved in the project with three end-user sites in Cambridge, Madrid, and Paris.[1] The project was built around three sets of user trials. The first trial involved nonspecialist learners of French using the network locally in Cambridge; the second trial included learners of French and English in Paris and Cambridge, respectively; and the third trial brought together learners of English, French, and Spanish from all three end-user sites. In this chapter, we report on the first and second trials.

One of the major aims of the project was to assess the practicality of providing learners of various European languages with opportunities to collaborate with their peers in the target language community via a broadband telecommunications network. Reciprocal peer tutoring was to be one of the major features of the system.

The main questions the project attempted to answer were:

- How well do high-bandwidth networks support collaborative learning?
- How well is a task-based approach suited to the network environment?
- What facilities are required to support network-based learning?

One of the major challenges of the project was to develop an effective network-based learning methodology and to identify which factors were

---

1 Working in partnership were: CAP SESA Télécom (France), and Software BV (Netherlands), ASCOM Tech AG (Switzerland), GEC-Marconi Limited (United Kingdom), University of Cambridge (United Kingdom), VTT Technical Research (Finland), Institut National de Télécommunication (France), and UPM (Spain).

most important in determining its effectiveness. External constraints such as the short duration of the trials and the complexity (and at times fragility) of the system made this a difficult task.

We begin with a brief outline of the theoretical assumptions on which the project's methodology was based, followed by a description of the methods, a discussion of the results, and some preliminary conclusions.

Theoretical background

Work on second language acquisition tends to take one of two fundamentally different positions. Researchers in the tradition of cognitive science focus on the mental processing of the individual engaged in language learning, the general conditions of learnability, and the internal structures and representations involved in language learning. The importance of the context in which learning takes place and its effect on learning are often played down because of a belief that environmental stimuli are not sufficiently rich to explain the structure of our internal representations and the cognitive processes that work on them. Researchers in the tradition of cultural psychology, on the other hand, usually stress the importance of seeing all learning as socially and culturally situated, as *inter*mental rather than *intra*mental processes. As Wertsch (1991) puts it, "The basic goal of the socio-cultural approach to mind is to create an account of human mental processes that recognizes the essential relationship between these processes and their cultural, historical and institutional settings" (p. 6). In sociocultural approaches, then, the importance of the mind as a computational device that manipulates internal representations is minimized.

For researchers who feel that both approaches have some valuable insights to offer, it is difficult to find sufficient common ground between the two approaches on which to base their work. However, recent work by Frawley (1997) may offer a way forward. Frawley draws a distinction between nonconscious, conscious, and metaconscious processing, with the first two mainly involving the mind as a biological computational device, thus acknowledging the concerns of cognitive science. The concept of metaconsciousness, on the other hand, offers him a way of joining the computational and social domains; it is seen as the essential interface between the mind as the individual's computing device and the mind as a sociocultural phenomenon.

In this view, the metaconscious domain is concerned with high-level mental activities that include framing problem spaces, planning actions, monitoring performance, reflecting on outcomes, and negotiating meaning between cooperating individuals. These processes, by necessity, transcend the autonomous individual and involve him in interaction with other individuals in social and cultural settings. Collaborating individuals have to establish a level of intersubjectivity that sustains their cooperative efforts. They can do this only if they have some means at their disposal to construct joint frames of reference, to plan, monitor, and adjust their actions. They have to form external representations that are at least partly shared and that they can manipulate jointly.

This construction of shared external representations fulfills a fourfold role. First, it allows individuals to establish common goals and objectives. It enables them to plan and monitor a cooperative course of action and to evaluate the outcome of their activities. Second, by externalizing some aspects of cognitive processing, the individual shares the burden of cognitive processing with others. A shared problem space is constructed that makes it possible for individuals to share their problem-solving strategies and learn from one another. Third, the process of externalizing symbolic representations implies an element of reflexivity; the individual gains some distance over the immediacy of internal cognitive processing and thus obtains explicit control over some of his cognitive operations. He can take the position of an external controller over his own actions. Fourth, and for our purpose most important, the individual who is a newcomer to a given social and cultural domain has a way of integrating himself or herself into that domain by internalizing the existing external representation and making it part of his or her own thinking. This is a true process of integration – not just a matter of apprehending or transferring the external representation to the internal mind.

It has been claimed that any intervention to change an individual's subjectivity (and learning clearly implies such an intervention) takes place at the metaconscious level (Neisser, 1992). Who the instigator of the intervention is – the individual himself or herself, or some external agent, such as a peer or a mentor – does not matter in this respect. In this view, learning implies that the learner is placed in some environment where he can engage in metaconscious activities with other collaborating individuals. The collaboration does not need to be intentionally pedagogical.

Vygotsky's zone of proximal development is an attempt to describe more precisely the conditions under which such learning takes place. Vygotsky (1978) describes the zone of proximal development as "the distance between the actual development level as determined by independent problem solving and the level of potential development as determined through problem solving under adult guidance or in collaboration with more capable peers" (p. 86). The crucial features of the zone of proximal development are intersubjectivity and asymmetry. For intersubjectivity to be established, the cooperating individuals must share some symbolic external representations, usually, but not necessarily or exclusively, construed via a common language. Furthermore, for development to take place, one of the individuals must have internalized more of the relevant external representations and show greater competence in manipulating these representations. He or she is thus able to provide the guidance necessary for the learner to acquire such representations and to manipulate them.

The fact that external representations in this process are mostly represented through speech implies that in some sense most learning also includes some form of "language learning," albeit usually in the native language. The difference in second language learning is that the means of mediating socially and culturally conventional representations itself becomes the focus of the learning activity.

In this view, language learning, as a deliberate and controlled activity, is essentially an intermental (social and cultural) process situated at the metaconscious level. This is not to deny that processes at the conscious and nonconscious levels are also involved. The metaconscious level, after all, is seen as resting on these other levels and extending the internal computational device into the external world. Moreover, the learning practice will itself shape automatic processes at the conscious level and to a lesser degree at the nonconscious level. However, learning as an intersubjective activity with possibilities of control and intervention has to focus on the metaconscious level and is thus mainly concerned with issues of problem framing, focus, negotiation of meaning, planning, monitoring, and evaluation. Put differently, both the fact and the outcome of learning will turn on the successful establishment of a zone of proximal development for the learner.

Research questions

Based on the preceding theoretical orientation, the LEVERAGE project involved designing and implementing a network-based language learning environment. Our research attempted to answer a range of questions: Did the environment and the tasks provided offer sufficient common ground for learners and their collaborators in the learning process to establish a shared frame of reference, to map out the problem space, and to work together toward a common goal? Were there sufficient opportunities for learners to construct new concepts through the negotiation of new meanings? Did the learners, by externalizing their thinking, share the cognitive burden with other, more competent, collaborators and also engage in a process of reflection on their thinking, allowing them ultimately to gain greater control over their thinking? In general, did the environment offer opportunities for planning, monitoring, and evaluation of learners' activities?

Method

Subjects

The subjects consisted of twenty-eight university students in Cambridge, England, who were learners of French and sixteen university students in Paris, France, who were learners of English. All subjects were volunteers, and none knew each other before the study.

The Cambridge students' proficency in French varied, but all had reached at least high school standard (British A-level, or equivalent). The range of their specializations ranged from engineering to law and history. The Parisian students were all engineering students studying telecommunications and taking English as a subsidiary and compulsory part of their main degree program. They all attended traditional classroom-based tutorials in addition to participating in the LEVERAGE project.

Computer literacy among the subjects varied greatly, from the highly experienced user to the near novice with difficulties using a mouse and moving windows in a graphic user environment. Both the observation of the students and the postobservation interviews indicated that the level of computer literacy had little impact on how effectively the system was used. Even the inexperienced subjects acquired the necessary skills quickly and easily.

An attempt was made to establish the students' general educational and linguistic background through a questionnaire administered at the outset of the study. One significant area of variabilty that became evident only during the study itself was the wide range in learning styles exhibited by individual users. These ranged along two axes: First, some students showed a clear preference for close guidance and almost continuous supervision, whereas others preferred to learn independently, following a less prescriptive and more exploratory path. Second, some students preferred working on their own, whereas others clearly appreciated and enjoyed the collaborative learning experience.

The first trial involved only Cambridge-based students (N = 16), whereas the second trial involved students from both Cambridge (N = 12) and Paris (N = 16).

Tasks

For both trials, the students were organized in small groups of three or four working from different sites over a computer network that provided opportunities for real-time multipoint video and audio as well as access to shared applications and exercise modules.[2] The capacity for real-time

---

2 One server (Windows NT) offered Web services and handled the user management; another server (Sun) took care of the multipoint conferencing unit and functioned as

written chatting was added in the second trial.[3] An adviser assisted as necessary from yet another site.

Over a period of 6 weeks, the groups worked on a given task. A task-based approach suggested itself for the natural way it fit both the theoretical orientation and the practical constraints of the project. The aim of the tasks was to design an environment that would require the students to engage in a series of metaconscious processes, including planning, monitoring, and the negotiation of meaning. The goal-oriented nature of task-based learning helps students to frame the problem space. Exploration of the problem space, in turn, entails students' negotiating new meanings with their collaborators or tutors. Students need to plan, monitor, modify, and evaluate their actions in the problem space and internalize the newly encountered external and culturally shared representations. The typical elements of zones of proximal development, such as collaboration, speech as the medium of interaction, and the externalization of thinking, all occur naturally in task-based learning. Nonnative/native speaker peer tutoring also offered a strong element of asymmetry, which, it was hoped, would foster scaffolding.

For each trial, LEVERAGE provided a large-scale task, which was divided into a number of clearly identified subtasks. In the first trial (Cambridge students only), learners were asked to assume the role of a British advertising agency bidding for a contract to represent the French Nord Pas-de-Calais area in the United Kingdom. Students worked in groups of three (one per remote site) and were given four weeks to complete their task. The final objective was a 20-minute oral presentation in French explaining the chosen marketing strategy and the production of material supporting the presentation. Documents leading into the task (initial letter, memos, and authentic information about the area) were available on the system, as was access to an on-line adviser who was able to help with task-related, language-related, and technical issues. The main aim of the

a video server. All work stations had a 133-MHz processor, a 17-inch color monitor, a 1.6-Gb hard disk, and 16 Mb of RAM. They were equipped with a sound card, an MPEG-capable graphics card, and a special card for video-conferencing. All machines had headphones, a microphone, and a video camera attached. All workstations ran Windows 95 and had Netscape and Microsoft Office installed. The network connectivity was provided by 25 Mbits ATM network cards. All work stations were connected to an ATM switch. These switches were connected via access nodes to a double ring running at 625 Mbits. The two servers were connected directly to the access nodes (156-Mbits link).

3 The transnational link was a 10-Mbit constant bit rate ATM connection allowing high-quality videoconferencing and audioconferencing, as well as the running of shared applications. Access to the system was through a Web browser running on all workstations. The resources were either available as HTML documents or as audio or video files, which could be played from within the browser. There was also direct access from within the browser to the multipoint videoconferencing and audioconferencing system, shared applications, exercise modules, and so on.

task was to provide a context for language learning that reproduced some of the conditions and requirements the students were likely to face later in their professional life and thus to offer an important element of realism. The small-group arrangement with a joint presentation as the ultimate goal was intended to foster intensive collaboration involving all students. The nature of the task suggested a short but intensive period of collaborative work rather than a longer period of intermittent work – a characteristic that fit the external constraints of limited system availability.

The second trial (involving both Cambridge and Paris students) was based on a simulation related to the Channel tunnel. Students took on the role of English and French engineers who were preparing a joint presentation to the Canadian Institute of Engineering. This presentation was to last 20 minutes, and the students had the choice either to work on-line and deliver the presentation off-line or to do both the preparation and the presentation on-line. The planned duration of the task was again 6 weeks, but technical difficulties reduced the actual time spent on collaborative work to 5 weeks with one 2-hour session per week. All work was carried out in groups of three to four students, with either two English and two French native speakers or one English and two French native speakers. A French native speaker was available as an on-line adviser throughout the trial. The students in France additionally had access to an adviser who was physically present at their location. However, almost all reciprocal peer tutoring occurred between native/nonnative pairs.

The data

Data about the subjects' interaction with each other and and the system was collected in a number of ways. All students were given a pretrial questionnaire in order to assess their general education, language background, and expectations. A posttrial questionnaire allowed comparison with initial expectations and asked participants for opinions and suggestions. After each trial, the participants were interviewed and asked a range of questions about their impression of the usability of the system. These interviews were tape-recorded and transcribed. A number of sessions were recorded on videotape (with the camera looking at the screen and the audio signal from all participants in the group recorded). These sessions were later transcribed for analysis. The system itself tracked a range of user statistics, including the use of particular modules such as videoconferencing, the users' access to resources, and their time on the system.

In evaluating the LEVERAGE system, the major focus lay on determining whether the infrastructure was able to support intensive collaborative learning and whether those elements identified as indicative of effective zones of proximal development could be discovered. To this end, students were asked directly about their experience with the system and were observed working on their own and interacting with each other (mediated by the system). In this way, it was possible to use both subjective and objective data in the evaluation.

It should be noted that the trials were plagued by a number of technical problems. In the first trial, the audio quality of the videoconferencing/audioconferencing was not of the desired standard, with excessive line noise. This problem was overcome in the second trial, which instead suffered from the occasionally unreliable transnational connection. The effects of these problems not only were obvious from the session recordings but were commented on by the students in posttrial interviews. The results of the evaluation, therefore, have to be seen at least partly in the light of these problems.

Results

The first trial

The first trial was organized among sixteen of the Cambridge students, with none of the French students participating. Thus, there was no native speaker/nonnative speaker reciprocal peer tutoring. Students were allowed to use either English or French in their negotiation and planning. Although most of the interaction took place in English, the negotiation provided some interesting observations about the effectiveness of collaborative learning in general and a useful comparison for the second trial, with its much heavier emphasis on native/nonnative speaker interaction. The main features we looked for in the data from the first trial were the typical signs of metaconscious processing: framing, planning, and interaction.

The students had been given a brief description of their task. It was left to the individual groups to establish a framework, to identify specific goals, and to plan their work accordingly. The effect of this approach varied considerably from group to group. In the posttrial interview, some students commented on the focus the task provided and its integrative effect:

S1: The presentation is a good idea because it's the group work side and everybody can discuss who is going to do what and things like that.

S2: Because it was focused and we did actually have to do something at the end of it, I felt I was *actually using language* (emphasis added).

S3: It's a very good way of integrating language. Quite often the traditional approach to language is that it is taught in bits and pieces and people also think of applying it in bits and pieces and don't think of it as an all-round learning experience, whereas that gave you the entire sort of range of how you would be using it, and how you would be expected to use a language and how you would experience it, which was a very, very good idea.

It is significant that these students understood the importance of settling on a particular goal for establishing a joint conceptual framework that supports the collaborative work on the task and enables individuals to plan, share, and integrate their activities. S2 also reported subjectively that she experienced this form of language learning as more authentic, and thus more socially and culturally situated than traditional forms of teaching centered on specific decontextualized functional or grammatical units.

However, not all groups managed the initial stage of establishing and structuring the problem space with equal success:

S3: Everyone was a bit vague on the actual aim. I think it needed to be set out in English like . . . this what you've got to do, one, two, three, before we went on the computer. . . . An introductory meeting to assert exactly where you're going to be at the end.

This student did not experience the need to establish a common task goal with her collaborators as an important part of structuring her learning experience. Instead, she was left in a state of disorientation. She obviously expected the structure of her work to be imposed externally and was unable to engage in a constructive discourse with the other group members on how to frame the problem and how to develop a strategy for achieving the given goal.

What is significant about this student is that she belonged to a group that for technical reasons was not able do a videoconference with the on-line adviser (who might have provided the support required to overcome the initial framing problem). Although the students had other means of contacting the adviser (e.g., by e-mail), they did not make use of them. It appears that the failure of the major communication channel prevented the students from seeking support – instead, they remained for a considerable time in a state of drift.

In groups where the students successfully agreed on what the problem space was, what goal they wanted to settle on, and how they were going to achieve it, a high degree of intersubjectivity occurred. For example, in one typical audiovisual conference, three students at different sites discussed how they should plan their report. In this there were signs of meta-conscious processing, such as negotiation of meaning:

S5: I had a look at the thing we have to fill in. I can't remember what it is called.
S6: The tender form.
S5: Yes, I think that is what it was called.

probing the problem space:

S4: What are we up to?
S5: I think the object of the exercise is . . .
S6: What are we supposed to choose? What section of industry . . .

S5: From what I gather, we just need to write a short report about how great the Lilloise region is. . . .

shared orientation:

S5: There is stuff about how easy it is to move to the area – isn't there?
S6: Yeah – There is a whole section on how good a region it is. With lots of little things on how good we are at this and that; which we could recycle. . . .
S5: Where is the thing we have to fill in?
S4: I think . . .
S5: Basically, we have to fill in that form.
S6: Yeah.
S6: Where is this form anyway? . . .
S5: The submission thing at the bottom. It is a form.
S5: You can click it.
S6: Okay, yeah.

and tentatively establishing a strategy for working on the task:

S6: I think we can basically title the project . . .
S6: All we can do is fill it in.
S6: In the process of filling it in we will get some ideas. . . .

At each turn, all participants took great care in establishing and maintaining consensus among themselves, and no one tried to impose a particular view or course of action on the others.

Overall, the network-based learning environment offering videoconferencing and audioconferencing allowed high-level metaconscious processing to take place. The students in general were able to arrive at a consensus of what constituted the task, to plan a series of intermediate stages to achieve the task objective, and to support each other in the accomplishment of the task.

During the initial phase of establishing the task goal and an appropriate course of action, there was heavy reliance on direct communication between the members of the group; but even after this phase, when the group members tended to explore the available resources individually, learning as a collaborative effort continued. Consider the following comment from a posttrial interview:

S9: I think the audioconference was useful at different stages of the task as somebody would say, "oh look, I've found a page here," and you could then go to it. I don't think it's necessary to meet together all the time, but while we were there during our 2 hours it was more or less necessary to go on audioconferencing all the time, not because you always needed to, but because there would always be a point in the session when you wanted to ask a question or whatever . . .

Reciprocal peer tutoring emerged quite naturally out of the context of the task without any explicit form of tutoring/teaching. Because the tutoring function was linked to finding interesting and relevant bits of information in the system, it passed from participant to participant and was not permanently tied to one individual simply on the basis of his or her greater linguistic or content knowledge. This is not to say that at other points – for example, in the preparation of the joint presentation – greater competence in the target language or greater experience in giving presentations did not predispose one or the other individual for the tutor role.

Evidence of intersubjectivity and close collaboration should not, however, be taken to imply that audioconferencing and videoconferencing create the same environment for collaborative learning as traditional face-to-face peer-group learning. There are still significant differences. A number of students remarked, for example, on the lack of a shared physical work space:

S10: Well, I found working at a distance was a difficulty because you couldn't, like, although you could see the person's face you couldn't, like, give them notes and things . . .

This comment points to an important aspect of collaborative learning that must not be overlooked in network-based learning environments: the need of learners to externalize their thinking by means of writing, drawing, sketching, and sharing these auxiliary artifacts with their peers and/or tutor. Processes of externalization are important in establishing both a degree of intersubjectivity with collaborators and an opportunity for the learner to reflect on his or her own thinking and acting. The immediacy of speech means that there is little room for this kind of reflection. Both aspects are reflected in the following comments of a student:

S9: In the end, writing things down is better than just speaking. . . . If they are speaking another language and however much you try you just can't understand them, then writing is the sure way of getting the message across.

Other forms of network-based communication, either synchronous such as a shared notepad or asynchronous such as e-mail, appear to offer some opportunities in this direction but were not explored in the first trial. A shared editor and chat tool were introduced as part of the second trial, and their use is mentioned in the next section.

Interestingly, limitations in the available communication bandwidth offer novel opportunities for learners to engage in dialogue, and ultimately to promote their language proficiency. This point was demonstrated in one lengthy on-line conference in French involving two of the Cambridge students and their adviser. The students, who had encountered a technical problem with a piece of software, had to explain to the adviser what the problem was. The physical distance and bandwidth limitation made it impossible for the students to show the problem directly to the adviser. They thus had to find verbal ways of helping the adviser to conceptualize the problem. The exchanges between the students and the adviser show how, mediated through talk in the foreign language, a shared understanding of the problem space slowly emerges. Hesitations, confirmation, backtracking, and asking for clarification are typical features of these kinds of discourse – a discourse that arises quite naturally out of the task-oriented setting.

This same session showed another dynamic that we observed elsewhere – an exacerbation of inequality in foreign language participation. When the above-mentioned two students worked together as a pair, with most of their work in English, S7 (a male, with good proficiency in French) spoke only slightly more than S8 (a female, with less knowledge of French than S7). But when they conversed together with the adviser in French, S8 spoke much less frequently. Of course, a similar outcome could have occurred in a face-to-face interaction, but it appears that network-based oral communication poses additional problems for more reticent personalities specific to the communication medium. Less forceful participants seem to find it difficult to join an ongoing discourse.[4] Possible reasons might be:

- Difficulties in signaling the intention to take the turn. In face-to-face situations, participants have a range of signals, eye contact, facial expressions, body language, and so on, to indicate their intention. Over the network, most of these clues are not available. The visual channel is quite restricted because of the nature of desktop videoconferencing (no direct eye contact, maybe not all participants are visible, and so on), so the only alternative is direct verbal intervention. The inhibitory effect of these features was commented on by a number of students in the posttrial interviews.
- Videoconferencing offers limited visual feedback. The reaction of the other partners in the discourse is not available to the current speaker, or only to a limited degree. People who rely strongly on visible feedback from their partners in a discourse situation find the absence of such feedback disconcerting. Insecurity and lack of confidence are possible consequences.

Transmission delays, which are not noticeable during continuous speech but are obvious during dialogues with rapid turn taking, interfere with the natural turn-taking rhythm. It becomes difficult to know if the partner's turn has ended or if he or she intends to continue. This can lead to a number of false starts and start-up collisions.

These are problems that clearly warrant further investigation. It must

---

4 This contrasts with on-line written communication, where research findings suggest that learners who are reticent in face-to-face interaction often participate more actively (e.g., Bump, 1990; Kern, 1995).

not be forgotten that desktop videoconferencing in language learning is very new and that the students did not yet have time to adapt completely to this new communication medium.

The second trial

Based on the task of preparing a joint presentation on the Channel tunnel to the Canadian Institute of Engineering, the second trial involved the remaining twelve students in Cambridge and the sixteen students in France. The native/nonnative speaker interaction and the reciprocal peer tutoring made the second trial a richer environment for language learning than the first. Among the questions raised were: How would the students negotiate the choice of language? How would they collaborate? Would there be evidence of planning, work sharing, and so on? Would there be clear signs of peer tutoring and where would it occur: in the lexical or grammatical domain or at the level of discourse and planning? How would they use the various communication facilities? Would one communication channel be chosen to the exclusion of the others?

The decision about language choice during the collaborative sessions was left entirely to the students themselves. Logically, three possibilities presented themselves: (1) each student speaking his or her native language; (2) each student speaking the language he/she is learning; or (3) the use of one language only, perhaps alternating after a certain period of time. Of these choices, the second one clearly dominated. Interestingly, the choice of language appeared to be uncontroversial and almost automatic. Concerns of the teaching staff that one language might dominate were not borne out. The fact that most students preferred to practice the foreign language indicates that the opportunity to speak the foreign language was perceived to be the most important aspect of this form of collaborative work. The opportunity to listen to a native speaker was obviously perceived to be of lesser importance, despite the fact that in their post-trial interviews most students stated that the opportunity to communicate with a native speaker was the most important aspect of the trial. Perhaps a clue to this apparent contradiction lies in the observation of one student who stated that talking to a peer in the foreign language was much less stressful than talking to a tutor or teacher who is a native speaker. The social standing of the participants, and their relative roles in the institutional setting, clearly played an important part in how intersubjectivity between native and nonnative speakers was established and experienced.

One of the most significant aspects of the observed instances of peer tutoring was their integration into the collaborative process. Overt tutoring occurred not as a distinct and separate interactional unit but naturally and spontaneously out of the task. The most directly observable instances of peer tutoring were seen at the lexical level. There were numerous examples, from the simple asking for an equivalent term, to straightforward corrections, negotiation of meaning, and semantic and syntactic issues:

Asking for an equivalent term
E1: Je crois que . . . que c'est, err . . . il faut err . . . de . . . qu'est-ce que c'est "record"?
[I believe that . . . that it is . . . err . . . it is necessary . . . err . . . what is the word for "record"?]
F1: Enregistrer.
[Record.]
E1: Enregistrer, OK.

Correction
E1: OK . . . Oui-oui, parce que je n'ai pas le déjeuner. Parce que mon . . . ma . . . mes . . . mes lectures finit à une heure . . . à une heure Angleterre?
[OK . . . Yeah-yeah, because I did not go to lunch. Because my "lectures" [*lectures* are actually "readings" in French] finished at one o'clock, one o'clock in England?]
F1: Cours . . . mes cours!
[Lectures . . . my lectures!]
E1: Cours, pardon. Mes cours finit à . . . à une heure Angleterre, c'est deux heures France, donc . . .
[Lectures, sorry. My lectures finished at . . . at one o'clock in England, that's two o'clock in France, so . . .

Negotiation of meaning
F2: When is your next holidays . . . euh . . . E1?
E1: Err . . . Five weeks time.
F1: Ouh!
F2: Ouh!
F1: Very long.
E1: It's fourteenth of March, but we have five or six weeks.
F2: Five or six!
E1: Oui . . . oui c'est seulement . . . err . . . trois terms? . . . C'est ça? Terms? Qu'est-ce que c'est en français?
[Yes . . . yes it is only err . . . three 'terms'? Isn't it? "Terms"? What is it in French?]
F1: Terms . . . Terms c'est the "trimestre."
[Terms . . . terms, it is a "trimester."]
E1: Yeah, c'est seulement trois trimestres de huit semaines. Donc ce n'est pas beaucoup.
[Yes, it is only three trimesters of eight weeks. So it's not very much.]
F1: But trimestre in French is the third of one year.
E1: Pardon?
F1: Non, euh . . . trimestre in French is three months. [A trimester in France is three months.]
E1: Three months.
F1: Yeah.
E1: Oh, it's a quarter of a year. Yeah.

F1: Three-mestre! [TRI-mester!]
E1: Oh, OK!
F1: A fourth of the year.

Semantic issues
E1: Qu'est-ce que c'est "fut" f-u-t?
   [What is "was" "w-a-s"?]
F2: Euh . . . C'est le verbe être au passé . . .
   [Oh . . . It's the verb "to be" in the past tense . . .]
E1: OK . . . OK.
F2: Euh . . . Je fus . . . travailleur quand j'étais jeune à l'école . . .
   [Eh . . . I was . . . a hard worker when I was young at school . . .]

Syntactic issues
E1: Ce n'est pas temps ancien? Je ne sais pas, je suis enrhumé. J'ai cru que les
   adjectifs . . . parce que sometimes it's les temps anciens et . . . is it?
   [It's not "temps ancien"? I don't know, I have a cold. I thought that adjec-
   tives . . . because sometimes it is "temps ancien" and . . . is it?]
F2: Oui, mais dans le temps ancien, non. On dit plutôt l'ancien temps . . .
   dans ce cas-là.
   [Yes, but not in "le temps ancien." We'd rather say "l'ancien temps" . . .
   in this case.
E1: OK, oui.

Generally, the transcripts of the working sessions were dominated by
discourse centered on collaboration and coordination. The focus ranged
from the simple arrangement of the next session and the resolution of
timing issues to the discussion of available material.

As in more conventional teaching situations, there were instances of
misunderstandings and errors. In one excerpt, for example, a French native speaker mistook "tender" for "contender," believing that his English partner was speaking about the participants in the process and not
the legal document. However, these misunderstandings usually got resolved in the subsequent discourse and often gave rise to further elaborations and negotiation of meaning. The following is a good example of
how this kind of discourse can extend over many turns:

F1: Because he wants us to . . . to keep a . . . to keep a . . . a mark, a trace . . .
   to keep a . . . hmm, how can we say? Comment on dit une empreinte? To
   keep something.
E1: Log? Yeah, oui, un log. Yes. To keep a log or a record?
F1: A print? Non, a record or . . . something . . .
E1: A log. A record, yeah.
F1: A lock? . . . How do you . . . A lock, how do you write it? So, do you
   know how work . . . how works SIESTA? [F1 is inquiring about the
   shared editor to work out the spelling.]
E1: Non.
F1: No. Did you open it?
E1: Oui, oui.
F1: You have it.

E1: Yeah. Oui.

F1: "A log", yeah. So, all that kind of . . . of a . . . all that kind of . . . E1, yes you're right. You get it.

E1: Do I? Oh . . .

F1: Yeah, now you can write on it.

E1: Est-ce que vous pouvez . . . ? Oui, vous pouvez voir ça?
[Can you . . . ? Yes, can you see it?]

F1: Hello. Yes. Yes, I can see "Hello."

E1: Et ça comme ça?
[And this like this?]

F1: A-A!

E1: Oui, lettre . . . deux lettres. Ah, OK, c'est bon.
[Yes, two letters, two letters, that is OK.]

F1: I want, I want . . . Now I'm asking you for the . . . Now I can write in and I can correct what you have written. Yeah, you know!

E1: Oh oui, OK, c'est bon. Ah oui c'est bon!
[Oh yes, OK, that's good. Yes, that's good!]

F1: That's perfect! And I can put . . .

E1: Oui. Eh . . . Oh oui, c'est vrai.
[Yes, eh . . . Oh yes, that's true.]

F1: So, what, a "log"?

E1: A log. En anglais c'est bien? Est-ce que vous sais qu'est-ce que c'est "a log"?
[A log. In English, is it OK? Do you know what's a log?]

F1: Yes, I'm asking you!

E1: OK. En anglais s'il vous plaît?
[OK. In English please?]

F1: Yes, en anglais if you want to.

E1: All right. A log is . . . it's if you've . . . C'est une "empreinte" je crois, mais je ne connais pas "empreinte" donc c'est difficile de . . .
[. . . It is a "mark," I think, but I don't know "mark," so it is difficult to . . .]

F1: "Empreinte"? It's a "fingerprint," it's "a print," "fingerprint" you know? Digital, digital print?

E1: Fingerprint?

F1: Euh, you know what is a fingerprint, no?

E1: Oui, oui je connais un fingerprint, mais . . .
[Yes, yes, I know "fingerprint," but . . .]

F1: . . . For the police . . . There's a mark . . .

E1: . . . mais en contexte? Oh, oui, oui OK.
[. . . but in this context? Oh, yes, yes, OK.]

F1: You put something that's stay . . . that's stay . . . that's re . . . No, what, another word to stay?

E1: Pardon?

F1: Another word, in English, for 'to stay'?

E1: "To stay" . . .

F1: Yes. "To rest" yeah, no? Another word . . .

E1: "Stay" comme ça?

F1: Where are you? You're writing on LECHE? [LECHE is the chat tool.]

E1: On LECHE, oui.

F1: Yes, "to stay," another word "to stay"? But something will not change and will . . . non . . .
E1: Err . . . "Remain"?
F1: Remain, yes, remain. I was looking for that word. Yes! So, is this a "print"? An "empreinte"? It's something that remain and that . . .
E1: Oui, ah, mais ce n'est pas un "fingerprint." Or, c'est exactement un "fingerprint" . . .
   Yes, ah, but it's not a "fingerprinting." Or, it's exactly a "fingerprint" . . .]
F1: A fingerprint, yeah. A fingerprint is something that . . .
E1: Oui, pardon. Does "une empreinte" mean "fingerprint"?
   [Yes, sorry. . . .]
F1: "Fingerprint" is . . . mean "une empreinte." Yes, but in French we use it . . . we use that word "empreinte" to make . . . to signify that we . . . it's something that will remain . . . we can use it then . . . to analyze it or . . .
E1: OK? "A log," oui, "a branch"?
F1: Yeah . . . Un peu d'un arbre? A branch, yeah.
   [Yes, part of a tree? . . .]
E1: Mais, je crois que beaucoup d'ans . . . err . . . depuis beaucoup d'ans il . . . A long time ago it came to mean, you know, sort of "a record."
   [Yes, but I believe that many years . . . err . . . many years ago . . . .]
F1: Yes, "a record." We can . . . Stop it! Let's stop it and we'll say . . . So, that my teacher wants, my teacher wants to us to keep something of "a log" or "a print" . . . as you wish . . . of our conversation and then I will be able to make a report or something like that. You know?

As the excerpts show, videoconferencing was clearly the main channel of communication, but the text-based chat tool (LECHE) played a significant role too. It was often used in exchanges about lexical meanings to resolve spelling issues and the like, and it provided a degree of permanence in the planning phase with one student jotting down some ideas and the others changing and amending them. This seems to indicate that the availability of some visual reference with a degree of permanence is an important element in language task performance. It allows the collaborators to externalize their ideas and thus make them the subject for reflection and negotiation.

Conclusion

Both the data obtained through the observation of collaborative working sessions and the subjective response of the students in the posttrial interviews provide clear evidence that the LEVERAGE system was effective in supporting collaborative learning. The tasks engaged students in establishing a common understanding of what the problem space was and provided planning, monitoring, and evaluation opportunities. Peer-to-peer support was provided throughout the collaborative work, both via the audio channel and, to a lesser degree, via the visual channel. The exchanges between the students show a number of features indicative of collaborative discourse, such as the negotiation of meaning, consensus building and maintenance, and repair. There is good evidence of externalization in the form of thinking aloud in front of other students and offering them opportunities to experience the other's thinking process and to participate in it; thinking was thus an intersubjective, collaborative process. Evidence of self-reflection can also be found, albeit to a much lesser degree and at a fairly shallow level. The short duration of the trials and the absence of a long-term follow-up make it impossible to say how effective this form of learning is in raising the subjects' ability to control their own thinking.

All in all, this leads to the conclusion that broadband telecommunications networks that are capable of offering high-quality audioconferencing and videoconferencing are able to support effective zones of proximal development. However, the provision of the sufficient communication bandwidth in itself is not enough: Students must be provided with the right setting to encourage collaborative work. First, students must be provided an appropriate, engaging task. Second, a means of externalizing and exchanging thoughts and ideas in written form (e.g., a shared scratch pad or similar tool) seems necessary, even in a task strongly oriented toward spoken communication. Third, support must be available to provide students with ready assistance in understanding the problem domain, in finding solutions, and in monitoring progress. To this end, the role of the adviser in the system is crucial. Carefully chosen tasks, a shared writing tool, and access to an adviser together can help maximize the potential benefits of audiovisual conferencing for collaborative interaction and language learning.

References

Bump, J. (1990). Radical changes in class discussion using networked computers. *Computers and the Humanities, 24*(1–2), 49–65.

Frawley W. (1997). *Vygotsky and cognitive science: Language and the unification of the cognitive and social mind.* Cambridge: Harvard University Press.

Kern, R. G. (1995). Restructuring classroom interaction with networked computers: Effects on quantity and quality of language production. *Modern Language Journal, 79,* 457–476.

Neisser, U. (1992). The development of consciousness and the acquisition of the self. In F. Kessel, P. Cole, & D. Johnson (Eds.), *Self and consciousness: Multiple perspectives* (pp. 1–18). Hillsdale, NJ: Lawrence Erlbaum Associates.

Vygotsky, L. S. (1978). *Mind in society.* Cambridge: Harvard University Press.

Wertsch, J. (1991) *Voices of the mind.* Cambridge: Harvard University Press.

10 *Is network-based learning CALL?*

Carol A. Chapelle

In his overview, Levy defines computer-assisted language learning (CALL) broadly as "the search for and study of applications of the computer in language teaching and learning" (Levy, 1997a, p. 1). In Chapter 1 of this volume, Kern and Warschauer describe network-based language teaching (NBLT) as "language teaching that involves the use of computers connected to one another in either local or global networks." On the basis of these broad definitions, it appears that network-based learning might be considered one type of CALL. Consistent with this expectation, the essays in this volume raise many of the same issues that have appeared in the CALL literature since the early 1980s – issues such as evaluation and the role of the teacher.

Despite superficial appearances, however, one cannot be satisfied to consider NBLT the same as pre-network CALL simply because computers play a role in both types of activities.[1] From the perspective of second language acquisition, it is significant that learners often interact with a computer program in pre-network CALL activities, but they usually interact with other people in NBLT activities. Drawing a sharp distinction between the "impoverished" interactions afforded by pre-network CALL and those of NBLT, Debski (1997b) points out that "until recently, very few teachers looked to the potential of computer technology to enrich the foreign language classroom through fostering human to human communication and creative endeavour" (p. 46). From a historical perspective, Kern and Warschauer (this volume) explain that theoretical foundations for network-based learning are social as well as cognitive in nature and that uses of computer-mediated communication have mainly focused on creating discourse communities. The current literature continues to reflect these historical roots. The NBLT literature displays the language of "activity," "collaboration," "creativity," "experiential learning," and even "social computing" (e.g., Debski, Gassin, & Smith, 1997). The pre-network CALL literature reflects different perspectives through language

---

1 CALL that does not require networking is referred to as "pre-network CALL," even though, as Patrikis (1997) points out, approaches to computer-based teaching accumulate and coexist rather than progressing in a linear fashion replacing old (pre-network CALL) with new (NBLT).

such as "effective and ineffective uses," "meta-analytic research," and "consistent findings" (e.g., Dunkel, 1991). These language differences may reflect the divergent approaches of those concerned with pre-network CALL and NBLT, but do they actually denote critical distinctions?

To what extent is it useful to consider network-based learning the same as pre-network CALL? This question is important given the tendency of work in CALL to rediscover the same instructional practices and problems with each generation of computer hardware and software – a tendency that has stifled evolutionary progress. Some of the same software designs appeared on the mainframe computers of the 1970s, the microcomputers of the 1980s, and the World Wide Web of the 1990s – not necessarily because they were shown to be effective, but because some members of each generation were satisfied to reinvent rather than determined to evolve. If NBLT is CALL, one would hope that design and evaluation of Web-based learning would productively draw on past work in CALL. If network-based activities are different from pre-network CALL, their development and study should implicate a different set of issues from those familiar in the CALL of the 1970s and 1980s.

In this chapter, I would like to suggest that grounds for making a useful distinction between network-learning and pre-network CALL do not exist at this time. I will first discuss the type of empirically based research that would help to make meaningful distinctions among different types of CALL activities. I will then review recurring themes evident throughout the CALL literature and suggest that these themes are relevant to NBLT. Finally, I will outline the contributions that the study of NBLT offers in the evolution of CALL.

Defining types of CALL activities

To address the question of similarity between NBLT and pre-network CALL, it is necessary to have a means – beyond the broad definitions already cited – for distinguishing computer-based activities from one another. If the superficial definition "use of computers in language teaching" is inadequate, what pedagogical or analytic criteria should be brought to bear on defining types of CALL activities?

How can CALL activities be categorized?

Historically, categorization of CALL has been attempted on the basis of global judgments made by teachers and CALL developers – judgments about the intended role of the computer, the role of the target language, or a cluster of descriptive features. For example, one approach focusing on the role of the computer relative to the learner in the CALL activity suggested that the salient feature of an activity would be whether the computer played the role of "magister" directing the student's learning or "pedagogue" assisting the student's learning (Higgins, 1988). An approach targeting the role of the target language distinguished between communicative and noncommunicative CALL activities (Underwood, 1984). Levy (1997a) reviews a number of such schemes for conceptualizing CALL that were developed primarily for pre-network CALL. Many of these suggest that CALL programs can be described through multiple features such as "language difficulty" and "activity type" (Phillips, 1985). Description of NBLT activities, in contrast, typically includes just two features of the hardware and software configurations: (1) whether the activity takes place over a local area network or a wide area network such as the Internet, and (2) whether the communication takes place synchronously (i.e., in real time) or asynchronously (i.e., with delay, such as in e-mail).

These approaches to description have provided the conceptual apparatus for teachers and CALL developers to describe and expand the methodological techniques underlying CALL design. At the same time, they fall short of what is needed in three ways, as I pointed out in 1990:

First, descriptions based on a single view of an entire CALL activity do not account for the details of student-computer interaction. . . . A second problem with general descriptions of CALL activities is that they characterize what students can or should do while working on a computer activity, failing to describe what they actually do. . . . [Third, w]hen a CALL activity is described in terms devised and defined exclusively for that [activity], it is not clear how the [activity] is similar to or different from other CALL or classroom activities. (Chapelle, 1990, p. 204)

To move beyond a superficial level of description, activities need to be defined on the basis of a description of the language that learners use through their interactions during the activity.

CALL texts

CALL text refers to the observable record of the process of learners' work on CALL activities (Chapelle, 1994). CALL texts are the data used by researchers to document the language and interactions relevant for empirically based descriptions of CALL. Table 1 illustrates the dichotomy of text types that one might associate with pre-network CALL and NBLT.

The most important differences evident in these two texts are in the function that the target language performs in each. In the pre-network CALL text (the drill and practice dialogue), the learner uses the target language to display ability to translate into French. The computer uses one word of French (i.e., to express incorrectness with *Non*) to judge the learner's performance. In the Spanish NBLT activity, the learners use the

TABLE I. EXAMPLE CALL TEXTS FROM PRE-NETWORK CALL AND NBLT

Drill and practice dialogue (pre-network CALL, Marty, 1981, p. 34)		*CMC dialogue (NBLT, Pellettieri, this volume)*	
Computer	Translate: I returned the money to you six months ago.	*Learner 1*	. . . si yo pienso, cosas para ayudan el aprendier . . . yo no se.
Learner	J'ai rendu à vous cette argent six mois il y a.	*Learner 2*	cosas que ayudan a aprender
Computer	Non.	*Learner 1*	si, lo siento.

target language to communicate with each other and negotiate meaning. Attempting to express something during the course of the conversation, Learner 1 stumbles over a grammatical form (translated by Pellettieri as "yes, I think, things for helping the learning . . . I don't know." The other learner recognizes the error and suggests a correction (i.e., "things that help you to learn"), to which Learner 1 responds, "yes, I'm sorry."

An empirically based definition of CALL activities

The dichotomy illustrated by the two texts in Table 1 reflects a simplistic, but popular, view of pre-network CALL versus NBLT, but it is misleading for addressing the question of similarity between pre-network CALL and NBLT. In reality, pre-network CALL consists of a variety of pedagogical activities that include software such as microworlds (Papert, 1980; Coleman, 1985), grammar checkers (Hull, Ball, Fox, Levin, & McCutchen, 1987), pronunciation feedback systems (Pennington, 1991; Anderson-Hsieh, 1994), intelligent tutoring systems (Chanier, Pengelly, Twidale, & Self, 1992), concordancer programs (Johns, 1986; Tribble & Jones, 1990), and word processing (Pennington, 1993), to name a few. Similarly, a variety of activities can be carried out through NBLT (Warschauer, 1995). Given the variety – as opposed to dichotomy – of activities that can be devised in pre-network CALL and NBLT, what is needed is a means of defining types of CALL based on observation, description, and analysis of CALL texts, that is, an empirically based procedure. An empirically based definition of CALL needs to be developed through two levels of analysis: description of CALL texts (i.e., what learners are doing with language) and explanation of activity features likely to be responsible for the significant aspects of the texts (i.e., why the activity influences the language as it does).

Descriptive research plays an important role in the study of technology

TABLE 2. EXAMPLES OF CALL TEXTS FROM A VARIETY OF CALL ACTIVITIES

Interaction between . . .	CALL text	Setting
Learner–computer	Drulla [Computer]: Play, please! Student: Okay. Drulla: Thank you. What should I do? Student: You should tell me where the glass is. Drulla: The glass is on the table. Student: Try laying it inside the fridge. Drulla: Very good.	An individual learner's output of commands to computer and computer's responses (Murray, 1995, p. 248)
Learners–computer	Computer: I have learned quite large number of words. Is there an error in this sentence? R: I have learned quite large number of words. Is there an error in this sentence? M: quite large number R: I have learned quite large number. M: quite large number, quite large number	Learners sit together in front of a computer reading from the screen and discuss their responses to questions (Abraham & Liou, 1991, p. 105)
Learner–learner	Kang: Alda, est-ce que tes parents parle à toi en chinois et tu parle aux parents en anglais? Moi, mes parents ne me parle pas en anglais, mais je leur parle en anglais en meme temps. C'est un peu bizarre. Billy: Alda, est-ce que vous êtes chinoise? Si vous êtes chinoise, avez-vous célebré la nouvelle anneé chinoise hier? Avez-vous reçu beaucoup d'argent de votre famille? Kang: Alda, pourquoi "tu n'aime pas trop" de traditions chinois? Que penses-tu a la NOUVELLE ANNEE de Chinois?	Learners discuss the topic "intergenerational differences" through computer-mediated communication (Kern, 1995, pp. 458–459)

and learning (Knupfer & McLellan, 1996) and in studies of second language classroom learning (Seliger & Long, 1983; Day, 1986; Allwright, 1988; Chaudron, 1988; van Lier, 1988; Allwright & Bailey, 1991; Johnson, 1995). The application of descriptive methodologies to CALL requires examination of CALL texts as illustrated in Table 1. If texts for a variety of CALL activities were documented, one could begin to analyze ways in which they were similar and different. For example, Table 2 illustrates texts from several other CALL activities. The first one comes from an activity based on a microworld in which the language is used for communicating meaning and in which interactions are constructed through language – the language of both the learner and the computer. "Drulla" is a Poltergeist character in an interactive computer game. The second text illustrates an activity in which learners work together collaboratively through oral language and the computer program contributes written language. The third is constructed through NBLT in which the learners communicate through computers connected in a local area network. Description of these additional texts would add complexity to the simple dichotomy of language use that was illustrated earlier by the texts in Table 1. Description of such texts might include their syntactic complexity, the types of functions used (e.g., commands in the first one, and repetitions in the second), and their linguistic accuracy.

On the basis of text description, explanatory features of the activities might be developed to account for their significant features. For example, one significant feature would be the role of the "participants" in the CALL activity (e.g., the learner[s], the instructor, other people, and the computer). Rather than defining participants' roles in terms of the role of the computer, however, role is defined in terms of how responsibility for controlling various facets of the activity is distributed among participants. Teachers and researchers working with NBLT are expanding the set of possible descriptors for CALL. For example, the term "agentive" is introduced as a concept for explaining the type of activity perceived to be associated with the "contextually and linguistically impoverished" language of pre-network CALL (Debski, 1997b, p. 45). Additional empirical data are needed, however, to provide evidence for what such "impoverished" language use consists of within the computer uses that the author would term "agentive." An empirically based definition of CALL activities with theoretically and empirically motivated features might support a distinction between NBLT and pre-network CALL. Support would come from description of the CALL texts in both network and nonnetwork CALL activities. Such descriptions might show systematic differences in the texts whose explanation could be found in typical features of network-based activities. However, until empirically based distinctions are made, it may be useful to consider themes from CALL that appear to continue to evolve through NBLT.

Recurring themes through generations of CALL

The NBLT-related issues raised in this volume are familiar to those who have participated in pre-network CALL. Difficult issues of evaluation, exacerbated by the temptation to equate the computer with a method of instruction, have persisted throughout CALL's history. This conceptual "computer method" trap presents a problem for CALL research because it locks researchers into framing questions in terms of differences between computer-assisted learning activities and other classroom activities. Nevertheless, some researchers have moved beyond this trap by investigating the effects of specific features of CALL activities and by looking for guidance to research in second language acquisition (SLA), which has pointed to avenues such as the need to investigate the classroom context of CALL and the sociocultural factors related to CALL.

The need for CALL evaluation

The concern for evaluation extends back to the 1960s and 1970s when CALL was an innovative and expensive departure from other classroom practices. But then, like now, the focus of many CALL developers was on the *technology* rather than on technology *use*. Summarizing more than 10 years of experience with CALL in the PLATO project at the University of Illinois, Hart's overview of CALL activities on PLATO included the following comment on evaluation:

It is obvious that the developers of computer-based language materials have given far too little attention to evaluation. . . . If the issues are so complex that conventional procedures (e.g., those employing group mean differences) are inappropriate for providing an answer, then we should present clear arguments why that is so and provide alternative analyses (e.g., based on individualization or optimization features). (Hart, 1981, p. 16)

The point was then – as it is now – that CALL needs to be evaluated and that more than one method is needed to do so. However, with the quickly changing technology of the 1980s and an academic community preoccupied with construction rather than evaluation, little progress was made in CALL evaluation.[2]

In the 1990s, CALL evaluation began to receive more attention. Dunkel's words, written 10 years after Hart's, reflect exactly the same theme:

Systematic evaluation of the effectiveness of all aspects of CALL must continue; however, new focuses as well as methods of research inquiry will need to be developed if we are to gauge correctly the power of the computer to affect different aspects of second language acquisition. (Dunkel, 1991, pp. 23–24)

In the same 1991 volume, concrete suggestions were made for "new focuses and methods" such as process-oriented studies, ethnographic research, and discourse analysis. About the same time, an important study of CALL use in Germany included a variety of methodologies for CALL evaluation, such as discourse analysis for evaluation of learners' use of

---

2 Despite overall trends, several papers addressing evaluation issues did appear during the 1980s (e.g., Doughty, 1987; Pedersen, 1987; Chapelle & Jamieson, 1989).

simulation programs and qualitative methods from cognitive psychology for evaluation of text reconstruction programs (Legenhausen & Wolff, 1990). Reflecting on their methodological choices, Legenhausen and Wolff reported the following:

It seems quite obvious that computer software, serving several diverse functions in the foreign language classroom, cannot be evaluated according to any single methodological principle. What we are trying to do, therefore, is to systematically vary the evaluative principles and techniques according to different CALL software types. (1990, p. 2)

Whether or not one agrees that the program should influence the choice of research methodology, it is important to note that researchers were attempting to move beyond the traditional quasi-experimental methods. At the same time, some researchers have found it appropriate to assess the particular outcomes relevant to the goals of their CALL activities (e.g., Doughty, 1991; Nagata, 1993; Hsu, 1994). When the approaches to CALL evaluation are viewed from the perspective of traditions of second language classroom research, it is apparent that CALL researchers face conceptually similar – even if technically unique – issues in their investigations (Chapelle, Jamieson, & Park, 1996).

Despite evolution of CALL evaluation methods, the editorial comments in a 1995 issue of *Computer Assisted Language Learning* reflect the continued need for careful consideration of the research methods applied to CALL:

Validation and evaluation are extremely important aspects of any project and researchers should remember that if their papers are going to carry any weight, their findings have to be substantiated with the support of usage and validation. A number of submissions to this journal have been brilliant in their conception but have had to be returned because . . . the project had been poorly evaluated. (Cameron, 1995, p. 294)

Why do evaluation issues continue to plague CALL researchers? Perhaps one of the thorniest problems in evaluating CALL, which is as evident in NBLT as it is in pre-network CALL, is the temptation to equate the computer with a method of instruction.

The myth of "CALL method"

The most intuitively logical method of evaluation for CALL is comparison of the linguistic or cognitive outcomes between learners who have used CALL and those who have not. This intuitive approach to evaluation, which treats the computer as a method of instruction, has been problematic in CALL evaluation for at least two reasons. First, the focus on outcomes neglects important evidence for the quality of instruction in second language learning. As second language classroom researchers have pointed out, assessment of outcomes alone fails to document the many contextual factors influencing the process of learning (Seliger & Long, 1983; Day, 1986; Allwright, 1988; Chaudron, 1988; van Lier 1988; Allwright and Bailey, 1991; Johnson, 1995). Other researchers in educational technology working within the social constructivist paradigm echo this concern, arguing, for example, that "the whole educational context that is created online . . . needs to be the focus of analysis" in research on computer use (Riel & Harasim, 1994, p. 92) and that "computer use in and of itself is hardly a conceptually satisfying variable likely to have consistent and predictable results" (Schofield, 1995, pp. 6–7).

The second problem with method comparison studies is that they rest on the faulty assumption that the computer itself constitutes a method of instruction. Clark (1985, 1994) argues that in such research "instructional methods [have] been confounded with media" and that "it is the methods which influence learning" (Clark, 1994, p. 22). Clark defines "methods" as the "structural" characteristics of tasks for learners that engender the processes and strategies necessary for learning; he contrasts methods with "media," a means of delivering methods to learners. His argument can be challenged on a number of grounds, including his assumption that media and methods can be distinguished, yet Clark succeeds in questioning any general claims about the effects of *the computer* on learning. Moreover, his argument helps to point out that, rather than studies focused on "the computer," there is a need for studies that attempt to isolate and investigate the relevant "structural" task features in computer-assisted learning environments.

Doughty (1992) develops this general argument for the specific case of second language learning and CALL, pointing out that CALL activities should attempt to operationalize those features that are theorized to facilitate instructed SLA. The object of investigation, then, changes from the effects of the computer to the learners' interactions and outcomes involving particular features. The challenge in this promising line of research, both for pre-network CALL and for NBLT, is to identify the features that should be developed in CALL activities and to identify appropriate methods for investigating their effects.

Significant features of activities

Past CALL research has examined specific aspects of CALL activities such as the role of the linguistic input to learners and the type of interaction supported. For example, Schaeffer (1981) compared what he called "meaningful" versus "nonmeaningful" input in German grammar lessons and found the "meaningful" input better. Doughty (1991) compared the effects of two different types of explicitly salient ESL input with input that was not explicitly flagged to direct learners' attention. The learners receiving the salient input performed better on posttests on the relative clauses that had been made salient. A study comparing the value of different levels of interactivity in a CALL program for retention of German found that the interactive video condition was the one in which the subjects best remembered the material (Schrupp, Busch, & Mueller, 1983). Another study investigated the effects of various types of response-contingent feedback to learners of Japanese (Nagata, 1993) and found that learners who received "intelligent" feedback about their use of particles performed significantly better on both posttests and end-of-semester tests than did those students who had received only an indication of where they had made an error.

Results of such research are obviously useful for informing the development and use of CALL tasks, but they can also contribute to the broader research on instructed SLA if the task variables are chosen in view of theory-based hypotheses about the relationship between task features and SLA (e.g., Doughty, 1991). Such hypotheses have been formulated by researchers studying SLA from an interactionaist perspective (e.g., Pica, 1994). Based on a review of this research, Pica, Kanagy, and Falodun (1993) summarized the features that had proven significant in previous research and organized them under two variables, *interactionist activity* and *communication goal*. The features are intended to define the characteristics of an L2 task that can be expected to influence learners' texts in significant ways. The "significant ways" within the tradition of interactionist research refers to production of signals and modified output, for example, which are evident during negotiation of meaning. Another set of variables and features was developed by Skehan (1996, 1997), who was interested in identifying the task features accounting for accuracy, complexity, and fluency in learners' task-related texts. The three general categories in this task framework are *code complexity, cognitive complexity,* and *communication stress*.

The empirical basis for these sets of features makes them particularly useful for L2 research and perhaps for CALL. Their descriptive utility, however, is confined to the particular types of tasks that have been used in this research. In order to attempt to expand the scope of this work to CALL, a relevant task framework needs to be developed. An attempt should be made to be systematic about including all of the variables expected to affect learners' performance significantly. For example, in any given task, would the desired negotiations occur if the participants were not of equal status? How would the text differ if the communication were not face-to-face and oral, but instead were conducted in writing over the Internet? Work in NBLT makes apparent the need to look beyond the cognitive and interactive focus of SLA research to identify a fuller set of relevant variables (e.g., status relationship and medium) for defining and investigating the types of features involved in NBLT.

The need to link to SLA research

Some of the CALL literature also attempts to link evaluation methods to research in SLA, specifically including studies of interlanguage, individual differences (Skehan, 1989), strategies (Wenden & Rubin, 1987; Oxford, 1990; O'Malley & Chamot, 1991), and classroom discourse (Chaudron, 1988). I will briefly summarize these CALL/SLA connections below. The CALL studies working within the tradition of interlanguage research have used the computer to collect linguistic data from language learners. Examples of such work include studies of ESL spelling errors (Chapelle & Jamieson, 1981), acquisition of German syntax (Garrett, 1982), and learners' lexical development (Bland, Noblitt, Armington, & Gay, 1990). In the latter study, the researchers used learners' queries to an on-line dictionary during completion of a writing assignment as an indicator of their lexical development. Because the linguistic data were collected while learners were focused on constructing meaningful texts in a class assignment, one might argue for the ecological validity of the data. By supporting a variety of activities or language use, NBLT affords unique opportunities to expand computer-based interlanguage research to the study of pragmatic competence.

The individual-differences research in SLA has provided some guidance for the study of CALL. Because individual differences are known to play a role in language teaching and learning and because CALL activities offer a viable means of providing individual instruction, research might ideally help to identify CALL activities that are beneficial for specific types of learners. Despite the apparent richness of this line of research, as of the late 1990s few studies had taken up the suggestion. One that did (Abraham, 1985) found that field-independent learners performed better on posttests when they had used a rule-presentation (deductive) approach and field-dependent learners performed better after using a lesson presenting examples of the structure (inductive approach). Investigating the same learner variable, Chapelle and Jamieson (1986) found that field-independent ESL students tended to have a more negative attitude toward the CALL under investigation, while the field-dependent students had more positive attitudes. A third study found that impulsive students performed better on an oral sentence-construction task in Spanish when the program required them to wait before responding (Meredith, 1978). This initial research is the beginning of what might prove to be an important line of inquiry – one that has begun to be taken up by NBLT researchers (e.g., Meunier, 1996).

Studies of strategies have been conducted to address two research objectives: investigating psycholinguistic questions about language processing, and studying conditions of learning (Chapelle, Jamieson, & Park, 1996). Examples of psycholinguistic investigations are studies of EFL learners' reading processes through data gathered as they worked with an on-line dictionary (Hulstijn, 1993), learners' automaticity as inferred from response-time data in grammaticality judgment tasks (Hagen, 1994), and monitoring strategies through collection of error correction data from a dictation task (Jamieson & Chapelle, 1987). In each of these cases, inferences were made about learners' ability to address psycholinguistic questions about L2 processing.

Research investigating pedagogical questions relies on process data to act as evidence about the quality of a CALL activity in meeting an instructional goal. For example, Goodfellow and Laurillard (1994) reported the results of a case study investigating learners' use of a CALL program for vocabulary acquisition in Spanish. The program allowed learners to select, group, and practice vocabulary contained in on-line texts in order to achieve the pedagogical goals of learning the selected vocabulary. The researchers examined learning processes by observing the choices they made during use of the program and think-aloud protocols. The results indicated that learners were not able to use the program effectively for vocabulary learning, and that they needed more training if they were to use the software tools effectively – a result that has been found in other pedagogically oriented CALL research as well (Hsu, Chapelle, & Thompson, 1993).

A fourth connection with SLA research has called on methods of discourse analysis for describing the interactions within learning activities (e.g., Long, 1980; Allwright, 1988; Chaudron, 1988; van Lier, 1988; Allwright & Bailey, 1991). In CALL research, Esling (1991) suggested that it may be valuable to examine the oral and written texts that learners produce during CALL use:

One area in the evaluation of the effectiveness of CALL with immediate and potentially powerful research possibilities involves the assessment of the types of discourse generated during a CALL activity, and its similarities and differences to the discourse found in non-CALL classroom activities. (Esling, 1991, p. 114)

Esling's idea was that such research would improve understanding of the instructional value of various types of CALL activities by viewing them through the lens of familiar discourse types as outlined by Brown and Yule (1983). Fruitful work in using these methods has demonstrated, for example, that the discourse functions that students produce orally while working on CALL depend, in part, on the type of program the students work with (Piper, 1986; Abraham & Liou, 1991) and that context-embedded, cognitively demanding discourse can occur in such activities (Mohan, 1992).

Chapelle (1990) extended Esling's basic idea by applying classroom discourse analysis (Sinclair & Coulthard, 1975) to the "communication"

(Luff, Gilbert, & Frohlich, 1990; Hirst, 1991) that occurs between the learner and the computer program:

> Depending on the program, the interaction allowed can render possible a variety of functional acts. A precise description of an activity could be formulated by specifying the types of acts possible within a given CALL program, which acts can be used as each type of move, how moves fit together to form legal exchanges, until a grammar of the CALL activity is defined. This grammar, then, provides an unambiguous statement of the parameters of student–computer interaction within a CALL program. The grammar of possible discourse forms a framework for describing actual acts of the students as they work, as well as a basis for comparison with the acts allowed in other CALL and classroom activities. (Chapelle, 1990, p. 207)

Renie and Chanier (1995) take a similar approach in their description of a computer program by conceptualizing it as a collaborator with a French learner who participates in goal-directed scenarios such as making a reservation at a restaurant. Their approach to understanding the collaboration between learner and computer is to characterize the nature of the utterances (i.e., the acts) each can contribute to the collaboration. They are then able to speculate on the potential value of particular collaborative sequences for second language acquisition, on the basis of a Vygotskyan theory of collaboration and "exolingual interaction" theory, which hypothesizes the nature of "potentially acquisitional sequences" of interaction during collaboration.

These functional perspectives on learner–computer interaction provide a means for connecting CALL research to research on SLA tasks. For example, Hsu (1994) conducted a focused discourse analysis of interactions between learners and the computer to identify functions of interest for SLA (e.g., requests for modified input within a listening comprehension program). The normal interaction in this part of the program consisted of learners' requests for continuation of a story with accompanying pictures on one computer screen after another. The researcher counted as "interactional modification" sequences in which this normal interaction was interrupted by the learners' requests for modified input (which could be in the form of repetitions, written transcriptions, or written definitions for words in the input). Among the findings was a significant relationship between interactional modifications and acquisition of the specific lexical phrases with which the modifications had occurred.

Discourse analysis appears to be a useful tool for research on the language of NBLT. Investigating computer-assisted class discussion (i.e., written language transmitted over a network) in a first-year German class to seek evidence of the functions learners used, Chun (1994) found that learners used a number of interactional speech acts – for example, asking questions and requesting clarifications. She concluded that the computer-assisted class-discussion format created a context that was positive for the acquisition of these acts. Others have concluded on the basis of discourse analysis that learners take many turns in NBLT relative to some other classroom activities, that turn taking may be more evenly distributed, and that teacher control is diminished (Beauvois, 1992; Kelm, 1992; Kern, 1995; Warschauer, 1996; Ortega, 1997).

The classroom context of CALL

In 1991, Johnson pointed out the CALL research of the 1980s needed to evolve beyond investigation of the linguistic and cognitive facets of development:

The bulk of research on computers and learning in educational environments has focused on the cognitive aspects of learning. Yet, theory in second language acquisition and research in second language acquisition classrooms indicate that the social interactional environments of the classroom are also crucial factors that affect language learning in important ways. (Johnson, 1991, p. 62)

Johnson's suggestion to expand CALL research to social interactional environments is consistent with the ethnographic tradition of classroom research that investigates the classroom contexts in which second language acquisition occurs (Watson-Gegeo, 1988). Moreover, a qualitative study of CALL conducted in an L1 classroom prior to 1991 pointed to the value of examining the role the computer plays within the larger culture of the classroom (Cazden, Michaels, & Watson-Gegeo, 1987).

Relatively little work has been done so far to probe questions about the sociocultural and classroom contexts of CALL use. One study (Park, 1994) used qualitative methods to investigate the classroom culture of ESL learners using hypermedia language learning software in an intensive English program in the United States. The research revealed the role of factors in the language program and classroom culture in shaping the learners' experiences with CALL. A second study (Edwards, 1994), conducted in an intensive program in the United States, used survey research methods to investigate how the teachers' attitudes and knowledge of CALL influenced their CALL use. Sanaoui and Lapkin's (1992) qualitative study observed the nature of the language that ESL and FSL (French as a second language) learners in Canada produced and the quality of instructional experience that learners and teachers perceived as they worked collaboratively with peers from the target language across a computer network. Research on NBLT (including the studies in this volume) helps to reveal how CALL can work within the classroom context.

Sociocultural issues of CALL

The classroom-based studies that have been cited offer insight into some of the sociocultural issues related to CALL use. Critical perspectives on technology and society (e.g., Bowers, 1988), however, point to the need to raise fundamental questions about the culturally bound ideologies associated with educational technology. Hart and Daisley (1994) present their speculation on this issue based on their experience at an educational technology conference in Japan, but much work remains to be done. The accessibility of the Internet has increased the impact of the socio-political domain on the interplay between language and computers in all realms, including education (e.g., Murray, 1995).

It is clear that research in CALL must include cross-cultural perspectives. Even CALL researchers who wish to remain within the tradition of educational technology find that work in that area has evolved to include a number of different perspectives, including "a cultural constructivist approach" (Scott, Cole, & Engel, 1992; Crook, 1994). This approach has roots in Vygotskyan cultural psychology (Wertsch, 1985), which "makes sense of 'learning' by reference to the social structure of activity – rather than by reference to the mental structure of individuals" (Crook, 1994, p. 78). The perspective emphasizes that the values and priorities of a culture influence decisions concerning issues such as technology use within classrooms (Olson, 1987), and therefore affect learners' linguistic experiences.

None of the six themes described in this section has yet been fully developed. CALL research is just beginning to pull together the relevant questions, methods, and data. NBLT has arrived on the scene at a critical period to contribute to the evolution of CALL research.

Network learning: A critical role in CALL's evolution

Network learning significantly expands the scope of CALL activities and, as a consequence, critical investigation of NBLT offers fresh perspectives on CALL's familiar themes. NBLT has already added to current evolution in CALL and is likely to continue to do so.

The need for CALL evaluation is more evident to observers of NBLT than it has ever been. Teachers and researchers who critically observe the unique registers of Internet chat sessions (Werry, 1996) or on-line classroom discussions cannot help but ask about the effects on second language development. Such registers are characterized by a variety of features that do not appear in most forms of written language, such as partial sentences, invented words, and iconic symbols. Because NBLT activities move beyond the clear objectives and controlled instructional sequences of some pre-network CALL, the registers of language it produces can appear chaotic. Collombet-Sankey describes NBLT that she considered a success as follows:

No planned activity could have created better conditions for interaction in French. It unlocked the dynamics of the group because a new rapport among students was established based on criteria other than language competence. This reconfiguration of the culture of the language classroom which comprises a different system of socializing has to be regarded as a positive development in strategic language learning. (Collombet-Sankey, 1997, p. 149)

Despite the impression one might gain that such classroom dynamics are ideal for language learning, their success may be difficult to document in more concrete terms. When the goals of an activity are to create conditions for interaction and reconfiguration of classroom culture, methods of evaluation must focus on interactions within the classroom culture – slipperier objectives than those involving development of aspects of grammatical competence, for example.

NBLT *should be* more complex than pre-network CALL because network-based activities may attempt to develop a more complex set of abilities. Barson's description of a project-based methodology for NBLT is a good example of the types of learning goals that may be targeted by NBLT:

At the heart of the paradigm being proposed is the view that learning to act as oneself in a foreign language is the primary goal of the student, a goal involving a conciliation, over time, of self-identity with the linguistic code under assimilation. (Barson, 1997, p. 12)

Such goals may prove difficult for CALL evaluation. Past work has shown that the more concretely defined the outcomes, the more successfully they are assessed (Doughty, 1992; Nagata, 1993; Hsu, 1994). Researchers attempting to assess more complex outcomes, such as development of context-embedded and cognitively demanding language proficiency, have run into challenges in assessment (Mohan, 1992). Barson's targets for NBLT appear even more elusive, and therefore promise to challenge efforts in evaluation. Such challenges are needed, however, to push forward the scope of CALL use and evaluation.

The myth of "CALL method" is exposed in NBLT through the qualitative, process-oriented approaches in NBLT. Based on longitudinal interviews with students and teachers, audiotaping and videotaping of class sessions, analysis of electronic texts, and classroom observation, Warschauer (Chapter 3, this volume) reveals the dramatically different character of the activities in each class: "These four classes provided a powerful illustration to me that the Internet itself does not constitute a method, any more than books, or blackboards, or libraries constitute a method." In Warschauer's study, these differences in NBLT activities were interpreted as reflecting different teacher beliefs and institutional ideologies. Additional research on CALL may help to clarify the differences in the language of these activities that are related to the features of the activities that teachers design on the basis of their beliefs and institutional contexts.

The pursuit of significant activity features in NBLT extends beyond those proposed for pre-network CALL. In most NBLT activities, the software does not control the goals, the topics, or the duration of activities. The teacher can choose to specify these or not, and the learners – through their language – can play a significant role in shaping the activity. One study investigating the language of an international Internet discussion list interpreted results as follows:

With new teachers and students meeting in each virtual encounter, communication forms different from those anticipated by any model of structured community, whether of a Freirian community of co-investigators or a Foucauldian model of panopticon control, will develop. Tapping into the learning possible in this creative language environment is the next task for those interested in Internet-based education. (Warschauer & Lepeintre, 1997, p. 86)

The creativity afforded by an Internet discussion group such as the one Warschauer and Lepeintre describe demands that a framework of CALL activity features include the sociolinguistic factors known to influence context-contingent communication. Given the global community that can be created through the Internet, CALL research involving network learning promises to enrich the study of sociolinguistics and language acquisition.

Links between CALL and SLA are also strengthened by NBLT studies such as Pellettieri's (this volume), which draw on conceptual and empirical methods for investigating the language of L2 tasks. Given the principled basis for this research, the results address an important question about instructed SLA: To what extent do particular tasks provide opportunities for negotiation of meaning? Pellettieri describes the results of one such study:

The results of this study demonstrate that task-based synchronous NBC [network-based communication], such as chatting, can indeed foster the negotiation of meaning. Learners involved in NBC chats negotiate over all aspects of the discourse, which in turn pushes form-focused linguistic modifications. Additionally, learners provide and are provided corrective feedback, which was demonstrated to result in the incorporation of target-language forms. . . . (Pellettieri, this volume)

All forms of CALL have a dynamic relationship with the classrooms in which they are used, but approaches to design and research of NBLT have pushed the view of CALL to include the classroom context of CALL. Writing about NBLT, Patrikis (1997) notes that "a simple and often heard phrase like 'the integration of computers into the curriculum' is a false lead. Once introduced in any meaningful way, the computer

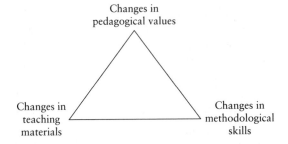

Figure 1 *The dimensions of curricular innovation (from Markee, 1997, p. 54).*

changes everything" (p. 175). Similarly, Debski (1997b) calls the relationship of language teaching and technology "ecological change" because "any significant change in one of its components may lead to changes in the remaining factor" (p. 41).

These observations are consistent with Markee's (1997) characterization of innovation in second language teaching. As illustrated in Figure 1, changes in materials do not occur independently. Instead, they must co-occur with changes in methodological teaching skills and philosophical values. The findings of NBLT studies have begun to demonstrate the interplay among these facets of teaching. For example, in his study of the CALL of several different classrooms, Warschauer observed that the "implementation of new technologies varied from classroom to classroom, influenced by the general institutional context and the particular beliefs of each individual teacher" (Warschauer, this volume). Similarly, Levy (1997b) describes how his project-based approach was influenced by institutional requirements for a syllabus at the beginning of the semester and formal evaluation of students – requirements reflecting particular pedagogical values. Other researchers have observed that when teachers do not have the values and skills that are consistent with NBLT activities, the types of changes introduced by NBLT can be "unsettling," in part because teachers' control is compromised and participation can appear "anarchistic" (Kern, 1995, p. 470).

NBLT also has much to add to the study of the sociocultural impact of CALL. Debski, for example, justifies the use of NBLT on the basis of societal values: "[I]t should be evident that current evolution of the society and the human self, and the role technology plays in shaping them, are in synchrony with the basic tenets of an exploratory, experience-based approach to second or foreign language learning" (Debski, 1997a, pp. 213–214). In this volume, the chapters by Meskill and Ranglova and by Warschauer provide the clearest examples of how technology use is subject to and becomes part of the sociocultural environment. Perhaps the most compelling illustration of the convergence of L2 activity, cultural values, and the technology that put them together is offered in a qualitative study by Warschauer and Lepeintre (1997). They tell a vivid story of their experience with an Internet list designed for EFL practice. The topic of war atrocities was nominated because of a question about Japanese culture posed by a Japanese learner, and a heated political discussion between members of two ethnic and cultural groups followed:

[A]t some point, this profoundly successful discussion started to turn into its opposite. These students weren't just talking about the real world, but rather they were the real world: they were debating serious issues of international relations based on their own personal experiences with war and oppression. (Warschauer & Lepeintre, 1997, p. 83)

What could display a greater contrast to the types of pre-network CALL dialogues illustrated in Table 1? Observations such as these indicate that NBLT pushes CALL research beyond examining the impact of importing and exporting educational technology to the study of how education, technology, language, and culture are evolving together.

Is network-based learning CALL?

This question is important for conceptual development and evolution of CALL as a whole and network-based learning in particular. In an initial response to this question, I have suggested that a meaningful definition of CALL activities requires descriptive research documenting the language and interactions that learners engage in during CALL use. I examined six themes that have emerged throughout the evolution of CALL and suggested the degree of connectedness of network-based learning to each theme. Network-based learning – in part through the studies in this volume – contributes substantially to each theme and therefore to the evolution of CALL. It therefore seems that, at least for the time being, it is useful to consider network-based learning within the scope of CALL. Debski (1997b) suggests that "the use of linguistically enriched environments (i.e., network-mediated multimedia) . . . invites a serious reconsideration of computer-aided language teaching and all of its constitutive elements" (p. 47). However, given the existing themes identified in the past CALL literature and the contributions that NBLT makes, one might suggest that NBLT represents an expansion rather than a reconceptualization of CALL.

References

Abraham, R. (1985). Field independence-dependence and the teaching of grammar. *TESOL Quarterly, 19*, 689–702.

Abraham, R., & Liou, H.-C. (1991). Interaction generated by three computer programs: Analysis of functions of spoken language. In P. Dunkel (Ed.), *Computer-assisted language learning and testing: Research issues and practice*. (pp. 85–109). New York: Newbury House.

Allwright, D. (1988). *Observation in the language classroom*. London: Longman.

Allwright, D., & Bailey, K. M. (1991). *Focus on the language classroom: An introduction to classroom research for language teachers*. Cambridge: Cambridge University Press.

Anderson-Hsieh, J. (1994). Interpreting visual feedback on suprasegmentals in computer assisted pronunciation instruction. *CALICO Journal, 11*(4), 5–21.

Barson, J. (1997). Space, time and form in the project-based foreign language classroom. In R. Debski, J. Gassin, & M. Smith (Eds.), *Language learning through social computing*. Applied Linguistics of Australia Occasional Papers Number 16 (pp. 1–38). Parkville, Australia: Applied Linguistics Association of Australia.

Beauvois, M. H. (1992). Computer-assisted classroom discussion in the foreign language classroom: Conversation in slow motion. *Foreign Language Annals, 25*(5), 455–464.

Bland, S. K., Noblitt, J. S., Armington, S., & Gay, G. (1990). The naive lexical hypothesis: Evidence from computer-assisted language learning. *Modern Language Journal, 74,* 440–450.

Bowers, C. A. (1988). *The cultural dimensions of educational computing*. New York: Teachers College Press.

Brown, G., & Yule, G. (1983). *Discourse analysis*. Cambridge: Cambridge University Press.

Cameron, K. (1995). Editorial. *Computer Assisted Language Learning, 8*(4), 293–294.

Cazden, C. B., Michaels, S., & Watson-Gegeo, K. A. (1987). *Final report: Microcomputers and literacy project* (Grant No. G-83–0051). Washington, DC: National Institute of Education.

Chanier, T., Pengelly, M., Twidale, M., & Self, J. (1992). Conceptual modeling in error analysis in computer-assisted language learning systems. In M. L. Swartz & M. Yazdani (Eds.), *Intelligent tutoring systems for foreign language learning* (pp. 125–150). Berlin: Springer-Verlag.

Chapelle, C. A. (1990). The discourse of computer-assisted language learning: Toward a context for descriptive research. *TESOL Quarterly, 24,* 199–225.

Chapelle, C. A. (1994). CALL activities: Are they all the same? *System, 22*(1), 33–45.

Chapelle, C., & Jamieson, J. (1981). ESL spelling errors. *TESL Studies, 4,* 29–36.

Chapelle, C., & Jamieson, J. (1986). Computer-assisted language learning as a predictor of success in acquiring Enslish as a second language. *TESOL Quarterly, 20,* 27–46.

Chapelle, C., & Jamieson, J. (1989). Research trends in computer-assisted language learning. In M. Pennington (Ed.), *Teaching language with computers: The state of the art* (pp. 47–59). San Francisco: Athelstan.

Chapelle, C., Jamieson, J., & Park, Y. (1996). Second language classroom research traditions: How does CALL fit? In M. Pennington (Ed.), *The power of CALL* (pp. 33–53). Houston, TX: Athelstan.

Chaudron, C. (1988). *Second language classrooms: Research on teaching and learning*. Cambridge: Cambridge University Press.

Chun, D. M. (1994). Using computer networking to facilitate the acquisition of interactive competence. *System, 22*(1), 17–31.

Clark, R. E. (1985). Confounding in educational computing research. *Journal Educational Computing Research, 1*(2), 137–148.

Clark, R. E. (1994). Media will never influence learning. *Educational Technology Research and Development, 42*(2), 21–29.

Coleman, D. W. (1985). TERRI: A CALL lesson simulating conversational interaction. *System, 13*(3), 247–252.

Collombet-Sankey, N. (1997). Surfing the net to acquire communicative competence and cultural knowledge. In R. Debski, J. Gassin, & M. Smith (Eds.), *Language learning through social computing.* Applied Linguistics of Australia Occasional Papers Number 16 (pp. 141–158). Parkville, Australia: Applied Linguistics Association of Australia.

Crook, C. (1994). *Computers and the collaborative experience of learning.* London: Routledge.

Day, R. (Ed.) (1986). *Talking to learn: Conversation in second language acquisition.* Rowley, MA: Newbury House.

Debski, R. (1997a). From individualisation to socialisation: An essay on CALL with reflections on Sherry Turkle's *Life on the Screen.* In R. Debski, J. Gassin, & M. Smith, (Eds.), *Language learning through social computing.* Applied Linguistics of Australia Occasional Papers Number 16 (pp. 201–219). Parkville, Australia: Applied Linguistics Association of Australia.

Debski, R. (1997b). Support of creativity and collaboration in the language classroom: A new role for technology. In R. Debski, J. Gassin, & M. Smith (Eds.), *Language learning through social computing.* Applied Linguistics of Australia Occasional Papers Number 16, (pp. 39–65). Parkville, Australia: Applied Linguistics Association of Australia.

Debski, R., Gassin, J., & Smith, M. (Eds.) (1997). *Language learning through social computing.* Applied Linguistics of Australia Occasional Papers Number 16. Parkville, Australia: Applied Linguistics Association of Australia.

Doughty, C. (1987). Relating second-language acquisition theory to CALL research and application. In W. F. Smith (Ed.), *Modern media in foreign language education: Theory and implementation* (pp. 133–167). Lincolnwood, IL: National Textbook.

Doughty, C. (1991). Second language instruction does make a difference: Evidence from an empirical study of SL relativization. *Studies in Second Language Acquisition, 13,* 431–469.

Doughty, C. (1992). Computer applications in second language acquisition research: Design, description, and discovery. In M. Pennington & V. Stevens (Eds.), *Computers in applied linguistics: An international perspective* (pp. 127–154). Clevedon, UK: Multilingual Matters.

Dunkel, P. (1991). The effectiveness research on computer-assisted instruction and computer-assisted language learning. In P. Dunkel (Ed.), *Computer-assisted language learning and testing: Research issues and practice* (pp. 5–36). New York: Newbury House.

Edwards, C. (1994). Perception, proficiency and prowess: Factors that affect the diffusion of CALL among ESL teachers and students. Paper presented at the Computers in Applied Linguistics Conference, Ames, IA, July 8–13, 1994.

Esling, J. (1991). Researching the effects of networking: Evaluating the spoken and written discourse generated by working with CALL. In P. Dunkel (Ed.),

Computer-assisted language learning and testing: Research issues and practice (pp. 111–131). New York: Newbury House.

Garrett, N. (1982). In search of interlanguage: A study of second language acquisition of German syntax. Unpublished doctoral dissertation. University of Illinois at Urbana-Champaign.

Goodfellow, R., & Laurillard, D. (1994). Modeling learning processes in lexical CALL. *CALICO Journal, 11*(3), 19–46.

Hagen, L. K. (1994). Constructs and measurement in parameter models of second language acquisition. In E. E. Tarone, S. M. Gass, & A. D. Cohen (Eds.), *Research methodology in second-language acquisition* (pp. 61–87). Hillsdale, NJ: Lawrence Erlbaum Association.

Hart, B., & Daisley, M. (1994). Computers and composition in Japan: Notes on real and virtual literacies. *Computers and Composition, 11*, 37–47.

Hart, R. S. (1981). Language study and the PLATO system. In R. S. Hart (Ed.), *Studies in language learning. Special issue on the PLATO system and language study, 3* (pp. 1–24.). Urbana: Language Learning Laboratory, University of Illinois at Urbana-Champaign.

Higgins, J. (1988). *Language, learners, and computers.* London: Longman.

Hirst, G. (1991). Does conversation analysis have a role in computational linguistics? *Computational Linguistics, 17*(2), 212–227.

Hsu, J. (1994). Computer assisted language learning (CALL): The effect of ESL students' use of interactional modifications on listening comprehension. Unpublished doctoral dissertation. Department of Curriculum and Instruction, College of Education, Iowa State University, Ames.

Hsu, J., Chapelle, C., & Thompson, A. (1993). Exploratory environments: What are they and do students explore? *Journal of Educational Computing Research, 9*(1), 1–15.

Hull, G., Ball, C., Fox, J., Levin, L., & McCutchen, D. (1987). Computer detection of errors in natural language texts: Some research on pattern-matching. *Computers and the Humanities, 21*, 103–118.

Hulstijn, J. (1993). When do foreign language learners look up the meaning of unfamiliar words? The influence of task and learner variables. *Modern Language Journal, 77*(2), 139–147.

Jamieson, J., & Chapelle, C. (1987). Working styles on computers as evidence of second language learning strategies. *Language Learning, 37*, 523–544.

Johns, T. (1986). Micro-Concord, a language learner's research tool. *System, 14*(2), 151–162.

Johnson, D. (1991). Second language and content learning with computers: Research in the role of social factors. In P. Dunkel (Ed.), *Computer-assisted language learning and testing: Research issues and practice* (pp. 61–83). New York: Newbury House.

Johnson, K. E. (1995). *Understanding communication in second language classrooms.* Cambridge: Cambridge University Press.

Kelm, O. R. (1992). The use of synchronous computer networks in second language instruction: A preliminary report. *Foreign Language Annals, 25*(5), 441–454.

Kern, R. G. (1995). Restructuring classroom interaction with networked computers: Effects on quantity and characteristics of language production. *Modern Language Journal, 79*, 457–476.

Knupfer, N. N., & McLellan, H. (1996). Descriptive research methodologies. In

D. H. Jonassen (Ed.), *Handbook of research for educational communications and technology* (pp. 1196–1212). New York: Simon & Schuster Macmillan.

Legenhausen, L., & Wolff, D. (1990). CALL in use – use of CALL: Evaluating CALL software. *System, 18*(1), 1–13.

Levy, M. (1997a). *Computer-assisted language learning: Context and conceptualization.* Oxford: Clarendon Press.

Levy, M. (1997b). Project-based learning for language teachers: Reflecting on the process. In R. Debski, J. Gassin, & M. Smith (Eds.), *Language learning through social computing.* Applied Linguistics of Australia Occasional Papers Number 16 (pp. 179–199). Parkville, Australia: Applied Linguistics Association of Australia.

Long, M. (1980). Inside the "black box": Methodological issues in classroom research on language learning. *Language Learning, 30,* 1–42.

Luff, P., Gilbert, N., & Frohlich, D. (Eds.). (1990). *Computers and conversation.* London: Academic Press.

Markee, N. (1997). *Managing curricular innovation.* Cambridge: Cambridge University Press.

Marty, F. (1981). Reflections on the use of computers in second language acquisition. In R. S. Hart (Ed.), *Studies in language learning. Special issue on the PLATO system and language study, 3* (pp. 25–53). Urbana: Language Learning Laboratory, University of Illinois at Urbana-Champaign.

Meredith, R. (1978). Improved oral test scores through delayed response. *Modern Language Journal, 62,* 321–327.

Meunier, L. E. (1996). Human factors in a computer-assisted foreign language environment: The effects of gender, personality, and keyboard control. *CALICO Journal, 13*(2–3), 47–72.

Mohan, B. (1992). Models of the role of the computer in second language development. In M. Pennington, & V. Stevens (Eds.), *Computers in applied linguistics: An international perspective* (pp. 110–126). Clevedon, UK: Multilingual Matters.

Murray, D. E. (1995). *Knowledge machines: Language and information in a technological society.* London: Longman.

Nagata, N. (1993). Intelligent computer feedback for second language instruction. *Modern Language Journal, 77*(3), 330–339.

Olson, C. P. (1987). Who computes? In L. W. Livingstone (Ed.), *Critical pedagogy and cultural power* (pp. 179–204). South Hadley, MA: Bergin & Garvey.

O'Malley, J. M., & Chamot, A. U. (1990). *Learning strategies in second language acquisition.* Cambridge: Cambridge University Press.

Ortega, L. (1997). Processes and outcomes in networked classroom interaction: Defining the research agenda for L2 computer-assisted classroom discussion. *Language Learning and Technology, 1*(1), 82–93.

Oxford, R. L. (1990). *Language learning strategies: What every teacher should know.* New York: Newbury House.

Papert, S. (1980). *Mindstorms.* New York: Basic Books.

Park, Y. (1994). Incorporating interactive multimedia in an ESL classroom environment: Learners' interactions and learning strategies. Unpublished doctoral dissertation. Department of Curriculum and Instruction, College of Education, Iowa State University, Ames.

Patrikis, P. C. (1997). The evolution of computer technology in foreign language teaching and learning. In R. Debski, J. Gassin, & M. Smith (Eds.), *Language learning through social computing.* Applied Linguistics of Australia Occasional Papers Number 16 (pp. 159–177). Parkville, Australia: Applied Linguistics Association of Australia.

Pederson, K. M. (1987). Research on CALL. In W. F. Smith (Ed.), *Modern media in foreign language education: Theory and implementation* (pp. 99–131). Lincolnwood, IL: National Textbook.

Pennington, M. C. (1991). Computer-assisted analysis of English dialect and interlanguage prosodics. In P. Dunkel (Ed.), *Computer-assisted language learning and testing: Research issues and practice* (pp. 133–154). New York: Newbury House.

Pennington, M. C. (1993). Exploring the potential of word processing for nonnative writers. *Computers and the Humanities, 27,* 149–163.

Phillips, M. (1985). Educational technology in the next decade: An ELT perspective. In C. Brumfit, M. Phillips, & P. Skehan (Eds.), *Computers in English language teaching: A view from the classroom* (pp. 99–119). Oxford: Pergamon Press.

Pica, T. (1994). Research on negotiation: What does it reveal about second-language learning conditions, processes, and outcomes? *Language Learning, 44*(3), 493–527.

Pica, T., Kanagy, R., & Falodun, J. (1993). Choosing and using communication tasks for second language instruction. In G. Crookes & S. Gass (Eds.), *Tasks and language learning: Integrating theory and practice* (pp. 9–34). Clevedon, UK: Multilingual Matters.

Piper, A. (1986). Conversation and the computer: A study of the conversational spin-off generated among learners of English as a second language working in groups. *System, 14,* 187–198.

Renie, D., & Chanier, T. (1995). Collaboration and computer-assisted acquisition of a second language. *Computer Assisted Language Learning, 8*(1), 3–29.

Riel, M., & Harasim, L. (1994). Research perspectives on network learning. *Machine-Mediated Learning, 4*(2–3), 91–113.

Sanaoui, R., & Lapkin, S. (1992). A case study of an FSL senior secondary course integrating computer networking. *Canadian Modern Language Review, 48*(3), 525–552.

Schaeffer, R. H. (1981). Meaningful practice on the computer: Is it possible? *Foreign Language Annals, 14,* 133–137.

Schofield, J. W. (1995). *Computers and classroom culture.* Cambridge: Cambridge University Press.

Schrupp, D. M., Busch, M. D., & Mueller, G. A. (1983). Klavier im Haus – an interactive experiment in foreign language instruction. *CALICO Journal, 1*(2), 17–21.

Scott, T., Cole, M., & Engel, M. (1992). Computers in education: A cultural constructivist perspective. *Review of Research in Education, 18,* 191–251.

Seliger, H. W., & Long, M. H. (Eds.). (1983). *Classroom-oriented research in second language acquisition.* Rowley, MA: Newbury House.

Sinclair, J., & Coulthard, R. M. (1975). *Towards an analysis of discourse: The English used by teacher and pupils.* London: Oxford University Press.

Skehan, P. (1989). *Individual differences in second language acquisition.* London: Edward Arnold.

Skehan, P. (1996). A framework for implementation of task-based instruction. *Applied Linguistics, 17*(1), 38–62.

Skehan, P. (1997). *Language learners and language learning.* Oxford: Oxford University Press.

Tribble, C., & Jones, G. (1990). *Concordances in the classroom: A resource book for teachers.* Essex: Longman.

Underwood, J. (1984). *Linguistics, computers, and the language teacher.* Rowley, MA: Newbury House.

van Lier, L. (1988). *The classroom and the learner.* London: Longman.

Warschauer, M. (1996). Comparing face-to-face and electronic discussion in the foreign language classroom. *CALICO Journal, 13*(2–3), 7–26.

Warschauer, M. (Ed.) (1995). *Virtual connections: Online activities and projects for networking language learners.* Honolulu: Second Language Teaching and Curriculum Center, University of Hawaii.

Warschauer, M., & Lepeintre, S. (1997). Freire's dream on Foucault's nightmare? Teacher-student relations on an international computer network. In R. Debski, J. Gassin, & M. Smith (Eds.), *Language learning through social computing.* Applied Linguistics of Australia Occasional Papers Number 16 (pp. 67–89). Parkville, Australia: Applied Linguistics Association of Australia.

Watson-Gegeo, K. A. (1988). Ethnography in ESL: Defining the essentials. *TESOL Quarterly, 22,* 575–592.

Wenden, A., & Rubin, J. (Eds.). (1987). *Learner strategies in language learning.* Englewood Cliffs, NJ: Prentice Hall.

Werry, C. C. (1996). Linguistic and interactional features of internet relay chat. In S. C. Herring (Ed.), *Computer-mediated communication: Linguistic, social and cross-cultural perspectives* (pp. 47–63). Amsterdam: John Benjamins.

Wertsch, J. V. (1985). *Vygotsky and the social formation of the mind.* Cambridge: Harvard University Press.

Name index

Subject index

234

T-216
Dover
FO'00

WITHDRAWAL